A DESCRIPTION
OF THE
WESTERN ISLANDS OF SCOTLAND ca 1695
and
A LATE VOYAGE TO ST KILDA

Martin Martin

DESCRIPTION OF THE
OCCIDENTAL
i.e.
WESTERN
ISLANDS OF SCOTLAND

Donald Monro

BIRLINN

This edition published in 2018 by
Birlinn Limited
West Newington House
10 Newington Road
Edinburgh EH9 1QS

www.birlinn.co.uk

First published by Birlinn in 1999
Reprinted 2010, 2014

ISBN 978 1 78027 546 8
eBook ISBN 978 0 85790 288 7

British Library Cataloguing-in-Publication Data
A Catalogue record of this book is available from the British Library

Typeset by Geethik technologies, India
Printed and bound by MBM Print SCS Ltd, East Kilbride

CONTENTS

———➤●◄———

A DESCRIPTION OF
THE WESTERN ISLANDS
OF SCOTLAND CA. 1695

Martin Martin

A LATE VOYAGE TO ST KILDA

Martin Martin

DESCRIPTION OF THE OCCIDENTAL
i.e.
WESTERN ISLES OF SCOTLAND

Donald Monro

A DESCRIPTION
OF THE
WESTERN ISLANDS OF SCOTLAND ca 1695

Introduction

Charles W. J. Withers

Martin Martin's *A Voyage to St Kilda* (1698) and *A Description of the Western Isles of Scotland* (1703) are amongst the first printed works to describe the Hebrides and the culture and beliefs of the people of Scotland's Outer Isles. For this reason alone, they are noteworthy. Some modern commentators consider Martin's Hebridean narratives the definitive forerunner to those topographical accounts of Scotland in general and of the Highlands in particular that are so common from the later eighteenth century. Later travellers, it is true, were influenced by the works. Martin's *Description of the Western Isles* was given to Samuel Johnson by his father, a fact which roused the doctor's interest in Scotland and prompted his own tour with James Boswell. Influenced Johnson may have been: impressed he was not. 'No man', wrote Johnson, 'now writes so ill as Martin's account of the Hebrides is written.' Boswell was only slightly more charitable: 'His Book is a very imperfect performance; & he is erroneous as to many particulars, even some concerning his own Island. Yet as it is the only Book upon the subject, it is very generally known... I cannot but have a kindness for him, not withstanding his defects.' Earlier, the antiquarian and natural historian John Toland had noted of Martin's Hebridean works that 'The Subject of this book deserv'd a much better pen... [These] Islands afford a great number of materials for exercising the talents of the ablest antiquaries, mathematicians, natural philosophers, and other men of Letters. But the author wontes almost every quality requisite in a Historian (especially in a Topographer).'

What, then, are we to make of these early, and, seemingly, erroneous and imperfect yet influential texts? It is vital to recognise, of course, that Johnson, Boswell and Toland were judging Martin and his work from the standards of *their* time, not his. Seen in terms of that more precise rhetoric which informed later eighteenth-century literary and geographical description, Martin's texts might indeed be judged 'an imperfect performance'. He himself admitted to 'Defects' in 'my Stile and way of Writing', and confessed that 'he might have put these papers into the hands of some capable of giving them, what they really want, a politer turn of phrase'. It is not appropriate, however, to judge the products of one age by the standards of another. Further, given the existence of earlier accounts of the Western Isles, albeit that many survived only in manuscript form, from Dean Monro's 1549 *Description of the Western Isles of Scotland* – included here in full (pp. 315–378) – and other geographical documents dating from the 1640s, 1670s and 1680s, the view that Martin's accounts mark the beginning of topographical description of the Hebrides cannot be allowed to stand.

Judged in the context of their own time, Martin Martin's works have considerable significance and are of interest to the modern reader for three reasons. First, Martin Martin, as a Skye native and a Gaelic speaker, is *of* the places and peoples he writes about. His work is of importance, then, not just because it is an early account but, crucially, because it is by a native. What we get is a credible account of St Kilda and of the Hebrides from, as it were, 'the inside', and, in that regard, Martin's works are unlike virtually any other commentary on the Highlands and Islands.

Second, what Martin Martin gives us is a view of Hebridean culture and society before the Highlands and Islands of Scotland get invested with those false yet persistent images of tartanry, romance, Bonnie Prince Charlie and the aesthetic majesty of empty landscapes that so mark commentators' works from the end of the eighteenth century. In this regard, too, Martin's accounts of the lives of ordinary people and of their customs and beliefs do not seek, as was so common in many later writers concerned with their own moral authority as 'improvers', to judge the people he is writing about. This is not to say the world he was writing about should be seen either as some sort of authentic and timeless Hebrides, or that that world was untouched by things going on elsewhere. This was far from the case.

Third, Martin was both part of, and an agent for, a different and wider world altogether. His works were largely written at the behest of influential members of the Royal Society, the London-based institution that was, from its foundation in 1660, crucial to the development of 'modern' scientific methodology. It is also the case that they were written in the face of competition from other people, notably John Adair the map-maker. Further, Martin was bound up with those networks of natural knowledge at that time centring upon Sir Robert Sibbald, the Geographer Royal for Scotland, who was using local informants' information to pull together a geographical description of Scotland as a whole. Martin was, then, both a local man, and, by the terms of his own day, a practising scientist with national connections.

Science at this time, or natural philosophy as it should more properly be called, was greatly dependent upon traveller's reports of unknown lands and peoples. What was geographically 'unknown' at this time did not simply mean distant places and strange peoples far away. It included 'the foreign' near at hand. The Highlands and Islands of Scotland were certainly unknown to most people, even to other Scots. Martin commented on just this point: 'Foreigners, sailing thro the Western Isles, have been tempted, from the sight of so many wild Hills... and fac'd with high Rocks, to imagine the Inhabitants, as well as the Places of their residence, are barbarous;... the like is suppos'd by many that live in the South of Scotland, who know no more of the Western Isles than the Natives of Italy.' To members of the Royal Society – men like Robert Boyle who had published guidelines in 1692 to travellers on the sorts of things they should comment upon, and, indeed, on the proper ways for a gentleman abroad to conduct himself in making such enquiries – Hebridean Scotland was indeed unknown. All knowledge about such places was welcome, especially if one could get a reliable and trustworthy reporter.

It is a mistake, then, either to treat Martin's works as just about the Outer Isles in the late seventeenth century, or as the beginning of an unchanging topographical tradition, or to see Martin as just a social writer without understanding something of this background as to why they were written, and for whom. Martin's accounts appear at a time of change in both the Gaelic world and of important developments in scientific enquiry in understanding the world as a whole; developments in which geographical description of the foreign and the strange even within one's own country played an important part.

Martin signals exactly this sense of the wider importance of local knowledge in the *Preface* to his 1698 St Kilda book.

> If we hear at any time a Description of some remote Corner in the Indies Cried in our Streets, we presently conclude we may have some Divertisement in Reading of it; when in the mean time, there are a Thousand things nearer us that may engage our Thoughts to better purposes, and the knowledge of which may serve more to promote our true Interest, and the History of Nature. It is a piece of weakness and folly merely to value things because of their distance from the place where we are Born: Thus Men have Travelled far enough in the search of Foreign Plants and Animals, and yet continue strangers to those produced in their own natural climate.

Understanding these issues in order better to read Martin's works in turn demands that we know something of the man himself.

Martin Martin is first clearly identifiable in source material in 1681 in graduating MA from Edinburgh. It is thought he was one of three brothers, at least two of whom were also graduates of Edinburgh. Martin's father, Donald Martin, son of Gille-Mhàrtainn, son of Aonghas na Gaoithe, soldiered with the Mac-Donalds of Sleat under the Duke of Montrose, and, later, was chamberlain of Trotternish in Skye. He married Màiri, the daughter of Alasdair, brother of Domhall Gorm Òg of Sleat in Skye. Martin was, therefore, a cousin to the clan chiefs of his day, both Dòmhnall Breac, who died in 1692 and Dòmhnall a' Chogaidh, who died in 1718. Between 1681 and 1686, Martin was also a tutor to the latter, and, from 1686 to 1695, he was tutor and governor to Ruaraidh Òg MacLeod of Harris. Most of this latter period was spent in Edinburgh where the young chief attended university.

The years between 1695 and 1703 were formative in shaping Martin's texts because it is in that period that he was clearly seen by others as the ideal man to undertake work on the then unknown Highlands. As Sibbald noted in a letter of 1699 to Sloane, Martin had all the qualifications one could want: 'He was borne in the Isle of Sky, was Gobernour to ye Chieffs of ye Clans in ys isles and heth yt interest and favour with them, they will doe for him what they will do for no other, yr [their] Language is his Mother Language, and he is well acquainted with yr Maners and customes and is the person here most capable to Serve the Royall Society in the accounts of what relateth to ye description of ys Isles.' Between 1703 and 1707, Martin moved between the Highlands and London, before, in early 1708, moving to London permanently. Shortly thereafter, he became tutor to the third son of the Earl of Bradford and with his charge toured Italy before Martin relocated to the Low Countries. Martin studied at Leyden for his MD and returned to London in 1710 where, for the rest of his life, he lived and practised as a doctor. He contracted asthma in the winter of 1717. Despite a period of recovery, he died on 9th October 1718 and was buried three days later in St Martin's-in-the-Fields in London.

This background is important. It shows Martin to have come from and moved within Gaelic elite groups themselves moving as soldiers, professional men and scholars within the upper ranks of contemporary society. These are people, Martin included, we should think of as British and European Gaels. Further, in being in Edinburgh for a decade after 1686, Martin met with men such as Sir Robert Sibbald, an important figure in Scotland's intellectual life and someone whose contacts included a wide range of antiquarians and natural philosophers, in Scotland and beyond. In 1682, Sibbald had begun a plan to undertake and publish in two volumes a geographical description or atlas of Scotland, the first volume to cover the nation's ancient traditions, the second Scotland's present geography and history, including natural history. Sibbald was largely dependent for his information upon local information, chiefly from parish ministers, but also from members of Scotland's gentry and nobility. The two-volume work was never published, but many manuscripts survive describing the geography, natural history and antiquities of parts of Scotland.

Amongst the manuscripts in Sibbald's keeping was Donald Monro's account of the Western Isles of Scotland, written in 1549, which lists the main features and products of most of the Hebrides, including the Isle of Man and Arran. Munro's description should be understood as an annotated local geography, or, to give it its proper name, a chorography or regional description. Regional and antiquarian descriptions of this sort were increasingly common in Britain from the second half of the sixteenth century, as both Sibbald and Martin recognised, and it is likely that this earlier topographical enumeration by Dean Monro, together with Sibbald's insistent organisation of his project from the early 1680s, prompted Martin's own works. Certainly, Martin's first work was a short manuscript 'Description of Sky' [Skye] for Sibbald's project.

A probable further prompt was Martin's need for a regular income, following the death of the young MacLeod chief in late June 1695. From August 1695, Martin travelled to Holland, perhaps to visit his brother and seek employment, and spent some time in London. There he met, amongst others, the antiquarian, natural historian and collector Hans Sloane, then Secretary of the Royal Society. It was under Sloane's patronage that Martin undertook both a tour of Lewis in 1696, and, more importantly, his trip to St Kilda in May 1697, which was to provide the crucial basis to his 1698 *Voyage*. It was with Sloane's guidance and support that Martin published his 'Several Observations in the North Islands of Scotland', in the Royal Society's *Philosophical Transactions* in October 1697. Martin briefly discusses there twelve items of natural lore and the natural history of the Hebrides, ranging from the seasonality of egg-laying amongst sea birds, Highland medicinal practices, the coincidence of respiratory disorders on St Kilda with the arrival of the estate chamberlain, and the transient blindness of a Harris man who lost and regained his sight with each new moon and was known locally as the 'Infallible Almanac'. This work was clearly based upon earlier travels in the area, not his St Kilda trip. Martin was also collecting natural products such as shells and minerals, both because they were unknown and because they might have a use value, an economic potential beyond being, simply, curious. As Charles Preston, later to be Professor of Botany at Edinburgh, noted of Martin in a letter to Hans Sloane in November 1697, Martin 'spares no pains in Collecting things'. In a letter of September 1697 to Sloane, Martin wrote how he had by then about 100 'Curiosities' from Skye for the Royal Society, 'and near the Same number of Natural Observations'.

In one sense, we can take Martin's own words on trust in outlining as he does the motives behind his St Kilda book. Martin sailed for St Kilda, from Harris, on 29 May 1697 at 6 o'clock in the evening. He notes in the *Preface* to the work that he was 'Prompted by Description of the island by the present steward, and the products of the Island, which were brought to me, together with a Natural Impulse of Curiosity, [which] form'd such an Idea of it in my Mind, that I determined to satisfy my self with the first Occasion I had of going further'. But Martin is not here telling the whole story. For in another sense, as the above has shown, Martin was being pushed to go by others, men like Sibbald, Sloane, Preston and others keen to know about the unknown Scotland. On at least one of his voyages, he was accompanied by John Adair, the mapmaker, who, since 1681, had been mapping Scotland. The two plainly did not get on: in a letter to Sloane, Sibbald notes how Adair treated Martin 'scurvily'. Martin's own background, the fact that he regularly travelled between the Highlands and the Lowlands, the fact that he knew Gaelic and that people elsewhere were prepared to support his work all meant that he carried both individual capacities and general hopes and interests into the area. His books are travel books. Yet to read them properly, we must understand how, in general terms, Martin himself travelled within and between two worlds – the Gaelic world into which he was born, and that wider world to which he aspired and which provided, in so many ways, the real motivation for writing them at all.

Martin makes much of what we might call his informants' 'native knowledge'. It is clear, for example, notably from his discussion of 'The Diseases Known and not Known in Skye' (pp. 123–144 here) that plant lore is widespread and that herbs and simples, often in combination with butter or fat taken from sea birds, are used to cure wounds and treat ailments. Ingesting the wrong things could, of course, be bothersome, as Martin recounts of the Talisker man, Fergus Caird, who became ill through eating hemlock root rather than the white wild carrot. Local information – the native voice, as it were – is often accompanied by our hearing Martin's 'other voice', that of the scientist-cum-traveller who knows that his audience lies beyond the Hebrides. Martin shows us his own learning – he alludes to his having read John Locke, for example, and he incorporates others' notes in places, and makes mention of men like James Sutherland, then the Keeper of the Botanic Garden in Edinburgh – as he also places knowledge of the Hebrides on a comparable footing with knowledge of other places. In general, the picture we are given is of a society that values and understands the natural world even if, in properly scientific terms, it is not always understood why things have the effect they do. Local names are given to sea birds and, in one important sense, of course, notably on St Kilda, the locals are heavily reliant upon birds' eggs for their food. We should not, however, see the knowledge of Hebrideans or St Kildans as some sort of intuitive and innate Gaelic 'folk' knowledge: it is, rather, an intimate knowledge of nature and of the local environment that comes from being dependent upon one's natural resources.

In his 1703 *Description* in particular, Martin is concerned with the future condition of the Highlands and Islands as well as with the present state of life there and with past beliefs. His language and general tone is nowhere near as economistic as later commentators, but we underplay the work's significance if we do not also recognise the concern for improvement that runs through it. Martin's attention to the mineralogical wealth of Skye, for example, is both a description of what is there and, in outline terms, a rough catalogue of its future potential. Isolation from others – both geographically and, he hints, because of language – has meant that the natural advantages of the Hebrides' rich fish resources have not been fully utilised. 'The north-west isles are of all others most capable of improvement by sea and land [he writes]; yet by reason of their distance from trading towns, and because of their langauge, which is Irish [Gaelic], the inhabitants have never had any opportunity to trade at home or abroad, or to acquire mechanical arts and other science: so that they are still left to act by the force of their natural genius, and what they could learn by observation'. Neither Martin nor any of his contemporaries could possibly have foreseen, of course, the wholesale break-up of Highland life a century or so later, but his 1703 work is of all the more interest in giving us as it does an optimistic vision for a future that never was.

The greater part of these two books is taken up with the beliefs and practices of ordinary people: with diet, how many gull's eggs were caught in a day, with the dangers of collecting eggs, with songs, customs and superstitions. The fact that this is an unlettered knowledge is not important, at least to the islanders themselves. As Martin noted, 'The inhabitants of these islands do for the most part labour under the want of knowledge of letters and other useful arts and sciences; notwithstanding which defect, they seem to be better versed in the book of nature than many that have greater opportunities for improvement'. Nature and the natural world is being interpreted differently and we are afforded valuable insight into how people in the islands used natural portents and Nature's rhythms to make sense of their lives. In that regard, the belief of the inhabitants of Rona off Lewis, for example, that the cuckoo is heard there only upon the death of the Earl of Seaforth or of the local minister, or the St Kildans' belief that the cuckoo is seen only upon 'extraordinary occasions, such as the death, or the arrival of some notable stranger' is not a matter of humour – although Martin certainly found the latter laughable and was chastised for his reaction – but of our recognising now that natural knowledge then very closely influenced ordinary social conduct. Nowhere is this clearer than in his discussion of second sight, the place of prophecy and, loosely, fortune-telling from natural events. Martin's account of second sight – pp. 195–216 – what he termed the 'singular faculty of seeing an otherwise invisible object, without any previous means used by the person that sees it for that end', should be seen as a serious piece of scientific commentary. In the 'question and answer' format of his enquiry, Martin is effectively conducting a conversation with contemporary natural philosophers. What is important here is not our ability to explain the phenomena, but recognition that it happens, and, crucially, that it is believed in, by Hebrideans and by others. 'These accounts' [Martin tells us] 'I had from persons of as great integrity as any are in the world.'

His accounts do not easily separate, then, the natural from the social, and neither do they clearly distinguish between the facts of everyday life and the beliefs that sustain that life. His writings do not clearly conform to a strict order: neither the 1703

Description nor the 1698 *Voyage* can properly be termed a narrative. Yet it is just that rather hurried style, the way that Martin Martin moves from one topic to another in an almost breathless way that gives his books both an importance and an immediacy. We read things in much the jumbled way Martin collected them: as he was presented with information by locals, as he observed things for himself, as he moved between islands collecting, recording and asking what was of interest to know and why. What we should not forget, however, is for whom Martin was writing. Martin's attention to descriptions of islands, to solan geese, his comments upon local belief in natural portents and ancient monuments like 'Callerniss' as he terms it, is all new and valuable knowledge for those then seeking to know about the world. To us, his texts are, as it were, both geographically limited and a window upon a largely vanished world. To his audiences in Edinburgh and London and elsewhere, Martin's books were up-to-date scientific contributions, albeit that his emphasis upon the local and 'curious' meant that his reports might not always be easily understood by those who read them.

In doing these things, in describing Hebrideans' natural knowledge and in documenting the customs by which they lived and managed their lives, Martin faced the problem of many other travellers and reporters at this time, namely, how to trust what he is told by others, and, importantly, how to get others to take seriously what is, essentially, the knowledge of 'the vulgar sort'. Martin at one point calls them 'the credulous vulgar'. Martin is unusual, of course, as geographical author and as Highlander in being of the culture and society he writes about. Unlike many other natural philosophers keen to establish their reputation through working in unknown lands and reporting upon them, Martin does not have to translate what he is told, although, of course, he has to for his audiences. Indeed, in order to convince distant readers of the credibility of his own narratives and, thus, of the native knowledge on which they are based, Martin has to represent Gaelic as a legitimate language through which to assess Nature and conduct geographical enquiry. Martin Martin, in short, had to establish credibility: his own, that of Highlanders themselves, and importantly, of the accounts he gives of them. It is for this reason that he writes as he does in the *Preface* to his 1698 St Kilda work – a book dedicated, it should be noted, to Charles Montague, then President of the Royal Society:

> There is nothing related to the following Account, but what he vouches to be true, either from his own harmonious Testimony that was given him by the inhabitants; and they are a sort of People so Plain, and so little inclined to Impose upon Mankind, that perhaps no place in the World at this day, knows such Instances of true primitive Honor and Simplicity; a People who abhor lying tricks and Artifices, as they do the most poisonous Plants or devouring Animals.

In these terms, whilst Martin Martin was of the local world he writes so compellingly about, his 1698 *Voyage to St Kilda* and his 1703 *Description of the Western Isles of Scotland* were used by him as a warrant to secure acceptance in that more distant English-speaking and gentlemanly world of London's Royal Society. Yet it is precisely because Martin took seriously questions of reliability – his own and that of his informants – that we should treat his books with a similar seriousness and with a sensitivity to their time and not read them, as did Johnson, by the standards of another age.

I

The Isle of Lewis

<hr>

THE island of Lewis is so called from *leog*, which in the Irish language signifies water, lying on the surface of the ground; which is very proper to this island, because of the great number of freshwater lakes that abound in it. The isle of Lewis is by all strangers and seafaring men accounted the outmost tract of islands lying to the north-west of Scotland. It is divided by several narrow channels, and distinguished by several proprietors as well as by several names: by the islanders it is commonly called, the Long Island; being from south to north 100 miles in length, and from east to west from three to fourteen in breadth. It lies in the shire of Ross, and made part of the diocese of the Isles.

The isle of Lewis, properly and strictly so called, is thirty-six miles in length; viz., from the north point of Bowling-head to the south point of Hussiness in Harris; and in some places it is ten, and in others twelve miles in breadth. The air is temperately cold and moist, and for a corrective the natives use a dose of *trestarig* or *usquebaugh*. This island is for the most part healthy, especially in the middle from south to north. It is arable on the west side, for about sixteen miles on the coast; it is likewise plain and arable in several places on the east. The soil is generally sandy, excepting the heaths, which in some places are black, and in others a fine red clay; as appears by the many vessels made of it by their women; some for boiling meat, and others for preserving their ale, for which they are much better than barrels of wood. This island was reputed very fruitful in corn, until the late years of scarcity and bad seasons. The corn sown here is barley, oats, and rye; and they have also flax and hemp. The best increase is commonly from the ground manured with sea-ware: they fatten it also with soot; but it is observed the bread made of corn growing in the ground so fattened, occasions the jaundice to those that eat it. They observe likewise that corn produced in ground which was never tilled before, occasions several disorders in those who eat the bread, or drink the ale made of that corn; such as the headache and vomiting.

The natives are very industrious, and undergo a great fatigue by digging the ground with spades, and in most places they turn the ground so digged upside down, and cover it with sea-ware; and in this manner there are about 500 people employed daily for some months. This way of labouring is by them called *timiy*; and certainly produces a greater increase than digging or ploughing otherwise. They have little harrows with wooden teeth in the first and second rows, which break the ground; and in the third row they have rough heath, which smooths it. This light harrow is drawn by a man having a strong rope of horsehair across his breast.

Their plenty of corn was such, as disposed the natives to brew several sorts of liquors, as common *usquebaugh*, another called *trestarig*, id est, aqua vitae, three times distilled, which is strong and hot; a third sort is four times distilled, and this by the natives is called *usquebaugh-baul*, id est, *usquebaugh*, which at first taste affects all the members of the body: two spoonfulls of this last liquor is a sufficient dose; and if any man exceed this, it would presently stop his breath, and endanger his life. The *trestarig* and *usquebaugh-baul* are both made of oats.

There are several convenient bays and harbours in this island. Loch Grace and Loch Tua lying north-west, are not to be reckoned such; though vessels are forced in there sometimes by storm. Loch Stornvay lies on the east side in the middle of the island, and is eighteen miles directly south from the northernmost point of the same. It is a harbour well known by seamen. There are several places for anchoring about half a league on the south of this coast. About seven miles southward there is a good harbour, called the Birkin Isles; within the bay called Loch Colmkill, three miles further south, lies Loch Erisort, which hath an anchoring-place on the south and north: about five miles south lies Loch Seafort, having two visible rocks in the entry; the best harbour is on the south side.

About twenty-four miles south-west lies Loch Carlvay, a very capacious, though unknown harbour, being never frequented by any vessels: though the natives assure me that it is in all respects a convenient harbour for ships of the first rate. The best entrance looks north and north-west, but there is another from the west. On the south side of the island Bernera, there are small islands without the entrance, which contribute much to the security of the harbour by breaking the winds and seas that come from the great ocean. Four miles to the south on this coast is Loch Rogue, which runs in among the mountains. All the coasts and bays above mentioned, do in fair weather abound with cod, ling, herring, and all other sorts of fishes taken in the Western Islands.

Cod and ling are of a very large size, and very plentiful near Loch Carlvay; but the whales very much interrupt the fishing in this place. There is one sort of whale remarkable for its greatness, which the fishermen distinguish from all others by the name of the gallan whale; because they never see it but at the promontory of that name. I was told by the natives, that about fifteen years ago, this great whale overturned a fisher's boat, and devoured three of the crew; the fourth man was saved by another boat which happened to be near and saw this accident. There are many whales of different sizes, that frequent the herring bays on the east side: the natives employ many boats together in pursuit of the whales, chasing them up into the bays, till they wound one of them mortally, and then it runs ashore; and they say that all the rest commonly follow the track of its blood, and run themselves also on shore in like manner by which means many of them are killed. About five years ago there were fifty young whales killed in this manner, and most of them eaten by the common people, who by experience find them to be very nourishing food. This I have been assured of by several persons, but particularly by some poor meagre people, who became plump and lusty by this food in the space of a week: they call it seapork, for so it signifies in their language. The bigger whales are more purgative than these lesser ones, but the latter are better for nourishment.

The bays afford plenty of shellfish, as clams, oysters, cockles, mussels, limpets, whelks, spout-fish; of which last there is such a prodigous quantity cast up out of the sand of Loch Tua, that their noisome smell infects the air, and makes it very unhealthful to the inhabitants, who are not able to consume them, by eating or fattening their ground with them: and this they say happens most commonly once in seven years.

The bays and coasts of this island afford great quantity of small coral, not exceeding six inches in length, and about the bigness of a goose's quill. This abounds most in Loch Seafort, and there is coraline likewise on this coast.

There are a great many freshwater lakes in this island, which abound with trouts and eels. The common bait used for catching them is earthworms, but a handful of parboiled mussels thrown into the water attracts the trouts and eels to the place; the fittest time for catching them is when the wind blows from the south-west. There are several rivers on each side this island which afford salmons, as also black mussels, in which many times pearl is found.

The natives in the village Barvas retain an ancient custom of sending a man very early to cross Barvas river, every first day of May, to prevent any female crossing it first; for that they say would hinder the salmon from coming into the river all the year round; they pretend to have learned this from a foreign sailor, who was shipwrecked upon that coast a long time ago. This observation they maintain to be true from experience.

There are several springs and fountains of curious effects; such as that at Loch Carlvay, that never whitens linen, which hath often been tried by the inhabitants. The well at St Cowsten's Church never boils any kind of meat, though it be kept on fire a whole day. St Andrew's Well, in the village Shader, is by the vulgar natives made a test to know if a sick person will die of the distemper he labours under. They send one with a wooden dish to bring some of the water to the patient, and if the dish, which is then laid softly upon the surface of the water, turn round sun-ways, they conclude that the patient will recover of that distemper, but if otherwise, that he will die.

There are many caves on the coast of this island, in which great numbers of otters and seals do lie; there be also many land and sea-fowls, that build and hatch in them. The cave in Loch Grace hath several pieces of a hard substance in the bottom, which distil from the top of it. There are several natural and artificial forts on the coast of this island, which are called *dun,* from the Irish word *dain,* which signifies a fort. The natural forts here are Dun-owle, Duncoradil, Dun-eisten.

The castle at Stornvay village was destroyed by the English garrison, kept there by Oliver Cromwell. Some few miles to the north of Brago there is a fort composed of large stones; it is of a round form, made taperwise towards the top, and is three storeys high: the wall is double, and hath several doors and stairs, so that one may go round within the wall. There are some cairns, or heaps of stones, gathered together on heaths, and some of them at a great distance from any ground that affords stones, such as Cairnwarp, near Mournagh Hill, etc. These artificial forts are likewise built upon heaths, at a considerable distance also from stony ground. The Thrusel Stone, in the parish of Barvas, is above twenty feet high, and almost as much in breadth. There are three erected stones upon the north side of Loch Carlvay, about twelve feet high each. Several other stones are to be seen here in remote places, and some of them standing on one end. Some of the ignorant vulgar say, they were men by enchantment turned into stones; and others say, they are monuments of persons of note killed in battle.

The most remarkable stones for number, bigness, and order, that fell under my observation, were at the village of Classerniss, where there are thirty-nine stones set up six or seven feet high, and two feet in breadth each. They are placed in form of an avenue, the breadth of which is eight feet, and the distance between each stone six; and there is a stone set up in the entrance of this avenue. At the south end there is joined to this range of stone a circle of twelve stones of equal distance and height with the other thirty-nine. There is one set up in the centre of this circle, which is thirteen feet high, and shaped like the rudder of a ship: without this circle there are four stones standing to the west, at the same distance with the stones in the circle; and there are four stones set up in the same manner at the south and east sides. I enquired of the inhabitants what tradition they had from their ancestors concerning those stones; and they told me, it was a place appointed for worship in the time of heathenism, and that the chief druid or priest stood near the big stone in the centre, from whence he addressed himself to the people that surrounded him.

Upon the same coast also there is a circle of high stones standing on one end, about a quarter of a mile's distance from those above-mentioned.

The shore in Egginess abounds with many little smooth stones prettily variegated with all sorts of colours; they are of a round form, which is probably occasioned by the tossing of the sea, which in those parts is very violent.

The cattle produced here are cows, horses, sheep, goats, hogs. These cows are little, but very fruitful, and their beef very sweet and tender. The horses are considerably less here, than in the opposite continent, yet they plough and harrow as well as bigger horses, though in the springtime they have nothing to feed upon but sea-ware. There are abundance of deer in the Chase of Oservaul, which is fifteen miles in compass, consisting in mountains, and valleys between them: this affords good pasturage for

The Form of ye Heathen Temple

the deer, black cattle, and sheep. This forest, for so they call it, is surrounded with the sea, except about one mile upon the west side: the deer are forced to feed on sea-ware, when the snow and frost continue long, having no wood to shelter in, and so are exposed to the rigour of the season.

I saw big roots of trees at the head of Loch Erisort, and there is about a hundred young birch and hazel trees on the south-west side of Loch Stornvay, but there is no more wood in the island. There is great variety of land and sea-fowls to be seen in this and the lesser adjacent islands.

The amphibia here are seals and otters; the former are eaten by the vulgar, who find them to be as nourishing as beef and mutton.

The inhabitants of this island are well proportioned, free from any bodily imperfections, and of a good stature: the colour of their hair is commonly a light brown, or red, but few of them are black. They are a healthful and strong-bodied people, several arrive to a great age. Mr Daniel Morison, late minister of Barvas, one of my acquaintance, died lately in his eighty-sixth year.

They are generally of a sanguine constitution: this place hath not been troubled with epidemical diseases, except the smallpox, which comes but seldom, and then it sweeps away many young people. The chincough afflicts children too: the fever, diarrhoea, dysentery, and the falling down of the uvula, fevers, jaundice and stitches, and the ordinary coughs proceeding from cold are the diseases most prevalent here. The common cure used for removing fevers and pleurisies, is to let blood plentifully. For curing the diarrhoea and dysentery, they take small quantities of the kernel of the black Molucca beans, called by them *crospunk;* and this being ground into powder, and drunk in boiled milk, is by daily experience found to be very effectual. They likewise use a little dose of *trestarig* water with good success. When the cough affects them, they drink *brochan* plentifully, which is oatmeal and water boiled together, to which they sometimes add butter. This drink used at going to bed, disposeth one to sleep and sweat, and is very diuretic if it hath no salt in it. They use also the roots of nettles, and the roots of reeds boiled in water and add yeast to it, which provokes it to ferment; and this they find also beneficial for the cough. When the uvula falls down, they ordinarily cut it, in this manner – they take a long quill, and putting a horsehair double into it, make a noose at the end of the quill, and putting it about the lower end of the uvula, they cut off from the uvula all that is below the hair with a pair of scissors; and then the patient swallows a little bread and cheese, which cured him. This operation is not attended with the least inconvenience, and cures the distemper so that it never returns. They cure green wounds with ointment made of golden-rod, all-heal, and fresh butter. The jaundice they cure two ways – the first is by laying the patient on his face, and pretending to look upon his back bones, they presently pour a pale full of cold water on his bare back; and this proves successful. The second cure they perform by taking the tongs, and making them red hot in the fire; then pulling off the clothes from the patient's back, he who holds the tongs gently touches the patient on the vertebrae upwards of the back, which makes him furiously run out of doors, still supposing the hot iron is on his back, until the pain be abated, which happens very speedily, and the patient recovers soon after. Donald Chuan, in a village near Bragir, in the parish of Barvas, had by accident cut his toe at the change of the moon, and it bleeds a fresh drop at every change of the moon ever since.

Anna, daughter to George, in the village of Melbost, in the parish of Ey, having been with child, and the ordinary time of her delivery being expired, the child made its passage by the fundament for some years, coming away bone after bone. She lived several years after this, but never had any more children. Some of the natives, both of the island of Lewis and Harris, who conversed with her at the time when this extraordinary thing happened, gave me this account.

The natives are generally ingenious and quick of apprehension; they have a mechanical genius, and several of both sexes have a gift of poesy, and are able to form a satire or panegyric extempore, without the assistance of any stronger liquor than water to raise their fancy. They are great lovers of music; and when I was there they gave an account of eighteen men who could play on the violin pretty well without being taught: they are still very hospitable, but the late years of scarcity brought them very low, and many of the poor people have died by famine. The inhabitants are very dexterous in the exercises of swimming, archery, vaulting, or leaping, and are very stout and able seamen; they will tug at the oar all day long upon bread and water, and a snush of tobacco.

II

Of the Inferior Adjacent Islands

<hr/>

Without the mouth of Loch Carlvay lies the small island Garve; it is a high rock, about half a mile in compass, and fit only for pasturage. Not far from this lies the island Berinsay, which is a quarter of a mile in compass, naturally a strong fort, and formerly used as such, being almost inaccessible.

The island Fladda, which is of small compass, lies between Berinsay and the mainland. Within these lies the island called Bernera Minor, two miles in length, and fruitful in corn and grass. Within this island, in the middle of Loch Carlvay, lies the island Bernera Major, being four miles in length, and as much in breadth. It is fruitful also in corn and grass, and hath four villages. Alexander MackLenan, who lives in Bernera Major, told me that some years ago a very extraordinary ebb happened there, exceeding any that had been seen before or since; it happened about the vernal equinox, the sea retired so far as to discover a stone wall, the length of it being about forty yards, and in some parts about five, six or seven feet high. They suppose much more of it to be under water: it lies opposite to the west side of Lewis, to which it adjoins. He says that it is regularly built, and without all doubt the effect of human industry. The natives had no tradition about this piece of work, so that I can form no other conjecture about it, but that it has probably been erected for a defence against the sea, or for the use of fishermen, but came in time to be overflowed. Near to both Berneras lie the small islands of Kialisay, Cavay, Carvay, and Grenim.

Near to the north-west promontory of Carlvay Bay, called Galen-head, are the little islands of Pabbay, Shirem, Vacksay, Wuya, the Great and Lesser. To the north-west of Galen-head, and within six leagues of it, lie the Flannan Islands, which the sea-men call north-hunters; they are but small islands, and six in number, and maintain about seventy sheep yearly. The inhabitants of the adjacent lands of the Lewis, having a right to these islands, visit them once every summer, and there make a great purchase of fowls, eggs, down, feathers, and quills. When they go to sea, they have their boat well manned, and make towards the islands with an east wind; but if before or at landing the wind turn westerly, they hoist up sail, and steer directly home again. If any of their crew is a novice, and not versed in the customs of the place, he must be instructed perfectly in all the punctilioes observed here before landing; and to prevent inconveniences that they think may ensue upon the transgression of the least nicety observed here, every novice is always joined with another, that can instruct him all the time of their fowling: so all the boat's crew are matched in this manner. After their landing, they fasten the boat to the sides of a rock, and then fix a wooden ladder by laying a stone at the foot of it, to prevent its falling into the sea; and when they are got up into the island, all of them uncover their heads, and make a turn sunways round, thanking God for their safety. The first injunction given after landing, is not to ease nature in that place where the boat lies, for that they reckon a crime of the highest nature, and of dangerous consequence to all their crew; for they have a great regard to that very piece of rock upon which they first set their feet, after escaping the danger of the ocean.

The biggest of these islands is called Island More; it has the ruins of a chapel dedicated to St Flannan, from whom the island derives its name. When they are come within about twenty paces of the altar, they all strip themselves of their upper garments at once; and their upper clothes being laid upon a stone, which stands there on purpose for that use, all the crew pray three times before they begin fowling: the first day they say the first prayer, advancing towards the chapel upon their knees; the second prayer is said as they go round the chapel; the third is said hard by or at the chapel; and this is their morning service. Their vespers are performed with the like number of prayers. Another rule is that it is absolutely unlawful to kill a fowl with a stone, for that they reckon a great barbarity, and directly contrary to ancient custom.

It is also unlawful to kill a fowl before they ascend by the ladder. It is absolutely unlawful to call the island of St Kilda (which lies thirty leagues southward) by its proper Irish name Hirt, but only The High Country. They must not so much as once name the islands in which they are following by the ordinary name Flannan, but only The Country. There are several other things that must not be called by their common names, e.g., *visk,* which in the language of the natives signifies water, they call *burn*; a rock, which in their language is *creg,* must here be called *cruey,* i.e. 'hard'; 'shore' in their language, expressed by *claddach,* must here be called *vah,* i.e. a 'cave'; 'sour' in their language as expressed *gort*, but must be here called *gaire,* i.e. 'sharp'; 'slippery', which is expressed *bog,* must be called *soft*; and several other things to this purpose. They account it also unlawful to kill a fowl after evening prayers. There is an ancient custom by which the crew is obliged not to carry home any sheep suet, let them kill ever so many sheep in these islands. One of their principal customs is not to steal or eat anything unknown to their partner, else the transgressor (they say) will certainly vomit it up; which they reckon as a just judgment. When they have loaded their boat sufficiently with sheep, fowls, eggs, down, fish, etc., they make the best of their way homeward. It is observed of the sheep of these islands that they are exceeding fat, and have long horns.

I had this superstitious account not only from several of the natives of the Lewis, but likewise from two who had been in the Flannan islands the preceding year. I asked one of them if he prayed at home as often, and as fervently as he did when in the

Flannan Islands, and he plainly confessed to me that he did not: adding further, that these remote islands were places of inherent sanctity; and that there was none ever yet landed in them but found himself more disposed to devotion there, than anywhere else. The Island of Pigmies, or, as the natives call it, the Island of Little Men, is but of small extent. There has been many small bones dug out of the ground here, resembling those of human kind more than any other. This gave ground to a tradition which the natives have of a very low-statured people living once here, called *lusbirdan*, i.e., pigmies.

The island of Rona is reckoned about twenty leagues from the north-east point of Ness in Lewis, and counted but a mile in length, and about half a mile in breadth: it hath a hill in the west part, and is only visible from the Lewis in a fair summer's day. I had an account of this little island, and the custom of it, from several natives of Lewis, who had been upon the place; but more particularly from Mr Daniel Morison, minister of Barvas, after his return from Rona island, which then belonged to him, as part of his glebe.

Upon my landing [says he] the natives received me very affectionately, and addressed me with their usual salutation to a stranger: 'God save you, pilgrim, you are heartily welcome here; for we have had repeated apparitions of your person among us [after the manner of the second sight], and we heartily congratulate your arrival in this our remote country.' One of the natives would needs express his high esteem for my person, by making a turn round about me sunways, and at the same time blessing me, and wishing me all happiness; but I bid him let alone that piece of homage, telling him I was sensible of his good meaning towards me: but this poor man was not a little disappointed, as were also his neighbours; for they doubted not but this ancient ceremony would have been very acceptable to me; and one of them told me, that this was a thing due to my character from them, as to their chief and patron, and they could not, nor would not fail to perform it. They conducted me to the little village where they dwell, and in the way thither there were three enclosures; and as I entered each of these, the inhabitants severally saluted me, taking me by the hand, and saying, 'Traveller, you are welcome here.' They went along with me to the house that they had assigned for my lodging; where there was a bundle of straw laid on the floor, for a seat for me to sit upon. After a little time was spent in general discourse, the inhabitants retired to their respective dwelling-houses; and in this interval, they killed each man a sheep, being in all five, answerable to the number of their families. The skins of the sheep were entire, and flayed off so from the neck to the tail, that they were in form like a sack. These skins being flayed off after this manner, were by the inhabitants instantly filled with barley-meal; and this they gave me by way of a present; one of their number acted as speaker for the rest saying, 'Traveller, we are very sensible of the favour you have done us in coming so far with a design to instruct us in our way to happiness, and at the same time to venture yourself on the great ocean; pray be pleased to accept of this small present, which we humbly offer as an expression of our sincere love to you.' This I accepted, though in a very coarse dress; but it was given with such an air of hospitality and goodwill as deserved thanks. They presented my man also with some pecks of meal, as being likewise a traveller, the boat's crew having been in Rona before, were not reckoned strangers, and therefore there was no present given them, but their daily maintenance.

There is a chapel here dedicated to St Ronan, fenced with a stone wall round it; and they take care to keep it neat and clean, and sweep it every day. There is an altar in it, on which there lies a big plank of wood about ten feet in length; every foot has a hole in it, and in every hole a stone, to which the natives ascribe several virtues: one of them is singular as they say, for promoting speedy delivery to a woman in travail.

They repeat the Lord's Prayer, Creed, and Ten Commandments in the chapel every Sunday morning. They have cows, sheep, barley and oats, and live a harmless life, being perfectly ignorant of most of those vices that abound in the world. They know nothing of money or gold, having no occasion for either, they neither sell nor buy, but covet no wealth, being fully content and satisfied with food and raiment; though at the same time they are very precise in the matter of property among themselves; for none of them will by any means allow his neighbour to fish within his property; and every one must exactly observe not to make any encroachment on his neighbour. They have an agreeable and hospitable temper for all strangers; they concern not themselves about the rest of mankind, except the inhabitants in the north part of Lewis. They take their surname from the colour of the sky, rainbow, and clouds. There are only five families in this small island, and every tenant hath his dwelling-house, a barn, a house where their best effects are preserved, a house for their cattle, and a porch on each side of the door to keep off the rain or snow. Their houses are built with stone, and thatched with straw, which is kept down with ropes of the same, posed with stones. They were the same habit with those in Lewis, and speak only Irish. When any of them comes to the Lewis, which is seldom, they are astonished to see so many people. They much admire greyhounds, and are mightily pleased at the sight of horses; and one of them observing a horse to neigh, asked if that horse laughed at him. A boy from Rona perceiving a colt run towards him, was so much frighted at it, that he jumped into a bush of nettles, where his whole skin became full of blisters.

Another of the natives of Rona having had the opportunity of travelling as far as Coul, in the shire of Ross, which is the seat of Sir Alexander Mackenzie, everything he saw there was surprising to him; and when he heard the noise of those who walked in the rooms above him he presently fell to the ground, thinking thereby to save his life, for he supposed that the house was coming down over his head. When Mr Morison, the minister, was in Rona, two of the natives courted a maid with intention to marry her, and being married to one of them afterwards, the other was not a little disappointed, because there was no other match for him in this island. The wind blowing fair, Mr Morison sailed directly to Lewis; but after three hours' sailing was forced back to Rona by a contrary wind: and at his landing, the poor man that had lost his sweetheart was overjoyed, and expressed himself in these words: 'I bless God and Ronan that you are returned again, for I hope you will now make me happy, and give me a right to enjoy the woman every other year by turns, that so we both may have issue by her.' Mr Morison could not refrain from smiling at this unexpected request, chid the poor man for his unreasonable demand, and desired him to have patience for a year longer and he would send him a wife from Lewis, but this did not ease the poor man, who was tormented by the thoughts of dying without issue.

Another who wanted a wife, and having got a shilling from a seaman that happened to land there, went and gave this shilling to Mr Morison, to purchase him a wife in the Lewis, and send her to him, for he was told that this piece of money was a thing of extraordinary value; and his desire was gratified the ensuing year.

About fourteen years ago a swarm of rats, but none knows how, came into Rona, and in a short time ate up all the corn in the island. In a few months after, some seamen landed there, who robbed the poor people of their bull. These misfortunes, and the want of supply from Lewis for the space of a year, occasioned the death of all that ancient race of people. The steward of St Kilda being by a storm driven there, told me that he found a woman with her child on her breast, both lying dead at the side of a rock. Some years after, the minister (to whom the island belongeth) sent a new colony to this island, with suitable supplies. The following year a boat was sent by him with some more supplies, and orders to receive the rents; but the boat being lost, as it is supposed, I can give no further account of this late plantation.

The inhabitants of this little island say, that the cuckoo is never seen or heard here, but after the death of the Earl of Seaforth, or the minister.

The rock Soulisker lieth four leagues to the east of Rona; it is a quarter of a mile in circumference, and abounds with great numbers of sea-fowl, such as solan geese, guillemot, coulterneb, puffin, and several other sorts. The fowl called the colk is found here: it is less than a goose, all covered with down, and when it hatches it casts its feathers, which are of divers colours; it has a tuft on its head resembling that of a peacock, and a train longer than that of a house-cock, but the hen has not much ornament and beauty.

The island Siant, or, as the natives call it, Island More, lies to the east of Ushiness in Lewis, about a league. There are three small islands here; the two southern islands are separated only by springtides, and are two miles in circumference. Island More hath a chapel in it dedicated to the Virgin Mary, and is fruitful in corn and grass; the island joining to it on the west is only for pasturage. I saw a couple of eagles here: the natives told me that these eagles would never suffer any of their kind to live there but themselves, and that they drove away their young ones as soon as they were able to fly. And they told me likewise, that those eagles are so careful of the place of their abode, that they never yet killed any sheep or lamb in the island, though the bones of lambs, of fawns, and wildfowls, are frequently found in and about their nests; so that they make their purchase in the opposite islands, the nearest of which is a league distant. This island is very strong and inaccessible, save on one side where the ascent is narrow, and somewhat resembling a stair, but a great deal more high and steep; notwithstanding which the cows pass and repass by it safely, though one would think it uneasy for a man to climb. About a musket-shot farther north lies the biggest of the islands called More, being two miles in circumference; it is fruitful in corn and pasturage, the cows here are much fatter than any I saw in the island of Lewis. There is a blue stone in the surface of the ground here, moist while it lies there, but when dry, it becomes very hard; it is capable of any impression, and I have seen a set of tablemen made of this stone, prettily carved with different figures. There is a promontory in the north end of the island of Lewis, called Eoropy Point, which is supposed to be the farthest to north-west of any part in Europe.

These islands are divided into two parishes, one called Barvas, and the other Ey or Y; both which are parsonages, and each of them having a minister. The names of the churches in Lewis isles, and the saints to whom they were dedicated, are St Columkil, in the island of that name; St Pharaer in Kaerness, St Lennan in Sternvay, St Collum in Ey, St Cutchon in Garbost, St Aula in Grease, St Michael in Tollosta, St Collum in Garien, St Ronan in Eurobie, St Thomas in Habost, St Peter in Shanabost, St Clemen in Dell, Holy Cross Church in Galan, St Brigit in Barove, St Peter in Shiadir, St Mary in Barvas, St John Baptist in Bragar, St Marcel in Kirkibost, St Dondan in Little Berneray, St Michael in the same island, St Peter in Pabbay Island, St Christopher's Chapel in Uge, and Stornvay Church; all these churches and chapels were, before the Reformation, sanctuaries; and if a man had committed murder, he was then secure and safe when once within their precincts.

They were in greater veneration in those days than now: it was the constant practice of the natives to kneel at first sight of the church, though at a great distance from them, and then they said their Paternoster. John Morison of Bragir told me that when he was a boy, and going to the church of St Malvay, he observed the natives to kneel and repeat the Paternoster at four miles' distance from the church. The inhabitants of this island had an ancient custom to sacrifice to a sea god called Shony, at Hallowtide, in the manner following: The inhabitants round the island came to the church of St Malvay, having each man his provision along with him; every family furnished a peck of malt, and this was brewed into ale; one of their number was picked out to wade into the sea up to the middle, and carrying a cup of ale in his hand, standing still in that posture, cried out with a loud voice saying, 'Shony, I give you this cup of ale, hoping that you'll be so kind as to send us plenty of sea-ware for enriching our ground for the ensuing year'; and so threw the cup of ale into the sea. This was performed in the night-ime. At his return to land they all went to church, where there was a candle burning upon the altar, and then standing silent for a little time, one of them gave a signal, at which the candle was put out, and immediately all of them went to the fields, were they fell a-drinking their ale, and spent the remainder of the night in dancing and singing, etc.

The next morning they all returned home, being well satisfied that they had punctually observed this solemn anniversary, which they believed to be a powerful means to procure a plentiful crop. Mr Daniel and Mr Kenneth Morison, ministers in Lewis, told me they spent several years before they could persuade the vulgar natives to abandon this ridiculous piece of superstition; which is quite abolished for these thirty-two years past.

The inhabitants are all Protestants except one family, who are Roman Catholics. I was told that about fourteen years ago, three or four fishermen who then forsook the protestant communion, and embraced the Romish faith, having the opportunity of a popish priest on the place, they applied themselves to him for some of the holy water, it being usual for the priests to sprinkle it into the bays, as an infalliible means to procure plenty of herring, as also to bring them into those nets that are besprinkled with it. These fishers accordingly having got the water, poured it upon their nets before they dropped them into the sea; they likewise turned the inside of their coats outwards, after which they set their nets in the evening at the usual hour. The protestant fishers, who used no other means than throwing their nets into the sea, at the same time were unconcerned; but the papists being impatient and full of expectation, got next morning betimes to draw their nets, and being come to the place, they soon perceived that all their nets were lost; but the protestants found their nets safe, and full of herring: which was no small mortification to the priest and his proselytes, and exposed them to the derision of their neighbours.

The protestant natives observe the festivals of Christmas, Good Friday, Easter, and Michaelmas; upon this last they have an anniversary cavalcade, and then both sexes ride on horseback.

There is a village called Stornvay, at the head of the bay of that name; it consists of about sixty families; there are some houses of entertainment in it, as also a church and a school, in which Latin and English are taught. The steward of the Lewis hath his residence in this village. The Lewis, which was possessed by Macleod of Lewis for several centuries is, since the reign of King James VI, become the property of the Earl of Seaforth, who still enjoys it.

III

The Isle of Harris

———◆———

THE Harris being separated from Lewis is eighteen miles, from the Hushiness on the West Ocean to Loch Seafort in the east; from this bounding to the Point of Strond in the south of Harris, it is twenty-four miles; and in some places four, five and six miles in breadth. The soil is almost the same with that of Lewis, and it produces the same sorts of corn, but a greater increase.

The air is temperately cold, and the natives endeavour to qualify it by taking a dose of aquavitae, or brandy; for they brew no such liquors as *trestarig,* or *usquebaugh-baul.* The eastern coast of Harris is generally rocky and mountainous, covered with grass and heath. The west side is for the most part arable on the seacoast; some parts of the hills on the east side are naked without earth. The soil being dry and sandy, is fruitful when manured with sea-ware. The grass on the west side is most clover and daisy which in the summer yields a most fragrant smell. Next to Loch Seafort, which for some miles divides the Lewis from Harris, is the notable harbour within the island, by seafaring men called Glass, and by the natives Scalpa; it is a mile and a half long from south to north, and a mile in breadth. There is an entrance on the south and north ends of the isle, and several good harbours in each, well known to the generality of seamen. Within the isle of Loch Tarbat, running four miles west; it hath several small isles, and is sometimes frequented by

34

herring. Without the loch there is plenty of cod, ling, and large eels.

About half a league further on the same coast, lies Loch Stokness, which is about a mile in length: there is a freshwater lake at the entrance of the island, which affords oysters, and several sorts of fish, the sea having access to it at springtides.

About a league and a half farther south, is Loch Finisbay, an excellent, though unknown harbour, the land lies low, and hides it from the sight of seafaring men, till they come very near the coast. There are, besides this harbour, many creeks on this side, for barks and lesser boats.

Freshwater lakes abound in this island, and are well-stored with trout, eels, and salmon. Each lake has a river running from it to the sea, from whence the salmon comes about the beginning of May, and sooner if the reason be warm. The best time for angling for salmon and trout, is when a warm south-west wind blows. They use earthworms commonly for bait, but cockles attract the salmon better than any other.

There is a variety of excellent springs issuing from all the mountains of this island, but the wells on the plains near the sea are not good. There is one remarkable fountain lately discovered near Marvag houses, on the eastern coast, and has a large stone by it, which is sufficient to direct a stranger to it. The natives find by experience that it is very effectual for restoring lost appetite; all that drink of it become very soon hungry, though they have ate plentifully but an hour before: the truth of this was confirmed to me by those that were perfectly well, and also by those that were infirm; for it had the same effect on both.

There is a well in the heath, a mile to the east from the village Borve; the natives say that they find it efficacious against colics, stitches, and gravel.

There are several caves in the mountains, and on each side of the coast: the largest and best fortified, by nature, is that in the hill Ulweal, in the middle of a high rock; the passage leading to it is so narrow, that one only can enter at a time. This advantage renders it secure from any attempt; for one single man is able to keep off a thousand, if he have but a staff in his hand, since with the least touch of it he may throw the strongest man down the rock. The cave is capacious enough for fifty men to lodge in: it hath two wells in it, one of which is excluded from dogs; for they say if a dog do but taste of the water, the well presently drieth up: and for this reason, all such as have occasion to lodge there, take care to tie their dogs, that they may not have access to the water. The other well is called The Dogs Well, and is only drunk by them.

There are several ancient forts erected here, which the natives say were built by the Danes: they are of a round form, and have very thick walls and a passage in them by which one can go round the fort. Some of the stones that compose them are very large: these forts are named after the villages in which they are built, as that in Borve is called Down-Gorve, etc. They are built at convenient distances on each side of the coast, and there is a fort built in every one of the lesser isles.

There are several stones here erected on the end, one of which is in the village of Borve, about seven feet high. There is another stone of the same height to be seen in the opposite isle of Taransay. There are several heaps of stones, commonly called cairns, on the tops of hills and rising grounds on the coast, upon which they used to burn heath, as a signal of an approaching enemy. There was always a sentinel at each cairn to observe the seacoast; the steward of the isle made frequent rounds, to take notice of the sentinels, and if he found any of them asleep, he stripped them of their clothes, and deferred their personal punishments to the proprietor of the place. This isle produceth the same kind of cattle, sheep, and goats, that are on the Lewis. The natives gave me an account, that a couple of goats did grow wild on the hills, and after they had increased, they were observed to bring forth their young twice a year.

There are abundance of deer in the hills and mountains here, commonly called the forest; which is eighteen miles in length from east to west: the number of deer computed to be in this place is at least 2,000; and there is none permitted to hunt there without a licence from the steward to the forester. There is a particular mountain, and above a mile of ground surrounding it, to which no man hath access to hunt, this place being reserved for Macleod himself, who when he is disposed to hunt, is sure to find game enough there.

Both hills and valleys in the forest are well provided with plenty of good grass mixed with heath, which is all the shelter these deer have during the winter and spring: there is not a shrub of wood to be seen in all the forest; and when a storm comes, the deer betake themselves to the seacoast, where they feed upon the *Alga marina*, or sea-ware.

The mertrick, a four-footed creature, about the size of a big cat, is pretty numerous in this isle: they have a fine skin, which is smooth as any fur, and of a brown colour. They say that the dung of this animal yields a scent like musk.

The amphibia here are otters and seals; the latter are ate by the meaner sort of people, who say they are very nourishing. The natives take them with nets, whose ends are tied by a rope to the strong alga, or sea-ware, growing on the rocks.

This island abounds with variety of land and sea-fowl, and particularly with very good hawks.

There are eagles here of two sorts; the one is of a large size and grey colour, and these are very destructive to the fawns, sheep, and lambs.

The other is considerably less, and black, and shaped like a hawk, and more destructive to the deer, etc., than the bigger sort.

There are no venomous creatures of any kind here, except a little viper which was not thought venomous till of late, that a woman died of a wound she received from one of them.

I have seen a great many rats in the village Rowdil, which became very troublesome to the natives, and destroyed all their corn, milk, butter, cheese, etc. They could not extirpate these vermin for some time by all their endeavours. A considerable amount of cats was employed for this end, but were still worsted, and became perfectly faint, because overpowered by the rats, who were twenty to one. At length one of the natives, of more sagacity than his neighbours, found an expedient to renew his cat's strength and courage, which was by giving it warm milk after every encounter with the rats; and the like being given to all the other cats after every battle, succeeded so well, that they left not one rat alive, notwithstanding the great number of them in the place.

On the east-side of the village Rowdil, there is a circle of stone, within eight yards of the shore: it is about three fathoms under water, and about two stories high: it is in form broader above than below, like to the lower story of a kiln: I saw it perfectly on one side, but the season being then windy, hindered me from a full view of it. The natives say that there is such another circle of less compass in the pool Borodil, on the other side of the bay.

The shore on the west coast of this island affords variety of curious shells and walks; as tellinae and turbines of various kinds, thin patellae, streaked blue, various coloured pectenes, some blue, and some of orange colours.

The os-sepie is found on the sand in great quantities. The natives pulverise it, and take a cost of it in boiled milk which is found by experience to be an effectual remedy against the diarrhoea and dysentery. They rub this powder likewise, to take off the film on the eyes of sheep.

There is variety of nuts, called Molucca beans, some of which are used as amulets against witchcraft, or an evil eye, particularly the white one; and upon this account they are wore about children's necks, and if any evil is intended to them, they say the nut changes into a black colour. That they did change colour, I found true by my own observation, but cannot be positive as to the cause of it.

Malcolm Campbell, Steward of Harris, told me, that some weeks before my arrival there, all his cows gave blood instead of milk, for several days together: one of the neighbours told his wife that this must be witchcraft, and it would be easy to remove it, if she would but take the white nut, called the Virgin Mary's nut, and lay it in the pail into which she was to milk the cows. This advice she presently followed, and having milked one cow into the pail with the nut in it, the milk was all blood, and the nut changed its colour into dark brown: she used the nut again, and all the cows gave pure good milk, which they ascribe to the virtue of the nut. This very nut Mr Campbell presented me with, and I keep it still by me.

Some small quantity of ambergris hath been found on the coast of the island Bernera. I was told that a weaver in this island had burnt a lump of it, to show him a light for the most part of the night, but the strong scent of it made his head ache exceedingly, by which it was discovered.

An ancient woman about sixty years of age, here lost her hearing; and having no physician to give her advice, she would needs try an experiment herself, which was thus: She took a quill with which she ordinarily snushed her tobacco, and filling it with the powder of tobacco, poured it into her ear, which had the desired effect, for she could hear perfectly well next day. Another neighbour about the same age, having lost her hearing some time after, recovered it by the same experiment, as I was told by the natives.

The sheep which feed here on sandy ground, become blind sometimes, and are cured by rubbing chalk in their eyes.

A servant of Sir Norman Macleod's living in the island of Bernera, had a mare that brought forth a foal with both the hinder feet cloven, which died about a year after: the natives concluded that it was a bad omen to the owner, and his death, which followed in a few years after, confirmed them in their opinion.

The natives make use of the seeds of a white wild carrot, instead of hops, for brewing their beer, and they say that it answers the end sufficiently well, and gives the drink a good relish besides.

John Campbell, forester of Harris, makes use of this singular remedy for a cold: He walks into the sea up to the middle with his clothes on, and immediately after goes to bed in his wet clothes, and then laying the bedclothes over him procures a sweat, which removes the distemper, and this he told me is his only remedy for all manner of colds. One of the said John Campbell's servants having his cheek swelled, and there being no physician near, he asked his master's advice: he knew nothing proper for him, but however bid him apply a plaster of warm barley-dough to the place affected. This assuaged the swelling, and drew out of the flesh a little worm, about half an inch in length, and the bigness of a goose quill, having a pointed head, and many little feet on each side: this worm they call *fillan*, and it hath been found in the head and neck of several persons that I have seen in the isle of Skye.

Allium latisolium, a kind of wild garlic, is much used by some of the natives, as a remedy against the stone: they boil it in water, and drink the infusion, and it expels sand powerfully with great ease.

The natives told me, that the rock on the east side of Harris, in the sound of island Glass, hath a vacuity near the front, on the north-west side of the sound; in which they say there is a stone that they call the lunar stone, which advances and retires according to the increase and decrease of the moon.

A poor man born in the village of Rowdil, commonly called St Clements-blind, lost his sight at every change of the moon, which obliged him to keep his bed for a day or two, and then he recovered his sight.

The inferior islands belonging to Harris are as follows: the island Bernera is five miles in circumference, and lies about two leagues to the south of Harris. The soil is sandy for the most part, and yields a great product of barley and rye in a plentiful year, especially if the ground be enriched by sea-ware, and that there be rain enough to satisfy the dry soil. I had the opportunity to travel this island several times, and upon a strict enquiry I found the product of barley to be sometimes twenty fold and upwards, and at that time all the east side of the island produce thirty fold. This hath been confirmed to me by the natives, particularly by

Sir Norman Macleod, who possesses the island: he likewise confirmed to me the account given by all the natives of Harris and South Uist, viz. that one barley grain produceth in some places seven, ten, twelve and fourteen ears of barley; of which he himself being diffident for some time, was at the pains to search nicely the room of one grain after some weeks growth, and found that from this one grain many ears had been grown up. But this happens not, except when the season is very favourable, or in grounds that have not been cultivated some years before; which, if manured with sea-ware, seldom fail to produce an extraordinary crop. It is observed in this island as elsewhere, that when the ground is dug up with spades and the turfs turned upside down, and covered with sea-ware, it yields a better product than when it is ploughed.

There is a freshwater lake in this island, called Loch Bruist, in which there are small islands, abounding with land and sea-fowl, which build there in the summer. There is likewise plenty of eels in this lake, which are easiest caught in September, and then the natives carry lights with them in the night-time to the rivulet running from the lake, in which the eels fall down to the sea in heaps together.

This island in the summer is covered all over with clover and daisy, except in the cornfields. There is to be seen about the houses of Bernera, for the space of a mile, a soft substance, in show and colour exactly resembling the sea plant called slake, and grows very thick among the grass. The natives say, that it is the product of a dry hot soil; it grows likewise in the tops of several hills in the island of Harris.

It is proper to add here an account of several strange irregularities in the tides, on Bernera coast, by Sir Robert Murray, mentioned in the *Phil. Transactions*.

The tides increase and decrease gradually, according to the moon's age, so as about the third day after the new and full moon, in the Western Isles and continent, they are commonly at the highest, and about the quarter moons at the lowest (the former called springtides, the other neaptides). The tides from the quarter to the highest springtide increase in a certain proportion, and from the springtide to the quarter tide in like proportion; and the ebbs rise and fall always after the same manner.

It is supposed that the increase of tides is made in the proportion of sines; the first increase exceeds the lowest in a small proportion, the next in a greater, the third greater than that, and so on to the middlemost, whereof of the excess is the greatest; diminishing again from that to the highest springtide, so as the proportions before and after the middle do answer one another. And likewise from the highest springtide to the lowest neaptide, the decreases seem to keep the like proportions. And this commonly falls out when no wind or other accident causes an alteration. At the beginning of each flood on the coast, the tide moves faster, but in a small degree, increasing its swiftness till towards the middle of the flood, and then decreasing in swiftness again from the middle to the top of the high water. It is supposed that the inequal spaces of time, the increase and decrease of swiftness, and consequently the degrees of the risings and fallings of the same inequal spaces of time, are performed according to the proportion of sines. The proportion cannot hold precisely and exactly in regard of the inequalities that fall out in the periods of the tides, which are believed to follow certain positions of the moon in regard to the equinox, which are known not to keep a precise constant course; so that there not being equal portions of time between one new moon and another, the moon's return to the same meridian cannot be always performed in the same time. And the tides from new moon being not always the same in number, or sometimes but fifty-seven, sometimes fifty-eight, sometimes fifty-nine (without any certain order or succession) is another evidence of the difficulty of reducing this to any great exactness.

At the east end of this isle there is a strange reciprocation of the flux and reflux of the sea. There is another no less remarkable upon the west side of the Long Island. The tides which come from the south-west run along the coast northward; so that during the ordinary course of the tides the flood runs east in the firth, where Bernera lies, and the ebb west; and thus the sea ebbs and flows orderly, some four days before the full and change, and as long after (the ordinary springtides rising some fourteen or fifteen feet upright, and all the rest proportionably, as in other places); but afterwards, for four days before the quarter moons, and as long after, there is constantly a great and singular variation. For then (a southerly moon making there a full sea) the course of the tide being eastward, when it begins to flow, which is about nine and a half of the clock, it not only continues so about three and a half in the afternoon, that it be high water, but after it begins to ebb, the current runs on still eastwards during the whole ebb; so that it runs eastwards twelve hours together, that is, all day long, from about nine and a half in the morning till about nine and a half at night. But then when the night tide begins to flow, the current turns and runs westward all night, during both flood and ebb, for some twelve hours more, as it did eastward the day before. And thus the reciprocations continue, one flood and ebb running twelve hours eastward, and another twelve hours westward till four days before the full and new moon; and then they resume their ordinary regular course as before, running east during the six hours of flood, and west during the six of ebb.

There is another extraordinary irregularity in the tides, which never fail: That whereas between the vernal and autumnal equinox, that is, for six months together, the course of irregular tides about the quarter moons, is to run all day, twelve hours, as from about nine and a half to nine and a half or ten, exact eastward; all night, that is, twelve hours more westward: during the other six months, from the autumnal to the vernal equinox, the current runs all day westward, and all night eastward. I have observed the tides as above, for the space of some days both in April, May, July, and August. The natives have frequent opportunities to see this both day and night, and they all agree that the tides run as mentioned above.

There is a couple of ravens in this island, which beat away all ravenous fowls, and when their young are able to fly abroad, they beat them also out of the island, but not without many blows, and a great noise.

There are two chapels in this isle, to wit, St Asaph's and St Columbus's chapel. There is a stone erected near the former, which is eight feet high, and two feet thick.

About half a league from Bernera, to the westward lies the island Pabbay, three miles in circumference, and having a mountain in the middle. The soil is sandy, and fruitful in corn and grass, and the natives have lately discovered here a white marble. The west end of the island, which looks to St Kilda, is called the wooden harbour, because the sands at low water discover several trees that have formerly grown there. Sir Norman Macleod told me that he had seen a tree cut there, which was afterwards made into a harrow.

There are two chapels in this island, one of which is dedicated to the Virgin Mary, the other to St Muluag.

The steward of Kilda, who lives in Pabbay, is accustomed in time of storm to tie a bundle of puddings made of the fat of sea-fowl to the end of his cable, and lets it fall into the sea behind the rudder, this, he says, hinders the waves from breaking, and calms the sea; but the scent of the grease attracts the whales, which put the vessel in danger.

About half a league to the north of Pabbay lies the isle of Sellay, a mile in circumference, that yields extraordinary pasturage for sheep, so that they become fat very soon; they have the biggest horns that ever I saw on sheep.

About a league farther to the north lies the isle Taransay, very fruitful in corn and grass, and yields much yellow talk. It is three miles in circumference, and has two chapels, one dedicated to St Tarran, the other to St Keith.

There is an ancient tradition among the natives here, that a man must not be buried in St Tarran's, nor a woman in St Keith's, because otherwise the corpse would be found above ground the day after it is interred. I told them this was a most ridiculous fancy which they might soon perceive by experience if they would not put it to a trial. Roderick Campbell, who resides there, being of my opinion, resolved to embrace the first opportunity that offered, in order to undeceive the credulous vulgar, and accordingly a poor man in this island, who died a year after, was buried in St Tarran's chapel, contrary to the ancient custom and tradition of this place, but his corpse is still in the grave, from whence it is not like to rise until the general resurrection. This instance has delivered the credulous natives from this unreasonable fancy. This island is a mile distant from the mainland of Harris, and when the inhabitants go from this island to Harris with a design to stay for any time, they agree with those that carry them over, on a particular motion of walking upon a certain piece of ground, unknown to every body but themselves, as a signal to bring them back.

Three leagues to the westward of this island, lies Gasker, about half a mile in circumference; it excels any other plot of its extent for fruitfulness in grass and product of milk; it maintains eight or forty cows. The natives kill seals here, which are very big.

About two leagues farther north lies the island Scarp, two miles in circumference, and is a high land covered with heath and grass.

Between Bernera and the mainland of Harris lies the island Ensay, which is above two miles in circumference, and for the most part arable ground, which is fruitful in corn and grass: there is an old chapel here, for the use of the natives; and there was lately discovered a grave in the west end of the island, in which was found a pair of scales made of brass, and a little hammer, both which were finely polished.

Between Ensay and the mainland of Harris lie several small islands, fitter for pasturage than cultivation.

The little island Quedam hath a vein of adamant stone in the front of the rock. The natives say that mice do not live in this island, and when they chance to be carried thither among corn they die quickly after. Without these small islands there is a tract of small isles in the same line with the east side of the Harris, and North Uist. They are in all respects of the same nature with those two islands, so that the sight of them is apt to dispose one to think that they have been once united together.

The most southerly of these islands, and the nearest to North Uist, is Hermetra, two miles in circumference. It is moorish soil, covered all over almost with heath, except here and there a few plies of grass and the plant milkwort. Yet, notwithstanding this disadvantage, it is certainly the best spot of its extent for pasturage among these isles, and affords great plenty of milk in January and February beyond what can be seen in the other islands.

I saw there the foundation of a house built by the English, in King Charles I's time, for one of their magazines to lay up the cask, salt, etc., for carrying on the fishery, which was then begun in the Western Islands; but this design miscarried because of the civil wars which then broke out.

The channel between Harris and North Uist is above three leagues in breadth, and abounds with rocks as well under as above water: though, at the same time, vessels of 300 tons have gone through it from east to west, having the advantage of one of the natives for a pilot. Some sixteen years ago one Captain Frost was safely conducted in this manner. The Harris belongs in property to the Laird of Macleod. He and all the inhabitants are Protestants, and observe the festivals of Christmas, Good Friday, and St Michael's Day. Upon the latter they rendezvous on horseback, and make their cavalcade on the sands at low water.

The island of North Uist lies about three leagues to the south of the island of Harris, being in form of a semicircle, the diameter of which looks to the east, and is mountainous and full of heath, and fitter for pasturage than cultivation. The west side is of a quite different soil – arable and plain. The whole is in length from south to north nine miles, and about thirty in circumference.

There are four mountains in the middle, two lie within less than a mile of each other and are called South and North Lee.

All the hills and heath afford good pasturage, though it consists as much of heath as grass. The arable ground hath a mixture of clay in some places; and it is covered all over in summertime and harvest with clover, daisy, and variety of other plants, pleasant to the sight, and of a very fragrant smell; and abounds with black cattle and sheep. The soil is very grateful to the husbandman, yielding a produce of barley from ten to thirty fold in a plentiful year, provided the ground he manured with sea-ware and that it have rain proportionable to the soil. I have upon several occasions enquired concerning the produce of barley in this and the neighbouring islands, the same being much doubted in the south of Scotland, as well as in England; and, upon the whole, I have been assured by the most ancient and industrious of the natives that the increase is the same as mentioned before in Harris.

They told me likewise that a plot of ground which hath lain unmanured for some years, would in a plentiful season produce fourteen ears of barley from one grain; and several ridges were then showed me of this extraordinary growth in different places. The grain sown here is barley, oats, rye; and it is not to be doubted but the soil would also produce wheat. The way of tillage here is commonly by ploughing, and some by digging. The ordinary plough is drawn by four horses, and they have a little plough also called *ristle,* i.e., a thing that cleaves, the culter of which is in form of a sickle; and it is drawn sometimes by one and sometimes by two horses, according as the ground is. The design of this little plough is to draw a deep line in the ground, which otherwise would be much retarded by the strong roots of bent lying deep in the ground, that are cut by the little plough. When they dig with spades it produceth more increase. The little plough is likewise used to facilitate digging as well as ploughing. They continue to manure the ground until the tenth of June, if they have plenty of *braggir,* i.e. the broad leaves growing on the top of the *Alga Marina.*

About a league and a half to the south of the island Hermetra in Harris lies Loch Maddy, so-called from the three rocks without the entry on the south side. They are called *maddies* from the great quantity of big mussels, called *maddies,* that grows upon them. This harbour is capacious enough for some hundreds of vessels of any burden. It hath several isles within it, and they contribute to the security of the harbour for a vessel may safely come close to the quay. The seamen divide the harbour in two parts, calling the south side Loch Maddy, and the north side Loch Partan. There is one island in the south loch which for its commodiousness is by the English called Nonsuch. This loch hath been famous for the great quantity of herrings yearly taken in it within these fifty years last past. The natives told me, that in the memory of some yet alive, there had been 400 sail loaded in it with herrings at one season; but it is not now frequented for fishing, though the herrings do still abound in it; and on this coast every summer and harvest, the natives sit angling on the rocks, and as they pull up their hooks do many times brings up herrings. That they are always on the coast appears from the birds, whales, and other fishes that are their forerunners everywhere; and yet it is strange that in all this island there is not one herring net to be had; but if the natives saw any encouragement, they could soon provide them. Cod, ling, and all sorts of fish taken in these islands, abound in and about this lake.

In this harbour there is a small island called Vacksay, in which there is still to be seen the foundation of a house, built by the English, for a magazine to keep their casks, salt, etc., for carrying on a great fishery which was then begun there. The natives told me that King Charles I had a share in it. This lake, with the convenience of its fishings and islands, is certainly capable of great improvement; much of the ground about the bay is capable of cultivation, and affords a great deal of fuel, as turf, peats, and plenty of fresh water. It also affords a good quantity of oysters and clam shellfish; the former grow on rocks, and are so big that they are cut in four pieces before they are ate.

About half a minute further south is Loch Eport having a rock without the mouth of the entry, which is narrow. The lake penetrates some miles towards the west, and is a good harbour, having several small isles within it. The seals are very numerous here. In the month of July the springtides carry in a great quantity of mackerel, and at the return of the water they are found many times lying on the rocks. The vulgar natives make use of the ashes of burnt sea-ware, which preserves them for some time instead of salt.

About two miles to the south of Loch Eport lies the bay called the Kyle of Rona, having the island of that name (which is a little hill) within the bay; there is a harbour on each side of it. This place hath been found of great convenience for the fishing of cod and ling, which abound on this coast. There is a little chapel in the island Rona, called the Lowlanders' Chapel, because seamen who die in time of fishing are buried in that place.

There is a harbour on the south side of the island Borera. The entry seems to be narrower than really it is. The island and the opposite point of land appear like two little promontories off at sea. Some vessels have been forced in there by storm, as was Captain Peters, a Dutchman, and after him an English ship, who both approved of this harbour. The former built a cockboat there on a Sunday, at which the natives were much offended. The latter having landed in the island happened to come into a house where he found only ten women, and they were employed (as he supposed) in a strange manner viz., their arms and legs were bare, being five on a side; and between them lay a board, upon which they had laid a piece of cloth, and were thickening of it with their hands and feet, and singing all the while. The Englishman presently concluded it to be a little bedlam, which he did not expect in so remote a corner, and this he told to Mr John Maclean, who possesses the island. Mr Maclean answered he never saw any mad people in those islands; but this would not satisfy him, till they both went to the place where the women were at work, and then Mr Maclean having told him that it was their common way of thickening cloth, he was convinced, though surprised at the manner of it.

There is such a number of freshwater lakes here as can hardly be believed. I myself and several others endeavoured to number them, but in vain, for they are so disposed into turnings that it is impracticable. They are generally well stocked with trouts and eels, and some of them with salmon; and which is yet more strange, cod, ling, mackerel, etc., are taken in these lakes, into which they are brought by the springtides.

These lakes have many small islands, which in summer abound with variety of land and sea-fowls that build and hatch here. There be also several rivers here, which afford salmon; one sort of them is very singular, that is called marled salmon, or, as the natives call it, *ieskdruimin*, being lesser than the ordinary salmon, and full of strong large scales; no bait can allure it, and a shadow frights it away, being the wildest of fishes; it leaps high above water, and delights to be in the surface of it.

There is great plenty of shellfish round this island, more particularly cockles; the islands do also afford many small fish called eels, of a whitish colour, they are picked out of the sand with a small crooked iron made on purpose. There is plenty of lobsters on the west side of this island, and one sort bigger than the rest, having the toe shorter and broader.

There are several ancient forts in this island, built upon eminences, or in the middle of freshwater lakes.

Here are likewise several cairns or heaps of stones; the biggest I observed was on a hill near to Loch Eport. There are three stones erected about five feet high, at a distance of a quarter of a mile from one another, on eminences about a mile from Loch Maddy, to amuse invaders; for which reason they are still called false sentinels.

There is a stone of twenty-four feet long and four in breadth in the hill Criniveal: the natives say a giant of a month old was buried under it. There is a very conspicuous stone in the face of the hill above St Peter's village, above eight feet high.

There is another about eight feet high at Dunrossel, which the natives call a cross. There are two broad stones about eight feet high, on the hill two miles to the south of Valay.

There is another at the quay, opposite to Kirkibost, twelve feet high: the natives say that delinquents were tied to this stone in time of divine service.

There is a stone in form of a cross in the Row, opposite to St Mary's Church, about five feet high: the natives call it the Water Cross, for the ancient inhabitants had a custom of erecting this sort of cross to procure rain, and when they had got enough they laid it flat on the ground, but this custom is now disused. The inferior island is the island of Heiskir, which lies near three leagues westward of North Uist, is three miles in circumference, of a sandy soil, and very fruitful in corn and grass, and black cattle. The inhabitants labour under want of fuel of all sorts, which obliges them to burn cow's dung, barley-straw, and dried sea-ware; the natives told me that bread baked by the fuel of sea-ware relishes better than that done otherwise. They are accustomed to salt their cheese with the ashes of barley-straw, which they suffer not to lie on it above twelve hours time, because otherwise it would spoil it. There was a stone chest lately discovered there, having an earthen pitcher in it which was full of bones, and as soon as touched they turned to dust.

There are two small islands separated by narrow channels from the north-west of this island, and are of the same mould with the big island. The natives say that there is a couple of ravens there, which suffer no other of their kind to approach this island, and if any such chance to come this couple immediately drive them away with such a voice as is heard by all the inhabitants; they are observed likewise to beat away their young as soon as they be able to purchase for themselves. The natives told me that when one of this couple happened to be wounded by gunshot, it lay still in the corner of a rock for a week or two, during which time its mate brought provision to it daily until it recovered perfectly. The natives add further that one of these two ravens having died some time after the surviving one abandoned the island for a few days, and then was seen to return with about ten or twelve more of its kind, and having chosen a mate out of this number, all the rest went quite off, leaving these two in possession of their little kingdom. They do by a certain sagacity discover to the inhabitants any carcass, on the shore or in the fields, whereof I have seen several instances: the inhabitants pretend to know by their noise whether it be flesh or fish. I told them this was such a nicety that I could scarcely give it credit; but they answered me that they came to the knowledge of it by observation, and that they make the loudest noise for flesh. There is a narrow channel between the island of Heiskir and one of the lesser islands, in which the natives formerly killed many seals in this manner: They twisted together several small ropes of horsehair in form of a net, contracted at one end like a purse; and so by opening and shutting this hair net, these seals were caught in the narrow channel. On the south side of North Uist are the islands of Illeray, which are accessible at low water, each of them being three miles in compass, and very fertile in corn and cattle.

On the western coast of this island lies the rock Eousmil, about a quarter of a mile in circumference, and it is still famous for the yearly fishing of seals there, in the end of October. This rock belongs to the farmers of the next adjacent lands: there is one who furnisheth a boat, to whom there is a particular share due on that account, besides his proportion as tenant. The parish minister hath his choice of all the young seals, and that which he takes is called by the natives *cullen-mory,* that is, 'the Virgin Mary's seal'. The steward of the island hath one paid to him, his officer hath another, and this by virtue of their offices. These farmers man their boat with a competent number fit for the business, and they always embark with a contrary wind, for their security against being driven away by the ocean, and likewise to prevent them from being discovered by the seals, who are apt to smell the scent of them, and presently run to sea.

When this crew is quietly landed, they surround the passes, and then the signal for the general attack is given from the boat, and so they beat them down with big staves. The seals at this onset make towards the sea with all speed, and often force their passage over the necks of the stoutest assailants, who aim always at the forehead of the seals, giving many blows before they be killed; and if they be not hit exactly on the front, they contract a lump on their forehead, which makes them look very fierce; and if they get hold of the staff with their teeth, they carry it along to sea with them. Those that are in the boat shoot at them as they run to sea, but few are caught that way. The natives told me that several of the biggest seals lose their lives by endeavouring to save their young ones, whom they tumble before them towards the sea. I was told also that 320 seals, young and old, have been killed at one time in this place. The reason of attacking them in October is because in the beginning of this month the seals bring forth their young on the ocean side; but those on the east side, who are of the lesser stature, bring forth their young in the middle of June.

The seals eat no fish till they first take off the skin: they hold the head of the fish between their teeth, and pluck the skin off each side with their sharp-pointed nails; this I observed several times. The natives told me that the seals are regularly coupled, and resent an encroachment on their mates at an extraordinary rate: the natives have observed that when a male had invaded a female already coupled to another, the injured male, upon its return to its mate, would by a strange sagacity find it out, and resent it against the aggressor by a bloody conflict, which gives a red tincture to the sea in that part where they fight. This piece of revenge has been often observed by seal hunters, and many others of unquestionable integrity, whose occasions obliged them to be much on this coast. I was assured by good hands, that the seals make their addresses to each other by kisses: this hath been observed often by men and women as fishing on the coast in a clear day. The female puts away its young from sucking as soon as it is able to provide for itself; and this is not done without many severe blows.

There is a hole in the skin of the female, within which the teats are secured from being hurt as it creeps along the rocks and stones; for which cause nature hath formed the point of the tongue of the young one cloven, without which it could not suck.

The natives salt the seals with the ashes of burnt sea-ware, and say they are good food: the vulgar eat them commonly in the springtime with a long pointed stick instead of a fork, to prevent the strong smell which their hands would otherwise have for several hours after. The flesh and broth of fresh young seals is by experience known to be pectoral; the meat is astringent, and used as an effectual remedy against the diarrhoea and dysentery; the liver of a seal being dried and pulverised, and afterwards a little of it drunk with milk, aqua vitae, or red wine, is also good against fluxes.

Some of the natives wear a girdle of the sealskin about the middle, for removing the sciatica, as those of the shire of Aberdeen wear it to remove the chincough. This four-footed creature is reckoned one of the swiftest in the sea; they say likewise, that it leaps in cold weather the height of a pike above water, and that the skin of it is white in summer, and darker in winter, and that their hair stands on end with the flood, and falls again at the ebb. The skin is by the natives cut in long pieces, and then made use of instead of ropes to fix the plough to their horses, when they till the ground.

The seal, though esteemed fit only for the vulgar, is also eaten by persons of distinction, though under a different name, to wit, *ham*: this I have been assured of by good hands, and thus we see that the generality of men are as much led by fancy as judgment in their palates, as well as in other things. The popish vulgar in the islands southward from this, eat these seals in Lent instead of fish. This occasioned a debate between a Protestant gentleman and a Papist of my acquaintance: the former alleged that the other hand transgressed the rules of his church, by eating flesh in Lent: the latter answered that he did not; 'For,' says he, 'I have eat a sea-creature, which only lives and feeds upon fish.' The Protestant replied, that this creature is amphibious, lies, creeps, eats, sleeps, and so spends much of its time on land, which no fish can do and live. It hath also another faculty that no fish has, that is, it breaks wind backward so loudly, that one may hear it at a great distance. But the Papist still maintained that he must believe it to be fish, till such time as the Pope and his priests decide the question.

About three leagues and a half to the west, lie the small islands called Hawsker Rocks, and Hawsker Eggath, and Hawsker Nimannich, id est, 'monk's rock', which hath an altar in it. The first called so from the ocean, as being near to it; for *haw* or *thau* in the ancient language signifies the ocean: the more southerly rocks are six or seven big ones nicked or indented, for *eggath* signifies so much. The largest island, which is northward, is near half a mile in circumference, and it is covered with long grass. Only small vessels can pass between this and the southern rocks, being nearest to St Kilda of all the west islands: both of them abound with fowls as much as any isles of their extent to St Kilda. The coulterneb, guillemot, and scarts, are most numerous here; the seals likewise abound very much in and about these rocks.

The island of Valay lies on the west, near the mainland of North Uist; it is about four miles in circumference, arable and a dry, sandy soil, very fruitful in corn and grass, clover and daisy. It hath three chapels, one dedicated to St Ulton, and another to the Virgin Mary. There are two crosses of stone, each of them about seven feet high, and a foot and a half broad.

There is a little font on an altar, being a big stone, round like a cannon-ball, and having in the upper end a little vacuity capable of two spoonfuls of water. Below the chapels there is a flat thin stone called Brownie's Stone, upon which the ancient inhabitants offered a cow's milk every Sunday; but this custom is now quite abolished. Some thirty paces on this side is to be seen a little stone house under ground; it is very low and long, and having an entry on the seaside. I saw an entry in the middle of it, which was discovered by the falling of the stones and earth.

About a league to the north-east of Valay is the island of Borera, about four miles in circumference. The mould in some places is sandy, and in others black earth. It is very fruitful in cattle and grass. I saw a mare here, which I was told brought forth a foal in her second year.

There is a cow here that brought forth two female calves at once, in all things so very like one another, that they could not be distinguished by any outward mark, and had such a sympathy that they were never separate, except in time of sucking, and then they kept still their own side of their dam, which was not observed until a distinguishing mark was put upon one of their necks by the milkmaid. In the middle of this island there is a freshwater lake, well stocked with very big eels, some of them as long as cod or ling fish. There is a passage under the stony ground, which is between the sea and the lake, through which it is supposed the eels come in with the springtides. One of the inhabitants called MacVanich, i.e., 'monk's son', had the curiosity to creep naked through this passage.

This island affords the largest and best dulse for eating; it requires less butter than any other of this sort, and has a mellowish taste.

The burial place near the houses is called the Monks' Field, for all the monks that died in the islands that lie northward from Eigg were buried in this little plot. Each grave hath a stone at both ends, some of which are three and others four feet high. There are big stones without the burial place even with the ground. Several of them have little vacuities in them as if made by art; the tradition is that these vacuities were dug for receiving the monks' knees when they prayed upon them.

The island Lingay lies half a league south on the side of Borera. It is singular in respect of all the lands of Uist and the other islands that surround it, for they are all composed of sand, but this on the contrary is altogether moss, covered with heath, affording five peats in depth, and is very serviceable and useful, furnishing the island Borera, etc., with plenty of good fuel. This island was held as consecrated for several ages, insomuch that the natives would not then presume to cut any fuel in it.

The cattle produced here are horses, cows, sheep and hogs, generally of a low stature. The horses are very strong, and fit for pads, though exposed to the rigour of the weather all the winter and spring in the open fields. Their cows are also in the fields all the spring, and their beef is sweet and tender as any can be. They live upon sea-ware in the winter and spring, and are fattened by it, nor are they slaughtered before they eat plentifully of it in December. The natives are accustomed to salt their beef in a cow's hide, which keeps it close from air, and preserves it as well, if not better than barrels, and tastes, they say, best when this way used. This beef is transported to Glasgow, a city in the west of Scotland, and from thence (being put into barrels there) exported to the Indies in good condition. The hills afford some hundreds of deer who eat sea-ware also in winter and springtime.

The amphibia produced here are seals and otters. There is no fox or venomous creature in this island. The great eagles there fasten their talons in the back of fish, and commonly of salmon, which is often above water and in the surface. The natives, who in the summertime live on the coast, do sometimes rob the eagle of its prey after its landing.

Here are hawks, eagles, pheasants, moorfowls, ptarmigan, plover, pigeons, crows, swans, and all the ordinary sea-fowls in the West Islands. The eagles are very destructive to the fawns and lambs, especially the black eagle, which is of a lesser size then the other. The natives observe that it fixes its talons between the deer's horns, and beats its wings constantly about its eyes; which puts the deer to run continually till it fall into a ditch, or over a precipice, where it dies, and so becomes a prey to this cunning hunter. There are at the same time several other eagles of this kind, which fly on both sides of the deer which fright it extremely, and contribute much to its more sudden destruction.

The forester and several of the natives assured me that they had seen both sorts of eagles kill deer in this manner. The swans come hither in great numbers in the month of October with north-east winds, and live in the fresh lakes, where they feed upon trout and water plants till March, at which time they fly away again with a south-east wind. When the natives kill a swan it is common for the eaters of it to make a negative vow (i.e. they swear never to do something that is in itself impracticable) before they taste of the fowl.

The bird corn-craker is about the bigness of a pigeon, having a longer neck, and being of a brown colour, but blacker in harvest than in summer. The natives say it lives by the water, and under the ice in winter and spring.

The colk is a fowl somewhat less than a goose, hath feathers of divers colours, as white, grey, green, and black, and is beautiful to the eye. It hath a tuft on the crown of its head like that of a peacock, and a train longer than that of a house-cock. This fowl loseth its feathers in time of hatching, and lives mostly in the remotest islands, as Heiskir and Rona.

The *gawlin* is a fowl less than a duck. It is reckoned a true prognosticator of fair weather, for when it sings, fair and good weather always follows, as the natives commonly observe. The piper of St Kilda plays the notes which it sings, and hath composed a tune of them, which the natives judge to be very fine music.

The rain goose, bigger than a duck, makes a doleful noise before a great rain. It builds its nest always upon the brink of freshwater lakes, so as it may reach the water.

The *bonnivochill*, so called by the natives, and by the seamen bishop and carara, as big as a goose, having a white spot on the breast, and the rest partly coloured. It seldom flies, but is exceedingly quick in diving. The minister of North Uist told me that he killed one of them, which weighed sixteen pounds and an ounce. There is about an inch deep of fat upon the skin of it, which the natives apply to the hip bone, and by experience find it a successful remedy for removing the sciatica.

The bird *goylir*, about the bigness of a swallow, is observed never to land but in the month of January, at which time it is supposed to hatch. It dives with a violent swiftness. When any number of these fowls are seen together it is concluded to be an undoubted sign of an approaching storm; and when the storm ceases they disappear under the water. The seamen call them *mal-ifigies,* from mali-effigies, which they often find to be true.

The bird *sereachan-aittin* is about the bigness of a large mall, but having a longer body, and a bluish colour. The bill is of a carnation colour. This bird shrieks most hideously, and is observed to have a greater affection for its mate than any fowl whatsoever: for when the cock or hen is killed the surviving one doth for eight or ten days afterwards make a lamentable noise about the place.

The bird *faskidar*, about the bigness of a sea maw of the middle size, is observed to fly with greater swiftness than any other fowl in those parts, and pursues lesser fowls, and forces them in their flight to let fall the food which they have got, and by its nimble-ness catches it before it touch the ground.

The natives observe that an extraordinary heat without rain, at the usual time the sea-fowls lay their eggs, hinders them from lay-ing any eggs for about eight or ten days; whereas warm weather accompanied with rain disposes them to lay much sooner.

The wild geese are plentiful here, and very destructive to the barley, notwithstanding the many methods used for driving them away both by traps and gunshot. There are some flocks of barren fowls of all kinds, which are distinguished by their not joining with the rest of their kind, and they are seen commonly upon the bare rocks, without any nest.

The air is here moist and moderately cold, the natives qualify it sometimes by drinking a glass of *usquebaugh*. The moisture of this place is such that a loaf of sugar is in danger to be dissolved, if it be not preserved by being near the fire, or laying it among oatmeal, in some close place. Iron here becomes quickly rusty; and iron which is on the sea side of a house grows sooner rusty than that which is on the land side.

The greatest snow falls here with the south-west winds, and seldom continues above three or four days. The ordinary snow falls with the north and north-west winds, and does not lie so deep on the ground near the sea as on the tops of mountains.

The frost continues till the spring is pretty far advanced, the severity of which occasions great numbers of trouts and eels to die; but the winter frosts have not this effect, for which the inhabitants give this reason, viz. that the rains being more frequent in October do in their opinion carry the juice and quintessence of the plants into the lakes, whereby they think the fish are nourished during the winter, and there being no such nourishment in the spring, in regard of the uninterrupted running of the water, which carries the juice with it to the sea, it deprives the fish of this nourishment, and consequently of life. And they add further that the fish have no access to the superficies of the water, or to the brink of it, where the juice might be had. The natives are the more confirmed in their opinion that the fishes in lakes and marshes are observed to outlive both winter and spring frosts. The east-north-east winds always procure fair weather here, as they do in all the north-west islands; and the rains are most frequent in this place in October and February than at any other time of the year.

Fountain water drunk in winter is reckoned by the natives to be much more wholesome than in the spring; for in the latter it causeth the diarrhoea and dysentery.

The diseases that prevail here are fevers, diarrhoea, dysentery, stitch, cough, sciatica, migraine, the smallpox which commonly comes once in seventeen years' time. The ordinary cure for fevers is letting blood plentifully; the diarrhoea is cured by drinking aqua vitae, and the stronger the better. The flesh and liver of seals are used as abovementioned, both for the diarrhoea and dysentery. Milk, wherein hectic stone has been quenched, being frequently drunk, is likewise a good remedy for the two diseases last mentioned.

The kernel of the black nut found on the shore, being beat to powder and drunk in milk or aqua vitae is reckoned a good remedy for the said two diseases; stitches are cured sometimes by letting blood.

Their common cure for coughs is *brochan*, formerly mentioned, the case of the carrara-fowl, with the fat, being powdered a little and applied to the hip bone is an approved remedy for the sciatica. Since the great change of the seasons, which of late years is become more piercing and cold, by which the growth of the corn, both in the spring and summer seasons are retarded; there are some diseases discovered which were not known here before, viz., a spotted fever which is commonly cured by drinking a glass of brandy or aqua vitae liberally when the disease seizes them, and using it till the spots appear outwardly. This fever was brought hither by a stranger from the island of Mull, who infected these other islands. When the fever is violent the spots appear the second day, but commonly on the fourth day, and then the disease comes to a crisis the seventh day, but if the spots do not appear the fourth day, the disease is reckoned mortal; yet it has not proved so here, though it has carried off several in the other adjacent southern islands. The vulgar are accustomed to apply *Flamula Jovis* for evacuating noxious humours, such as cause the headache, and pains in the arms or legs; and they find great advantage by it. The way of using it is thus: They take a quantity of it, bruised small and put into a patella, and apply it so to the skin, a little below the place affected: in a small time it raises a blister about the bigness of an egg, which, when broke, voids all the matter that is in it; then the skin fills and swells twice again, and as often voids this matter. They use the sea-plant linarich to cure the wound, and it proves effectual for this purpose, and also for the migraine and burning.

The broth of a lamb, in which the plants *shunnish* and Alexander have been boiled, is found by experience to be good against consumptions. The green sea-plant linarich is by them applied to the temples and forehead to dry up defluxions, and also for drawing up the nostrils. Neil Macdonald in the island Heiskir is subject to the falling of the tonsils at every change of the moon, and they continue only for the first quarter. This infirmity hath continued with him all his days, yet he is now seventy-two years of age.

John Fake who lives in Pabble, in the parish of Kilmoor, alias St Mary's, is constantly troubled with a great sneezing a day or two before rain; and if the sneezing be more than usual, the rain is said to be the greater: therefore he is called the Rain Almanac. He has had this faculty these nine years past.

There is a house in the village called Ard-Nimboothin in the parish of St Mary's; and the house-cock there never crows from the tenth of September till the middle of March. This was told me two years ago, and since confirmed to me by the natives and the present minister of the parish.

The inhabitants of this island are generally well proportioned, of an ordinary stature, and a good complexion; healthful, and some of them come to a great age: several of my acquaintance arrived at the age of ninety, and upwards; John Macdonald of Griminis was of this number, and died lately in the ninety-third year of his age. Donald Roy, who lived in the isle of Sand, and died lately in the hundredth year of his age, was able to travel and manage his affairs till about two years before his death. They are a very charitable and hospitable people, as is anywhere to be found. There was never an inn here till of late, and now there is but one which is not at all frequented for eating, but only for drinking; for the natives by their hospitality render this new-invented house in a manner useless. The great produce of barley draws many strangers to this island, with a design to procure as much of this grain as they can; which they get of the inhabitants gratis, only for asking, as they do horses, cows, sheep, wool, etc. I was told some months before my last arrival there, that there had been ten men in that place at one time to ask corn gratis, and every one of these had some one, some two, and others three attendants; and during their abode there, were all entertained gratis, no one returning empty.

This is a great, yet voluntary tax, which has continued for many ages; but the late general scarcity has given them an occasion to alter this custom, by making acts against liberality, except to poor natives and objects of charity.

The natives are much addicted to riding, the plainness of the country disposing both men and horses to it. They observe an anniversary cavalcade on Michaelmas Day, and then all ranks of both sexes appear on horseback. The place for this rendezvous is a large piece of firm sandy ground on the seashore, and there they have horse-racing for small prizes, for which they contend eagerly. There is an ancient custom, by which it is lawful for any of the inhabitants to steal his neighbour's horse the night before the race, and ride him all next day, provided he deliver him safe and sound to the owner after the race. The manner of running is by a few young men, who use neither saddles or bridles, except to small ropes made of bent instead of a bridle, nor any sort of spurs, but their bare heels: and when they begin the race, they throw these ropes on their horses' necks, and drive them on vigorously with a piece of long sea-ware in each hand instead of a whip; and this is dried in the sun several months before for that purpose. This is a happy opportunity for the vulgar, who have few occasions for meeting, except on Sundays: the men have their sweethearts behind them on horseback, and give and receive mutual presents; the men present the women with knives and purses, the women present the men with a pair of fine garters of divers colours, they give them likewise a quantity of wild carrots. This isle belongs in property to Sir Donald Macdonald of Sleat: he and all the inhabitants are Protestants, one only excepted; they observe Christmas, Good Friday, and St Michael's Day.

IV

The Isle Benbecula

━━━━━◆●◆━━━━━

THE island of Benbecula lies directly to the south of North Uist, from which it is two miles distant; the ground being all plain and sandy between them, having two little rivers or channels no higher than one's knee at a tide of ebb: this passage is overflowed by the sea at every tide of flood, nor is it navigable except by boats. There are several small islands on the east side of this channel. This island is three miles in length from south to north, and three from east to west, and ten miles in compass. The east side is covered with heath; it hath a bay called Uiskway, in which small vessels do sometimes harbour and now and then herrings are taken in it.

The mountain Benbecula, from which the isle hath its name, lies in the middle of it; the eastern part of this island is all arable, but the soil sandy, the mould is the same with that of North Uist, and affords the same corn, fish, cattle, amphibia, etc. There is no venomous creature here. It hath several freshwater lakes well stocked with fish and fowl. There are some ruins of old forts to be seen in the small islands, in the lakes, and on the plain.

There are also some small chapels here, one of them at Baelnin-Killach, id est, 'nun's-town', for there were nunneries here in time of popery. The natives have lately discovered a stone vault on the east side of the town, in which there are abundance of small bones, which have occasioned many uncertain conjectures;

some said they were the bones of birds, others judged them rather to be the bones of pigmies. The proprietor of the town, enquiring Sir Norman Macleod's opinion concerning them, he told him that the matter was plain, as he supposed, and that they must be the bones of infants born by the nuns there. This was very disagreeable to the Roman Catholic inhabitants, who laughed it over. But in the meantime the natives out of zeal took care to shut up the vault that no access can be had to it since: so that it would seem they believe what Sir Norman said, or else feared that it might gain credit by such as afterwards had occasion to see them. This island belongs properly to Ranald Macdonald of Benbecula, who, with all the inhabitants, are Roman Catholics; and I remember I have seen an old lady Capuchin here, called in the language *brahir-brocht*, that is, 'poor brother', which is literally true, for he answers this character, having nothing but what is given him. He holds himself fully satisfied with food and raiment, and lives in as great simplicity as any of his order, his diet is very mean, and he drinks only fair water, his habit is no less mortifying than that of his brethren elsewhere; he wears a short coat, which comes no further than his middle, with narrow sleeves like a waistcoat; he wears a plaid above it girt about the middle, which reaches to his knee; the plaid is fastened on his breast with a wooden pin, his neck bare, and his feet often so too; he wears a hat for ornament, and the string about it is a bit of fisher's line made of horsehair. This plaid he wears instead of a gown worn by those of his order in other countries. I told him he wanted the flaxen girdle that men of his order usually wear. He answered me that he wore a leather one, which was the same thing. Upon the matter if he is spoken to when at meat, he answers again: which is contrary to the custom of his order. This poor man frequently diverts himself with angling of trouts. He lies upon straw; and had no bell (as others have) to call him to his devotion, but only his conscience, as he told me.

The speckled salmons, described in North Uist, are very plentiful on the west side of this island.

The island of South Uist lies directly two miles to the south of Benbecula, being in length one and twenty miles, and three in breadth, and in some places four. The east side is mountainous on the coast, and heathy for the most part. The west side is plain arable ground, the soil is generally sandy, yielding a good produce of barley, oats, and rye, in proportion to that of North Uist, and has the same sort of cattle. Both east and west sides of this island abound in freshwater lakes, which afford trouts and eels, besides variety of land and sea-fowls. The arable land is much damnified by the overflowing of these lakes in divers places, which they have not hitherto been able to drain, though the thing be practicable. Several lakes have old forts built upon the small islands in the middle of them. About four miles on the south-east end of this island is Loch Eynord. It reaches several miles westward, having a narrow entry, which makes a violent current, and within this entry there is a rock upon which there was staved to pieces a frigate of Cromwell's, which he sent there to subdue the natives. Ambergris hath been found by several of the inhabitants on the west coast of this island, and they sold it at Glasgow at a very low rate not knowing the value of it at first; but when they knew it they raised the price to the other extreme. Upon a thaw after a long frost the south-east winds cast many dead fishes on the shore. The inhabitants are generally of the same nature and complexion with those of the next adjacent northern islands. They wear the same habit, and use the same diet. One of the natives is very famous for his great age, being, so it is said, a hundred and thirty years old, and retains his appetite and understanding. He can walk abroad, and did labour with his hands as usually till within these three years, and for anything I know is yet living.

There are several big cairns of stone on the east side of this island, and the vulgar retain the ancient custom of making a religious tour round them on Sundays and holidays.

There is a valley between two mountains on the east side called Glenstyle, which affords good pasturage. The natives who farm it come thither with their cattle in the summertime, and are possessed with a firm belief that this valley is haunted by spirits, who by the inhabitants are called the great men; and that whatsoever man or woman enters the valley without making first an entire resignation of themselves to the conduct of the great men will infallibly grow mad. The words by which he or she gives up himself to these men's conduct are comprehended in three sentences, wherein the glen is twice named, to which they add that it is inhabited by these great men, and that such as enter depend on their protection. I told the natives that this was a piece of silly credulity as ever was imposed upon the most ignorant ages, and that their imaginary protectors deserved no such invocation. They answered that there had happened a late instance of a woman who went into that glen without resigning herself to the conduct of these men, and immediately after she became mad, which confirmed them in their unreasonable fancy.

The people residing there in summer say they sometimes hear a loud noise in the air like men speaking. I inquired if their priest had preached or argued against this superstitious custom. They told me he knew better things, and would not be guilty of dissuading men from doing their duty, which they doubted not he judged this to be; and that they resolved to persist in the belief of it until they found better motives to the contrary than have been shown them hitherto. The protestant minister hath often endeavoured to undeceive them, but in vain, because of an implicit faith they have in their priest; and when the topics of persuasion, though never so urgent, come from one they believe to be a heretic there is little hope of success.

The island Erisca, about a mile in length, and three in circumference, is partly heathy and partly arable, and yields a good produce. The inner side hath a wide anchorage, there is excellent cod and ling in it; the natives begin to manage it better but not to that advantage it is capable of. The small island near it was overgrown with heath, and about three years ago the ground threw up all that heath from the very root, so that there is not now one shrub of it in all this island. Such as have occasion to travel by land between South Uist and Benbecula, or Benbecula and North Uist, had need of a guide to direct them, and to observe the tide when low, and also for crossing the channel at the right fords, else they cannot pass without danger.

There are some houses underground in this island, and they are in all points like those described in North Uist; one of them is the South Ferry-Town, opposite to Barra. The cattle produced here are like those of North Uist, and there are above three hundred deer in this island: it was believed generally that no venomous creature was here, yet of late some little vipers have been seen in the south end of the island.

The natives speak the Irish tongue more perfectly here than in most of the other islands; partly because of the remoteness and the small number of those that speak English, and partly because some of them are scholars, and versed in the Irish language. They wear the same habit with the neighbouring islanders.

The more ancient people continue to wear the old dress, especially women. They are a hospitable, well-meaning people, but the misfortune of their education disposes them to uncharitableness, and rigid thoughts of their protestant neighbours; though at the same time they find it convenient to make alliances with them. The churches here are St Columba and St Mary's in Hoghmore, the most centrical place in the island; St Jeremy's chapels, St Peter's, St Bannan, St Michael, St Donnan.

There is a stone set up near a mile to the south of Columba's church, about eight feet high, and two feet broad: it is called by the natives the Bowing Stone; for when the inhabitants had the first sight of the church, they set up this stone, and there bowed and said the Lord's prayer. There was a buckle of gold found in Einort ground some twenty years ago, which was about the value of seven guineas.

As I came from South Uist, I perceived about sixty horsemen riding along the sands, directing their course for the east sea;

and being between me and the sun, they made a great figure on the plain sands. We discovered them to be natives of South Uist, for they alighted from their horses and went to gather cockles in the sands, which are exceeding plentiful there. This island is the property of Allan Macdonald of Moydart, head of the tribe of Macdonald, called Clanronalds; one of the chief families descended of Macdonald, who was lord and king of the islands. He and all the inhabitants are Papists, except sixty, who are Protestants. The Papists observe all the festivals of their church, they have a general cavalcade on All Saints Day, and then they bake St Michael's cake at night, and the family and strangers eat it at supper.

Fergus Beaton hath the following ancient Irish manuscripts in the Irish character, to wit, Avicenna, Averroes, Joannes de Vigo, Bernardus Gordonus, and several volumes of Hippocrates.

The island of Barra lies about two leagues and a half to the south-west of the island South Uist; it is five miles in length and three in breadth, being in all respects like the islands lying directly north from it. The east side is rocky, and the west arable ground, and yields a good produce of the same grain that both Uists do; they use likewise the same way for enriching their land with seaware. There is plenty of cod and ling got on the east and south sides of this island. Several small ships from Orkney come hither in summer, and afterward return laden with cod and ling.

There is a safe harbour on the north-east side of Barra, where there is great plenty of fish.

The rivers on the east side afford salmon, some of which are speckled like these mentioned in North Uist, but they are more successful here in catching them. The natives go with three several herring nets, and lay them crossways in the river where the salmon are most numerous, and betwixt them and the sea. These salmon at the sight or shadow of the people make towards the sea, and feeling the net from the surface to the ground, jump over the first, then the second, but being weakened, cannot get over the third net, and so are caught. They delight to leap above water and swim on the surface. One of the natives told me that he killed a salmon with a gun, as jumping above water.

They informed me also that many barrels of them might be taken in the river above mentioned, if there was any encouragement for curing and transporting them. There are several old forts to be seen here, in form like those in the other islands. In the south end of this island there is an orchard which produces trees, but few of them bear fruit, in regard of their nearness to the sea. All sorts of roots and plants grow plentifully in it. Some years ago tobacco did grow here, being of all plants the most grateful to the natives, for the islanders love it mightily.

The little island Kismul lies about a quarter of a mile from the south of this isle. It is the seat of Macneil of Barra; there is a stone wall round it two storeys high, reaching the sea, and within the wall there is an old tower and a hall, with other houses about it. There is a little magazine in the tower, to which no stranger has access. I saw the officer called the cockman, and an old cock he is; when I bid him ferry me over the water to the island, he told me that he was but an inferior officer, his business being to attend in the tower, but if (says he) the constable, who then stood on the wall, will give you access, I'll ferry you over. I desired him to procure me the constable's permission, and I would reward him; but having waited some hours for the constable's answer, and not receiving any, I was obliged to return without seeing this famous fort. Macneil and his lady being absent was the cause of this difficulty, and of my not seeing the place. I was told some weeks after that the constable was very apprehensive of some design I might have in viewing the fort, and thereby to expose it to the conquest of a foreign power, of which I supposed there was no great cause of fear. The natives told me there is a well in the village Tangstill, the water of which being boiled grows thick like puddle. There is another well not far from Tangstill, which the inhabitants say in a fertile year throws up many grains of barley in July and August. And they say that the Well of Kilbarr throws up embryos of cockles, but

I could not discern any in the rivulet, the air being at that time foggy. The church in this island is called Kilbarr, i.e. 'St Barr's church'. There is a little chapel by it, in which Macneil and those descended of his family are usually interred. The natives have St Barr's wooden image standing on the altar, covered with linen in form of a shirt; all their greatest asservations are by this saint. I came very early in the morning with an intention to see this image, but was disappointed; for the natives prevented me by carrying it away, lest I might take occasion to ridicule their superstition, as some Protestants have done formerly; and when I was gone it was again exposed on the altar. They have several traditions concerning this great saint. There is a chapel (about half a mile on the south side of the hill near St Barr's Church) where I had occasion to get an account of a tradition concerning this saint, which was thus: 'The inhabitants having begun to build the church, which they dedicated to him, they laid this wooden image within it, but was invisibly transported [as they say] to the place where the church now stands, and found there every morning.' This miraculous conveyance is the reason they give for desisting to work where they first began. I told my informer that this extraordinary motive was sufficient to determine the case, if true, but asked his pardon to dissent from him, for I had not faith enough to believe this miracle, at which he was surprised, telling me in the meantime that this tradition hath been faithfully conveyed by the priests and natives successively to this day. The southern islands are: (1) Muldonish, about a mile in circumference; it is high in the middle, covered over with heath and grass, and is the only forest here for maintaining the deer, being commonly about seventy or eighty in number. (2) The island Sandreray lies southerly of Barra, from which it is separated by a narrow channel, and is three miles in circumference, having a mountain in the middle. It is designed for pasturage and cultivation. On the south side there is a harbour convenient for small vessels, that come yearly here to fish for cod and ling, which abound on the coast of this island. (3) The island Sandreray, two miles in circumference, is fruitful in corn and grass, and separated by a narrow channel from Vattersay. (4) To the south of these lies the island Bernera, about two miles in circumference. It excels other islands of the same extent for cultivation and fishing. The natives never go a fishing while Macneil or his steward is in the island, lest seeing their plenty of fish, perhaps they might take occasion to raise their rents. There is an old fort in this island, having a vacuity round the walls, divided in little apartments. The natives endure a great fatigue in manuring their ground with sea-ware, which they carry in ropes upon their backs over high rocks. They likewise fasten a cow to a stake, and spread a quantity of sand on the ground, upon which the cow's dung falls, and this they mingle together, and lay it on the arable land. They take great numbers of sea-fowls from the adjacent rocks, and salt them with the ashes of burnt sea-ware in cows' hides, which preserves them from putrefaction.

There is a sort of stone in this island, with which the natives frequently rub their breasts by way of prevention, and say it is a good preservative for health. This is all the medicine they use. Providence is very favourable to them, in granting them a good state of health, since they have no physician among them.

The inhabitants are very hospitable, and have a custom, that when any strangers from the northern islands resort thither, the natives, immediately after their landing, oblige them to eat, even though they should have liberally eaten and drank but an hour before their landing there. And this meal they call *bieyta'v*, i.e. 'ocean meat'; for they presume that the sharp air of the ocean, which indeed surrounds them, must needs give them a good appetite. And whatever number of strangers come there, or for whatsoever quality or sex, they are regularly lodged according to ancient custom, that is, one only in a family; by which custom a man cannot lodge with his own wife, while in this island. Mr John Campbell, the present minister of Harris, told me, that his father being then parson of Harris, and minister of Barra (for the natives at that time were Protestants) carried his wife along with him, and resided in this island for some time, and they disposed of him, his wife and servants in manner above-mentioned; and suppose Macneil of Barra and his lady should go thither, he would be obliged to comply with this ancient custom.

There is a large root grows among the rocks of this island lately discovered, the natives call it *curran-petris*, of a whitish colour, and upwards of two feet in length, where the ground is deep, and in shape and size like a large carrot; where the ground is not so deep it grows much thicker, but shorter: the top of it is like that of a carrot.

The rock, Linmull, about half a mile in circumference, is indifferently high, and almost inaccessible, except in one place, and that is by climbing, which is very difficult. This rock abounds with sea-fowls that build and hatch here in summer, such as the guillemot, coulterneb, puffin, etc. The chief climber is commonly called *gingich*, and this name imports a big man having strength and courage proportionable. When they approach the rock with the boat, Mr Gingich jumps out first upon a stone on the rock-side, and then, by the assistance of a rope of horsehair, he draws his fellows out of the boat upon this high rock, and draws the rest up after him with the rope, till they all arrive at the top, where they purchase a considerable quantity of fowls and eggs. Upon their return to the boat, this *gingich* runs a great hazard by jumping first into the boat again, where the violent sea continually rages; having but a few fowls more than his fellows, besides a greater esteem to compensate his courage. When a tenant's wife in this or the adjacent islands dies, he then addresses himself to Macneil of Barra representing his loss, and at the same time desires that he would be pleased to recommend a wife to him, without which he cannot manage his affairs, not beget followers to Macneil, which would prove a public loss to him. Upon this representation, Macneil finds out a suitable match for him; and the woman's name being told him, immediately he goes to her, carrying with him a bottle of strong waters for their entertainment at marriage, which is then consummated.

When a tenant dies, the widow addresseth herself to Macneil in the same manner, who likewise provides her with a husband, and they are married without any further courtship. There is in this island an altar dedicated to St Christopher, at which the natives perform their devotion. There is a stone set up here, about seven feet high, and when the inhabitants come near it they take a religious turn round it.

If a tenant chances to lose his milk cows by the severity of the season, or any other misfortune; in this case Macneil of Barra supplies him with the like number that he lost.

When any case of these tenants are so far advanced in years that they are incapable to till the ground, Macneil takes such old men into his own family, and maintains them all their life after. The natives observe, that if six sheep are put a grazing in the little island Pabbay, five of them still appear fat, but the sixth a poor skeleton; but any number in this island not exceeding five are always fat. There is a little island not far from this called Micklay, of the same extent as Pabbay, and hath the same way of feeding sheep. These little islands afford excellent hawks.

The isles above-mentioned, lying near to the south of Barra, are commonly called the Bishop's Isles, because they are held of the bishop. Some isles lie on the east and north of Barra, as Fiaray, Mellisay, Buya Major and Minor, Lingay, Fuda; they afford pasturage, and are commodious for fishing; and the latter being about two miles in circumference is fertile in corn and grass. There is a good anchoring place next to the isle on the north-east side.

The steward of the Lesser and Southern Islands is reckoned a great man here, in regard of the perquisites due to him; such as a particular share of all the lands, corn, butter cheese, fish, etc., which these islands produce; the measure of barley paid him by each family yearly is an *omer*, as they call it, containing about two pecks.

There is an inferior officer, who also hath a right to a share of all the same products. Next to these come in course those of the lowest posts, such as the cockman and porter, each of whom hath his respective due, which is punctually paid.

Macneil of Barra and all his followers are Roman Catholics, one only excepted, viz. Murdock Macneil; and it may perhaps be thought no small virtue in him to adhere to the Protestant communion, considering the disadvantages he labours under by the want of his chief's favour, which is much lessened, for being a heretic, as they call him. All the inhabitants observe the anniversary of St Barr, being the 27th of September, it is performed riding on horseback, and the solemnity is concluded by three turns round St Barr's Church. This brings into my mind a story which was told me concerning a foreign priest and the entertainment he met with after his arrival there some years ago, as follows: This priest happened to land here upon the very day, and at the particular hour of this solemnity, which was the more acceptable to the inhabitants, who then desired him to preach a commemoration sermon to the honour of their patron St Barr, according to the ancient custom of the place. At this the priest was surprised, he never having heard of St Barr before that day; and therefore knowing nothing of his virtues, could say nothing concerning him: but told them, that if a sermon to the honour of St Paul or St Peter could please them, they might have it instantly. This answer of his was so disagreeable to them, that they plainly told him he could be no true priest, if he had not heard of St Barr, for the pope himself had heard of him; but this would not persuade the priest, so that they parted much dissatisfied with one another. They have likewise a general cavalcade on St Michael's Day, in Kilbarr village, and do then also take a turn round their church. Every family, as soon as the solemnity is ended, is accustomed to bake St Michael's cake, as above described; and all strangers, together with those of the family, must eat the bread that night.

This island, and the adjacent islands, belong in property to Macneil, being the thirty-fourth of that name by lineal descent that has possessed this island, if the present genealogers may be credited. He holds his lands in vassalage of Sir Donald Macdonald of Sleat, to whom he pays £40 per annum and a hawk, if required, and is obliged to furnish him a certain number of men upon extraordinary occasions.

V

The Ancient and Modern Customs of the Inhabitants of the Western Islands of Scotland

———⟫●⟪———

E VERY heir or young chieftain of a tribe was obliged in honour to give a public specimen of his valour before he was owned and declared governor or leader of his people, who obeyed and followed him upon all occasions.

This chieftain was usually attended with a retinue of young men of quality, who had not beforehand given any proof of their valour, and were ambitious of such an opportunity to signalise themselves.

It was usual for the captain to lead them, to make a desperate incursion upon some neighbour or other that they were in feud with; and they were obliged to bring by open force the cattle they found in the lands they attacked, or to die in the attempt.

After the performance of this achievement, the young chieftain was ever after reputed valiant and worthy of government, and such as were of his retinue acquired the like reputation. This custom being reciprocally used among them, was not reputed robbery; for the damage which one tribe sustained by this essay of the chieftain of another, was repaired when their chieftain came in his turn to make his specimen: but I have not heard an instance of this practice for these sixty years past.

The formalities observed at the entrance of these chieftains upon the government of their clans, were as follows: A heap of stones was erected in form of a pyramid, on the top of which the young chieftain was placed, his friends and followers standing in a circle round about him, his elevation signifying his authority over them, and their standing below their subjection to him. One of his principal friends delivered into his hands the sword worn by his father, and there was a white rod delivered to him likewise at the same time.

Immediately after, the chief druid (or orator) stood close to the pyramid, and pronounced a rhetorical panegyric, setting forth the ancient pedigree, valour, and liberality of the family as incentives to the young chieftain, and fit for his imitation.

It was their custom when any chieftain marched upon a military expedition, to draw some blood from the first animal that chanced to meet them upon the enemy's ground, and thereafter to sprinkle some of it upon their colours. This they reckoned as a good omen of future success.

They had their fixed officers who were ready to attend them upon all occasions, whether military or civil. Some families continue them from father to son, particularly Sir Donald Macdonald has his principal standard-bearer and quartermaster. The latter has a right to all the hides of cows killed upon any of the occasions mentioned above; and this I have seen exacted punctually, though the officer had no charter for the same, but only custom.

They had a constant sentinel on top of their houses called *gockmin*, or in the English tongue 'cockman', who was obliged to watch day and night, and at the approach of anybody to ask, 'Who comes there?' This officer is continued in Barray still, and has the perquisites due to his place paid him duly at two terms in the year.

There was a competent number of young gentlemen called *lucht-taeh* or '*guard de corps*', who always attended the chieftain at home and abroad. They were well trained in managing the sword and target, in wrestling, swimming, jumping, dancing, shooting with bows and arrows, and were stout seamen.

Every chieftain had a bold armour-bearer, whose business was always to attend the person of his master night and day, to prevent any surprise, and this man was called *galloglach*; he had likewise a double portion of meat assigned him at every meal. The measure of meat usually given him is called to this day *bieyfir*, that is, a man's portion, meaning thereby an extraordinary man, whose strength and courage distinguished him from the common sort.

Before they engaged the enemy in battle, the chief druid harangued the army to excite their courage. He was placed on an eminence, from whence he addressed himself to all of them standing about him, putting them in mind of what great things were performed by the valour of their ancestors, raised their hopes with the noble rewards of honour and victory, and dispelled their fears by all the topics that natural courage could suggest. After this harangue, the army gave a general shout, and then charged the enemy stoutly. This in the ancient language was called *brosnichiy kah,* i.e., an incentive to war. This custom of shouting aloud is believed to have taken its rise from an instinct of nature, it being attributed to most nations that have been of a martial genius – as by Homer to the Trojans, by Tacitus to the Germans, by Livy to the Gauls. Every great family in the isles had a chief druid, who foretold future events, and decided all causes, civil and ecclesiastical. It is reported of them that they wrought in the night-time, and rested all day. Caesar says they worshipped a deity under the name of Taramis, or Taran, which in Welsh signifies thunder, and in the ancient language of the Highlanders, Torin signifies thunder also.

Another God of the Britons was Belus or Belinus, which seems to have been the Assyrian god Bel or Belus; and probably from this pagan deity comes the Scots term of *Beltane*, the first day of May, having its first rise from the custom practised by the druids in the isles, of extinguishing all the fires in the parish until the tithes were paid; and upon payment of them the fires were kindled in each family, and never till then. In those days malefactors were burnt between two fires; hence when they would express a man to be in a great strait, they say, 'He is between two fires of Bel', which in their language they express thus, '*Edir da hin Veaul or Bel*'. Some object that the druids could not be in the isles because no oaks grow there. To which I answer, that in those days oaks did grow there, and to this day there be oaks growing in some of them, particularly in Sleat, the most southern part of the isle of Skye. The houses named after those druids shall be described elsewhere.

The manner of drinking used by the chief men of the isles is called in their language *streah*, i.e. a 'round'; for the company sat in a circle, the cup-bearer filled the drink round to then, and was all drunk out whatever the liquor was, whether strong or weak; they continued drinking sometimes twenty-four, sometimes forty-eight hours. It was reckoned a piece of manhood to drink until they became drunk, and there were two men with a barrow attending punctually on such occasions. They stood at the door until some became drunk, and they carried them upon the barrow to bed, and returned again to their post as long as any continued fresh, and so carried off the whole company one by one as they became drunk. Several of my acquaintance have been witnesses to this custom of drinking, but it is now abolished.

Among persons of distinction it was reckoned an affront put upon any company to broach a piece of wine, ale, or aqua vitae and not to see it all drunk out at one meeting. If any man chance to go out from the company, though but for a few minutes, he is obliged upon his return, and before he take his seat, to make an apology for his absence in rhyme; which, if he cannot perform, he is liable to such a share of the reckoning as the company think fit to impose; which custom obtains in many places still, and is called *beanchiy bard*, which in their language signifies the poet's congratulating the company.

It hath been an ancient custom in these isles, and still continues, when any number of men retire into a house, either to discourse of serious business, or to pass some time in drinking; upon these occasions the door of the house stands open, and a rod is put across the same, which is understood to be a sign to all persons without distinction not to approach; and if any should be so rude as to take up this rod, and come in uncalled, he is sure to be no welcome guest; for this is accounted such an affront to the company, that they are bound in honour to resent it; and the person offending may come to have his head broken, if he do not meet with a harsher reception.

The chieftain is usually attended with a numerous retinue when he goes a-hunting deer, this being his first specimen of manly exercise. All his clothes, arms, and hunting equipage are, upon his return from the hills, given to the forester, according to custom.

Every family had commonly two stewards, which in their language were called *marischal taeh*: the first of these served always at home, and was obliged to be well versed in the pedigree of all the tribes in the isles, and in the Highlands of Scotland; for it was his province to assign every man at table his seat according to his quality; and this was done without one word speaking, only by drawing a score with a white rod which this marshal had in his hand, before the person who was bid by him to sit down; and this was necessary to prevent disorder and contention; and though the marshal might sometimes be mistaken, the master of the family incurred no censure by such an escape; but this custom has been laid aside of late. They had also cup-bearers, who always filled and carried the cup round the company, and he himself drank off the first draught. They had likewise purse-masters, who kept their money. Both these officers had an hereditary right to their office in writing, and each of them had a town and land for his service: some of those rights I have seen fairly written on good parchment.

Besides the ordinary rent paid by the tenant to his master, if a cow brought forth two calves at a time, which indeed is extraordinary, or a ewe two lambs, which is frequent, the tenant paid to the master one of the calves or lambs; and the master on his part was obliged, if any of his tenants' wives bore twins, to take one of them, and breed him in his own family. I have known a gentleman who had sixteen of these twins in his family at a time.

Their ancient leagues of friendship were ratified by drinking a drop of each other's blood, which was commonly drawn out of the little finger. This was religiously observed as a sacred bond; and if any person after such an alliance happened to violate the same, he was from that time reputed unworthy of all honest men's conversation. Before money became current, the chieftains in the isles bestowed the cow's head, feet, and all the entrails upon their dependants; such as the physician, orator, poet, bard, musicians, etc., and the same was divided thus: the smith had the head, the piper had the, etc.

It was an ancient custom among the islanders to hang a he-goat to the boat's mast, hoping thereby to procure a favourable wind; but this is not practised at present; though I am told it hath been done once by some of the vulgar within these thirteen years last past.

They had a universal custom, of pouring a cow's milk upon a little hill, or big stone, where the spirit called Browny was believed to lodge: this spirit always appeared in the shape of a tall man, having very long brown hair. There was scarce any the least village in which this superstitious custom did not prevail. I inquired the reason of it from several well-meaning women, who, until of late, had practised it; and they told me, that it had been transmitted to them by their ancestors successfully, who believed it was attended with good fortune, but the most credulous of the vulgar had now laid it aside. It was an ordinary thing among the over-curious to consult an invisible oracle, concerning the fate of families, and battles, etc. This was performed three different ways; the first was by a company of men, one of whom being detached by lot, was afterwards carried to a river, which was the boundary between two villages; four of the company laid hold on him, and having shut his eyes, they took him by the legs and arms, and then tossing him to and again, struck his hips with force against the bank. One of them cried out, 'What is it you have got here?' Another answers, 'A log of birchwood.' The other cries again, 'Let his invisible friends appear from all quarters, and let them relieve him by giving an answer to our present demands': and in a few minutes after a number of little creatures came from the sea, who answered the question and disappeared suddenly. The man was then set at liberty, and they all returned home to take their measures according to the prediction of their false prophets; but the poor deluded fools were abused, for the answer was still ambiguous. This was always practised in the night, and may literally be called the works of darkness.

I had an account from the most intelligent and judicious men in the isle of Skye that about sixty-two years ago the oracle was thus consulted only once, and that was in the parish of Kilmartin, on the east side, by a wicked and mischievous race of people, who are now extinguished, both root and branch.

The second way of consulting the oracle was by a party of men who first retired to solitary places, remote from any house, and there they singled out one of their number, and wrapped him in a big cow's hide, which they folded about him; his whole body was covered with it except his head, and so left in this posture all night until his invisible friends relieved him by giving a proper answer to the question in hand, which he received, as he fancied, from several persons that he found about him all that time. His consorts returned to him at break of day, and then he communicated his news to them, which often proved fatal to those concerned in such unwarrantable enquiries.

There was a third way of consulting, which was a confirmation of the second above-mentioned. The same company who put the man into the hide took a live cat and put him on a spit; one of the number was employed to turn the spit, and one of his consorts inquired of him, 'What are you doing?' He answered, 'I roast this cat until his friends answer the question, which must be the same that was proposed by the man shut up in the hide.' And afterwards a very big cat comes, attended by a number of lesser cats, desiring to relieve the cat turned upon the spit, and then answers the question. If this answer proved the same that was given to the man in the hide, then it was taken as a confirmation of the other, which in this case was believed infallible.

Mr Alexander Cooper, present minister of North Uist, told me that one John Erach, in the isle of Lewis, assured him it was his fate to have been led by his curiosity with some who consulted this oracle, and that he was a night within the hide, as above mentioned; during which time he felt and heard such terrible things that he could express them: the impression it made on him was such as could never go off, and he said that for a thousand worlds he would never again be concerned in the like performance, for this had disordered him to a high degree. He confessed it ingenuously, and with an air of great remorse, and seemed to be very penitent under a just sense of so great a crime. He declared this about five years since, and is still living in the Lewis, for anything I know. The inhabitants here did also make use of a fire called *tin-egin*, i.e. 'a forced fire', or fire of necessity, which they used as an antidote against the plague or *murrain* in cattle; and it was performed thus: all the fires in the parish were extinguished, and then eighty-one married men, being thought the necessary number for effecting this design, took two great planks of wood, and nine of them were employed by turns, who by their repeated efforts rubbed one of the planks against the other until the heat thereof produced fire; and from this forced fire each family is supplied with new fire, which is no sooner kindled than a pot full of water is quickly set on it, and afterwards sprinkled upon the people infected with the plague, or upon the cattle that have the *murrain*. And this they all say they find successful by experience. It was practised in the mainland, opposite to the south of Skye, within these thirty years.

They preserve their boundaries from being liable to any debates by their successors, thus: they lay a quantity of the ashes of burnt wood in the ground, and put big stones above the same; and for conveying the knowledge of this to posterity, they carry some boys from both villages next the boundary, and there whip them soundly, which they will be sure to remember, and tell it to their children. A debate having arisen betwixt the villages of Ose and Groban in Skye, they found ashes as above mentioned under a stone, which decided the controversy. It was an ancient custom in the islands that a man should take a maid to his wife, and keep her the space of a year without marrying her, and if she pleased him all the while, he married her at the end of the year, and legitimated these children; but if he did not love her, he returned her to her parents, and her portion also; and if there happened to be any children, they were kept by the father: but this unreasonable custom was long ago brought into disuse.

It is common in these islands, when a tenant dies, for the master to have his choice of all the horses which belonged to the deceased; and this was called the *eachfuin horizeilda*, i.e. a 'lord's gift': for the first use of it was from a gift of a horse granted by all the subjects in Scotland for relieving the king from his imprisonment in England. There was another duty payable by all the tenants to their chief, though they did not live upon his lands; and this is called *calpich*: there was a standing law for it also, called *calpich* law; and I am informed that this is exacted by some in the mainland to this day.

Women were anciently denied the use of writing in the islands to prevent love intrigues: their parents believed that nature was too skilful in that matter, and needed not the help of education; and therefore that writing would be of dangerous consequence to the weaker sex.

The orators, in their language called *is-dane*, were in high esteem both in these islands and the continent; until within these forty years they sat always among the nobles and chiefs of families in the *streah* or circle. Their houses and little villages were sanctuaries, as well as churches, and they took place before doctors of physic. The orators, after the druids were extinct, were brought in to preserve the genealogy of families, and to repeat the same at every succession of a chief; and upon the occasion of marriages and births, they made epithalamiums and panegyrics which the poet or bard pronounced. The orators by the force of their eloquence had a powerful ascendant over the greatest men in their time; for if any orator did but ask the habit, arms, horse, or any other thing belonging to the greatest man in these islands, it was readily granted them, sometimes out of respect, and sometimes for fear of being exclaimed against by a satire, which in those days was reckoned a great dishonour: but these gentlemen becoming insolent lost ever since both the profit and esteem which was formerly due to their character, for neither their panegyrics nor satires are regarded to what they have been, and they are now allowed but a small salary. I must not omit to relate their way of study, which is very singular: they shut their doors and windows for a day's time, and lie on their backs, with a stone upon their belly, and plaids about their heads, and their eyes being covered, they pump their brains for rhetorical encomium or panegyric; and indeed they furnish such a style from this dark cell, as is understood by very few; and if they purchase a couple of horses as the reward of their meditation, they think they have done a great matter. The poet or bard had a title to the bridegroom's upper garb, that is, the plaid and bonnet; but now he is satisfied with what the bridegroom pleases to give him on such occasions.

There was an ancient custom in the island of Lewis to make a fiery circle about the houses, corn, cattle, etc., belonging to each particular family: a man carried fire in his right hand, and went round, and it was called *dessil*, from the right hand, which in the ancient language is called *dess*. An instance of this round was performed in the village Shader, in Lewis, about sixteen years ago (as I was told), but it proved fatal to the practiser, called MacCallum; for after he had carefully performed this round, that very night following he and his family were sadly surprised, and all his houses, corn, cattle, etc., were consumed with fire. This superstitious custom is quite abolished now, for there has not been above this one instance of it in forty years past.

There is another way of the *dessil,* or carrying fire round about women before they are churched after child-bearing; and it is used likewise about children until they be christened: both which are performed in the morning and at night. This is only practised now by some of the ancient midwives: I inquired their reason for this custom, which I told them was altogether unlawful; this disobliged them mightily, insomuch as they would give me no satisfaction. But others, that were of a more agreeable temper, told me the fire-round was an effectual means to preserve both the mother and the infant from the power of evil spirits, who are ready at such times to do mischief, and sometimes carry away the infant; and when they get them once in their possession, return them poor meagre skeletons: and these infants are said to have voracious appetites, constantly craving for meat. In this case it was usual with those who believed that their children were thus taken away, to dig a grave in the fields upon quarter day, and there to lay the fairy skeleton till next morning; at which time the parents went to the place, where they doubted not to find their own child instead of this skeleton. Some of the poorer sort of people in these islands retain the custom of performing these rounds sunways about the persons of their benefactors three times, when they bless them, and wish good success to all their enterprises. Some are very careful when they set out to sea that the boat be first rowed about sunways; and, if this be neglected, they are afraid their voyage may prove unfortunate. I had this ceremony paid me (when in the island of Islay) by a poor woman after I had given her an alms: I desired her to let alone that compliment, for I did not care for it; but she insisted to make these three ordinary turns, and then prayed that God and MacCharming, the patron saint of that island, might bless and prosper me in all my designs and affairs.

I attempted twice to go from Islay to Colonsay, and at both times they rowed about the boat sunways, though I forbade them to do it; and by a contrary wind the boat and those in it were forced back. I took a boat again a third time from Jura to Colonsay, and at the same time forbade them to row about their boat, which they obeyed, and then we landed safely at Colonsay, without any ill adventure, which some of the crew did not believe possible, for want of the round; but this one instance hath convinced them of the vanity of this superstitious ceremony. Another ancient custom observed on the second of February, which the Papists there yet retain, is this: The mistress and servants of each family take a sheaf of oats and dress it up in women's apparel, put it in a large basket, and lay a wooden club by it, and this they call *Briid's bed*; and then the mistress and servants cry three times, 'Briid is come, Briid is welcome.' This they do just before going to bed, and when they rise in the morning they look among the ashes, expecting to see the impression of Briid's club there; which if they do, they reckon it a true passage of a good crop and prosperous year, and the contrary they take as an ill omen.

It has been an ancient custom amongst the natives, and now only used by some old people, to swear by their chief or laird's hand.

When a debate arises between two persons, if one of them assert the matter by your father's hand they reckon it a great indignity; but if they go a degree higher, and out of spite say, by your father's and grandfather's hand, the next word is commonly accompanied with a blow.

It is a received opinion in these islands, as well as in the neighbouring part of the mainland, that women by a charm, or some other secret way, are able to convey the increase of their neighbour's cow's milk to their own use; and that the milk so charmed doth not produce the ordinary quantity of butter, and the curds made of that milk are so tough that it cannot be made so firm as other cheese, and is also much lighter in weight. The butter so taken away and joined to the charmer's butter is evidently discernible by a mark of separation, viz, the diversity of colours; that which is charmed by being still paler than that part of the butter which hath not been charmed; and if butter having these marks be found with a suspected woman, she is presently said to be guilty. Their usual way of recovering this loss, is to take a little of the rennet from all the suspected persons, and to put it in an eggshell full of milk; and when that from the charmer is mingled with it, it presently curdles, and not before.

This was asserted to me by the generality of the most judicious people in these islands; some of them having, as they told me, come to the knowledge of it to their cost. Some women make use of the root of groundsel as an amulet against such charms, by putting it among their cream.

Both men and women in those islands, and in the neighbouring mainland, affirm that the increase of milk is likewise taken away by trouts; if it happen that the dishes or pails wherein the milk is kept be washed in the rivulets where trouts are. And the way to recover this damage is by taking a live trout, and pouring milk into its mouth; which they say doth presently curdle, if it was taken away by trouts, but otherwise they say it is not.

They affirm, likewise, that some women have an art to take away the milk of nurses.

I saw four women, whose milk were tried that one might be chosen for a nurse; and the woman pitched upon was, after three days' suckling, deprived of her milk; whereupon she was sent away, and another put in her place; and on the third day after, she that was first chosen recovered her milk again. This was concluded to be the effect of witchcraft by some of her neighbours.

They also say that some have an art of taking away the increase of malt, and that the drink made of this malt hath neither life nor good taste in it; and, on the contrary, the charmer hath very good ale all this time. A gentleman of my acquaintance, for the peace of a year, could not have a drop of good ale in his house; and having complained of it to all that conversed with him, he was at last advised to get some yeast from every alehouse in the parish; and having got a little from one particular man, he put it among his wort, which became as good ale as could be drunk, and so defeated the charm. After which the gentleman in whose land this man lived, banished him thirty-six miles from thence.

They say there be women who have an art of taking a moat out of one's eye, though at some miles' distance from the party grieved; and this is the only charm these women will avouch themselves to understand, as some of them told me, and several of these men, out of whose eyes moats were then taken, confirmed the truth of it to me.

All these islanders, and several thousands on the neighbouring continent, are of opinion, that some particular persons have an evil eye, which affects children and cattle; this, they say, occasions frequent mischances, and sometimes death. I could name some who are believed to have this unhappy faculty, though at the same time void of any ill design. This hath been an ancient opinion, as appears from that of the poet: 'Nescio quis teneros oculus mihi fassinat Agnos.'

VI

Courts of Judicatory — Church Discipline — Forms of Prayer

A T the first plantation of these isles, all matters were managed by the sole authority of the heads of tribes, called in
the Irish, *thiarna*, which was the same with Tyrannus, and now
it signifies lord or chief; there being no standard of equity or
justice, but what flowed from them. And when their numbers
increased, they erected courts called *mode*, and in the English,
baron courts.

The proprietor has the nomination of the members of this
court; he himself is president of it, and in his absence his bailiff:
the minister of the parish is always a member of it. There are no
attorneys to plead the cause of either party, for both men and
women represent their respective causes; and there is always a
speedy decision, if the parties have their witnesses present, etc.

There is a peremptory sentence passed in court for ready payment, and if the party against whom judgment is given prove
refractory, the other may send the common officer, who has power to distrain, and at the same time to exact a fine of £20 Scots,
for the use of the proprietor, and about two marks for himself.

The heads of tribes had their offensive and defensive leagues,
called bonds of mandrate, and man-rent in the Lowlands; by
which each party was obliged to assist one another upon all

extraordinary emergencies. And though the differences between those chieftains involved several confederates in a civil war, yet they obliged themselves by the bond mentioned above to continue steadfast in their duty to their sovereign. When the proprietor gives a farm to his tenant, whether for one or more years, it is customary to give the tenant a stick of wood, and some straw in his hand: this is immediately returned by the tenant again to his master, and then both parties are as much obliged to perform their respective conditions as if they had signed a lease or any other deed.

Church Discipline

Every parish in the Western Isles has a church judicature, called the consistory, or kirk session, where the minister presides, and a competent number of laymen, called elders, meet with him. They take cognisance of scandals, censure faulty persons, and with that strictness, as to give an oath to those who are suspected of adultery or fornication; for which they are to be proceeded against according to the custom of the country. They meet after divine service; the chief heritor of the parish is present, to concur with them and enforce their acts by his authority, which is irresistible within the bounds of his jurisdiction.

A Form of Prayer Used by Many of the Islanders at Sea After the Sails Are Hoisted

[This form is contained in the Irish liturgy composed by Mr John Kerswell, afterwards Bishop of Argyll; printed in the year 1566, and dedicated to the Earl of Argyll. I have set down the original for the satisfaction of such readers as understand it.]

Modh Bendaighthe luinge ag dul diondsaidhe na fairrge
  Abradh aón do chách marso.
    An Stiuradóir:

Beandaighidh ar long.
   Fregra Cháich:
Go mbeandaighe Dia Athair i.
   An Stiuradóir:
Beandaidhidh ar long.
   Fregra:
Go mbeandaighe Iosa Criosd i.
   An Stiuradóir:
Beandaidhidh ar long.
Créd is eagail libh is Dia Athair libh.
   Fregra:
Ni heagal én ní.
   An Stiuradóir:
GD mbeandaighe an Sbiorad Naomhi.
Créd is eagil libh is Dia Athair libh.
   Fregra:
Ní heagal én ní.
   An Stiuradóir:
Créd is eagail libh is Dia an Sbiorod Naomh libh.
   Fregra:
Ní heagal én ní.
      An Stiuradóir:

*Dia Athair uile chumhachtach ar grádh a Mhic Iosa Criosd,
le comhshurtacht an Sbioraid Naomh, An taon Dia tug Cland
Israhél trid an Muir ruaigh go mírbhuileach, agas tug Iónás ad
tir ambroind an mhil mhoir, tug Pol Easpol, agas a long gona,
foirind ó onfadh iomarcach, agas o dheartan doininde dar sa
oradhne, agas dar sénadh, agas dar mbeandughadh, agas dar
mbreith lé sén, agas le soinind, agas lé sólas do chum chuain,
agas chaluidh do réir a thoile diadha féin.*
Ar ni iarrmoid air ag rádha.
Ar Nathairne atá ar Neamh, etc.
Abradh cách uile.
   Biodh Amhluidh.

The Manner of Blessing the Ship
When They Put to Sea

The Steersman says:
Let us bless our ship.
The answer by all the crew:
God the Father bless her.
Steersman:
Let us bless our ship:
Answer:
Jesus Christ bless her:
Steersman:
Let us bless our ship:
Answer:
The Holy Ghost bless her.
Steersman:
What do you fear since God the Father is with you?
Answer:
We do not fear anything.
Steersman:
What do you fear since God the Son is with you?
Answer:
We do not fear anything.
Steersman:
What are you afraid of since God the Holy Ghost is with you?
Answer:
We do not fear anything.
Steersman:
God the Father Almighty, for the love of Jesus Christ his Son, by the comfort of the Holy Ghost, the one God, who miraculously brought the children of Israel through the Red Sea and brought **Jonas** to land out of the belly of the whale, and the apostle St Paul and his ship to safety from the troubled raging sea and from

the violence of a tempestuous storm, deliver, sanctify, bless, and conduct us peaceably, calmly, and comfortably through the sea to our harbour, according to his divine will, which we beg, saying, Our Father, etc.

VII

A Description of the Isle of Skye

━━►●◄━━

SKYE (in the ancient language *skianach*, i.e., 'winged') is so called because the two opposite northern promontories (Vaterness lying north-west, and Trotterness north-east) resemble two wings. This isle lies for the most part half way in the western sea, between the mainland on the east, the shire of Ross, and the western isle of Lewis, etc.

This isle is very high land, as well on the coast as higher up in the country; and there are seven high mountains near one another, almost in the centre of the isle.

This island is forty miles in length from south to north, and in some places twenty, and in others thirty in breadth; the whole may amount to a hundred miles in circumference.

The channel between the south of Skye and opposite mainland (which is part of the shire of Inverness) is not above three leagues in breadth; and where the ferryboat crosseth to Glenelg it is so narrow that one may call for the ferryboat and be easily heard on the other side. This isle is a part of the sheriffdom of Inverness, and formerly of the diocese of the Isles, which was united to that of Argyll: a south-east moon causeth a springtide here.

The mould is generally black, especially in the mountains; but there is some of a red colour, in which iron is found. The arable land is for the most part black, yet affords clay of different colours, as white, red, and blue; the rivulet at Dunvegan church, and that of Nisbost, have fuller's earth.

The villages Borve and Glenmore afford two very fine sorts of earth, the one red, the other white; and they both feel and cut like melted tallow. There are other places that afford plenty of very fine white marl, which cuts like butter, it abounds most in Corchattachan, where an experiment has been made of its virtue: a quantity of it being spread on a sloping hill, covered with heath, soon after all the heath fell to the ground, as if it had been cut with a knife. They afterwards sowed barley on the ground, which, though it grew but unequally, some places producing no grain, because perhaps it was unequally laid on; yet the produce was thirty-five fold, and many stalks carried five ears of barley. This account was given me by the present possessor of the ground, Lauchlin Mackinnon.

There are marcasites black and white, resembling silver ore, near the village Sartle: there are likewise in the same place several stones, which in bigness, shape, etc., resemble nutmegs, and many rivulets here afford variegated stones of all colours. The Applesglen near Loch Fallart has agate growing in it of different sizes and colours; some are green on the outside, some are of a pale sky colour, and they all strike fire as well as flint: I have one of them by me, which for shape and bigness is proper for a sword handle. Stones of a purple colour flow down the rivulets here after great rains.

There is crystal in several places of this island, as at Portree, Quillin, and Mingis; it is of different sizes and colours, some are sexangular, as that of Quillin, and Mingis; and there is some in Mingis of a purple colour. The village Torrin in Strath affords a great deal of good white and black marble; I have seen cups made of the white, which is very fine. There are large quarries of freestone in several parts of this isle, as at Suisness in Strath, in the south of Borrie and isle of Raasay. There is abundance of limestone in Strath and Trotterness: some banks of clay on the east coast are overflowed by the tide, and in these grow the

Lapis ceranius, or *Cerna amomis*, of different shapes; some of the breadth of a crown-piece, bearing an impression resembling the sun; some are big as a man's finger, in form of a semicircle, and furrowed on the inner side; others are less, and have furrows of a yellow colour on both sides. These stones are by the natives called crampstones, because (as they say) they cure the cramp in cows, by washing the part affected with water in which this stone has been steeped for some hours. The velumnites grow likewise in these banks of clay; some of them are twelve inches long, and tapering towards one end: the natives call them bot stones, because they believe them to cure the horses of the worms which occasion that distemper, by giving them water to drink in which this stone has been steeped for some hours.

This stone grows likewise in the middle of a very hard grey stone on the shore. There is a black stone in the surface of the rock on Rigshore, which resembles goats' horns.

The *Lapis hecticus,* or white hectic stone, abounds here both in the land and water: the natives use this stone as a remedy against dysentery and diarrhoea; they make them red hot in the fire, and then quench them in milk, and some in water, which they drink with good success. They use this stone after the same manner for consumptions, and they likewise quench these stones in water with which they bathe their feet and hands.

The stones on which the scurf called *corkir* grows are to be had in many places on the coast, and in the hills. This scurf dyes a pretty crimson colour, first well dried, and then ground to powder, after which it is steeped in urine, the vessel being well secured from air, and in three weeks it is ready to boil with the yarn that is to be dyed. The natives observe the decrease of the moon for scraping this scurf from the stone, and say it is ripest in August.

There are many white scurfs on stone, somewhat like these on which the *corkir* grows, but the *corkir* is white and thinner than any other that resembles it.

There is another coarser scurf called *crostil*. It is of a dark colour, and only dyes a philamot.

The rocks in the village Ord have much talk growing on them like the Venice talk.

This isle is naturally well provided with variety of excellent bays and harbours. In the south of it lies the peninsula called Oronsa, alias island Dierman. It has an excellent place for anchorage on the east side, and is generally known by most Scotch seamen. About a league more easterly in the same coast there is a small rock, visible only at half low water, but may be avoided by steering through the middle of the channel. About a league more easterly in the same coast there is an anchorage pretty near the shore. Within less than a mile further is the narrow sound called the Kyle, in order to pass which it is absolutely necessary to have the tide of flood for such as are northward bound, else they will be obliged to retire in disorder, because of the violence of the current; for no wind is able to carry a vessel against it. The quite contrary course is to be observed by vessels coming from the north. A mile due east from the Kyle there is a big rock on the south side the point of land on Skye side, called Kaillach, which is overflowed by the tide of flood; a vessel may go near its outside. Above a mile further due north there are two rocks in the passage through the Kyle; they are on the castle side, and may be avoided by keeping the middle of the channel. About eight miles more to the northward, or the east of Skye, there is secure anchorage between the isle Scalpa and Skye, in the middle of the channel; but one must not come to it by the south entry of Scalpa; and in coming between Raasay and this isle there are rocks without the entry, which may be avoided best by having a pilot of the country. More to the north is Loch Sligachan, on the coast of Skye, where is good anchorage. The entry is not deep enough for vessels of any burden, except at high water, but three miles further north lies Loch Portree, a capacious and convenient harbour of above a mile in length.

The island Tulm, which is within half a mile of the northernmost point of Skye, has a harbour on the inside. The entrance between the isle and Duntulm Castle is the best.

On the west of the same wing of Skye, and about five miles more southerly, lies Loch Uig, about a mile in length, and a very good harbour for vessels of the greatest burden. About two miles on this coast further south is Loch Snizort. It is three miles in length and half a mile in breadth; it is free from rocks, and has convenient anchorage.

On the west side of the promontory, at the mouth of Loch Snizort, lies Loch Arnizort, being about two miles in length, and half a mile in breadth. There are two small isles in the mouth of the entry, and a rock near the west side, a little within the entry.

Some five miles to the west of Arnizort lies Loch Fallart; the entry is between Vaterness Head on the east side, and Dunvegan Head on the west side. The loch is six miles in length, and about a league in breadth for some miles; it hath the island Isa about the middle, on the east side. There is a rock between the north end and the land, and there vessels may anchor between the north-east side of the isle and the land; there is also good anchorage near Dunvegan Castle, two miles further to the southward.

Loch Brakadil lies two miles south of Loch Fallart; it is seven miles in length, and has several good anchoring places. On the north side of the entry lie two rocks called Macleod's Maidens. About three miles south-west is Loch Einard, a mile in length; it has a rock in the entry, and is not visible but at an ebb.

About two miles to the eastward there is an anchoring place for barks, between Skye and the isle Soa.

About a league further east lie Loch Slapan and Loch Essort. The first reaches about four miles to the north, and the second about six miles to the east.

There are several mountains in the isle of a considerable height and extent – as Quillin, Scornifiey, Bein-store, Bein-vore-scowe, Bein-chro, Bein-nin-Kaillach. Some of them are covered with snow on the top in summer, others are almost quite covered with sand on the top, which is much washed down with the great rains. All these mountains abound with heath and grass, which serve as good pasturage for lack cattle and sheep.

The Quillin, which exceeds any of those hills in height, is said to be the cause of much rain, by breaking the clouds that hover about it, which quickly after pour down in rain upon the quarter on which the wind then blows. There is a high ridge of one continued mountain of considerable height, and fifteen miles in length, running along the middle of the east wing of Skye called Trotterness, and that part above the sea is faced with a steep rock.

The arable ground is generally along the coast and in the valleys between the mountains, having always a river running in the middle. The soil is very grateful to the husbandman. I have been shown several places that had not been tilled for seven years before, which yielded a good product of oats by digging, though the ground was not dunged, particularly near the village Kilmartin, which the natives told me had not been dunged these forty years last. Several pieces of ground yield twenty, and some thirty, fold when dunged with sea-ware. I had an account that a small tract of ground in the village Skorybreck yielded a hundred fold of barley.

The isle of Altig, which is generally covered with heath, being manured with sea-ware, the owner sowed barley in the ground, and it yielded a very good product – many stalks had five ears growing upon them. In plentiful years Skye furnishes the opposite continent with oats and barley. The way of tillage here is after the same manner that is already described in the isles of Lewis, etc.; and digging doth always produce a better increase here than ploughing.

All the mountains in this isle are plentifully furnished with variety of excellent springs and fountains, some of them have rivulets with water-mills upon them. The most celebrated well in Skye is Loch Siant Well. It is much frequented by strangers, as well as by the inhabitants of the isle, who generally believe it to be a specific for several diseases – such as stitches, headaches, stone, consumptions, migraine. Several of the common people oblige themselves by a vow to come to this well and make the ordinary tour about it, called *dessil,* which is performed thus: They move thrice round the well, proceeding sunways from east to west, and so on. This is done after drinking of the water, and when one goes away from the well it is a never-failing custom to leave some small offering on the stone which covers the well. There are nine springs issuing out of the hill above the well, and all of them pay the tribute of their water to a rivulet that falls from the well. There is a little freshwater lake within ten yards of the said well. It abounds with trouts, but neither the natives nor strangers will ever presume to destroy any of them, such is the esteem they have for the water.

There is a small coppice near to the well, and there is none of the natives dare venture to cut the least branch of it, for fear of some signal judgment to follow upon it.

There are many wells here esteemed effectual to remove several distempers. The lightest and wholesomest water in all the isle is that of Toubir Tellibreck in Uig. The natives say that the water of this well and the sea plant called dulse would serve instead of food for a considerable time of war. I saw a little well in Kilbride, in the south of Skye, with one trout only in it. The natives are very tender of it and although they often chance to catch it in their wooden pails they are very careful to preserve it from being destroyed. It has been seen there for many years. There is a rivulet not far distant from the well, to which it hath probably had access through some narrow passage.

There are many rivers on all quarters of the isle. About thirty of them afford salmon, and some of them black mussels, in which pearl do breed, particularly the river of Kilmartin and the River Ord. The proprietor told me that some years ago a pearl had been taken out of the former valued at £20 sterling. There are several cataracts, as that in Sker-horen, Holm, Rig, and Tout. When a river makes a great noise in time of fair weather it is a sure prognostic here of rain to ensue.

There are many freshwater lakes in Skye, and generally well stocked with trout and eels. The common fly and the earthworms are ordinarily used for angling trout. The best season for it is a calm, or a south-west wind.

The largest of the freshwater lakes is that named after St Columba, on the account of the chapel dedicated to that saint. It stands in the isle, about the middle of the lake.

There is a little freshwater lake near the south side of Loch Einordstard, in which mussels grow that breed pearl.

This isle hath anciently been covered all over with woods, as appears from the great trunks of fir trees, etc., dug out of the bogs frequently, etc. There are several coppices of wood scattered up and down the isle. The largest, called Lettir-hurr, exceeds not three miles in length.

Herrings are often taken in most or all the bays mentioned above; Loch Essort, Slapan, Loch Fallart, Loch Scowsar, and the Kyle of Scalpa, are generally known to strangers, for the great quantities of herring taken in them. This sort of fish is commonly seen without the bays, and on the coast all the summer. All other fish follow the herring and their fry, from the whale to the least fish that swims; the biggest still destroying the lesser.

The fishers and others told me that there is a big herring almost double the size of any of its kind, which leads all that are in a bay, and the shoal follows it wherever it goes. This leader is by the fishers called the king of herring, and when they chance to catch it alive, they drop it carefully into the sea; for they judge it petty treason to destroy a fish of that name.

The fishers say that all sorts of fish, from the greatest to the least, have a leader, who is followed by all of its kind.

It is a general observation all Scotland over, that if a quarrel happen on the coast where herring is caught, and that blood be drawn violently, then the herring go away from the coast, without returning during that season. This, they say, has been observed in all past age, as well as at present; but this I relate only as a common tradition, and submit it to the judgment of the learned.

The natives preserve and dry their herring without salt, for the space of eight months, provided they be taken after the tenth of

September, they use no other art in it but take out their guts, and then tieing a rush about their necks, hang them by pairs upon a rope made of heath cross a house; and they eat well, and free from putrefaction, after eight months keeping in this manner. Cod, ling, herring, mackerel, haddock, whiting, turbot, together with all other fish that are in the Scots seas, abound on the coasts of this island.

The best time of taking fish with an angle is in warm weather, which disposes them to come near the surface of the water, whereas in cold weather, or rain, they go to the bottom. The best bait for cod and ling is a piece of herring, whiting, thornback, haddock, or eel. The greylord, alias blackmouth, a fish of the size and shape of a salmon, takes the limpet for bait. There is another way of angling for this fish, by fastening a short white down, and are easily caught. The greylord swims in the surface of the water, and then is caught with a spear, a rope being tied to the further end of it, and secured in the fisherman's hand.

All the bays and places of anchorage here abound with most kinds of shellfish. The Kyle of Scalpa affords oysters in such plenty that commonly a springtide of ebb leaves fifteen, sometimes twenty, horse load of them on the sands.

The sands on the coast of Bernstill village at the springtides afford daily such plenty of mussels, as is sufficient to maintain sixty persons per day: and this was a great support to many poor families of the neighbourhood, in the late years of scarcity. The natives observe that all shellfish are plumper at the increase then decrease of the moon; they observe likewise that all shellfish are plumper during a south-west wind, than when it blows from the north or north-east quarters.

The limpet being parboiled with a very little quantity of water, the broth is drunk to increase milk in nurses, and likewise when the milk proves astringent to the infants. The broth of the black periwinkle is used in the same cases. It is observed that limpets being frequently eaten in June are apt to occasion the jaundice;

the outside of the fish is coloured like the skin of a person that has the jaundice: the tender yellow part of the limpet, which is next to the shell, is reckoned good nourishment, and very easy of digestion.

I had an account of a poor woman who was a native of the isle of Jura, and by the troubles in King Charles I's reign was almost reduced to a starving condition; so that she lost her milk quite, by which her infant had nothing proper for its sustenance: upon this she boiled some of the tender fat of the limpets, and gave it to her infant, to whom it became so agreeable that it had no other food for several months together, and yet there was not a child in Jura, or any of the adjacent isles, wholesomer than this poor infant, which was exposed to so great a strait.

The limpet creeps on the stone and rock in the night-time, and in a warm day; but if anything touch the shell it instantly clings to the stone, and then no hand is able to pluck it off without some instrument; and therefore such as take them have little hammers, called limpet hammers, with which they beat it from the rock; but if they watch its motion and surprise it, the least touch of the hand pulls it away: and this that is taken creeping, they say, is larger and better than that which is pulled off by force. The motion, fixation, taste and feeding, etc., of this little animal is very curious.

The pale whelk, which in length and smallness exceeds the black periwinkle, and by the natives called *gil-fiunt,* is by them beat in pieces, and both shell and fish boiled. The broth being strained, and drank for some days together, is accounted a good remedy against the stone. It is called a 'dead man's eye' at Dover. It is observed of cockles and spout-fish that they go deeper in the sands with north winds than any other, and, on the contrary, they are easier reached with south winds, which are still warmest.

It is a general observation of all such as live on the sea coast that they are more prolific than any other people whatsoever.

*

The Sea Plants Here are as Follows:

Linarich, a very thin small green plant, about eight, ten, or twelve inches in length. It grows on stone, on shells, and on the bare sand. This plant is applied plaster-wise to the forehead and temples to procure sleep for such as have a fever, and they say it is effectual for this purpose.

The linarich is likewise applied to the crown of the head and temples for removing the migraine, and also to heal the skin after a blister plaster of *Flamula Jovis*.

Slake, a very thin plant, almost round, about ten or twelve inches in circumference, grows on the rocks and sands. The natives eat it boiled, and it dissolves into oil. They say that if a little butter be added to it, one might live many years on this alone, without bread or any other food, and at the same time undergo any laborious exercise. This plant, boiled with some butter, is given to cows in the spring, to remove costiveness.

Dulse is of a reddish brown colour, about ten or twelve inches long, and above half an inch in breadth. It is eaten raw, and then reckoned to be loosening and very good for the sight; but if boiled, it proves more loosening if the juice be drank with it. This plant applied plaster-wise to the temples is reckoned effectual against the migraine. The plant boiled and eaten with its infusion is used against the colic and stone; and dried without washing it in water, pulverised and given in any convenient vehicle fasting, it kills worms. The natives eat it boiled with butter, and reckon it very wholesome. The dulse recommended here is that which grows on stone, and not that which grows on the *Alga marina*, or sea tangle: for though that be likewise eaten, it will not serve in any of the cases above-mentioned.

The *Alga marina* or sea tangle or, as some call it, sea-ware, is a rod about four, six, eight or ten feet long, having at the end a blade commonly slit into seven or eight pieces, and about a foot and a half in length. It grows on stone. The blade is eaten by the vulgar natives. I had an account of a young man who had lost his appetite and taken pills to no purpose; and being advised to boil the blade of the alga and drink the infusion boiled with a little butter, was restored to his former state of health.

There is abundance of white and red coral growing on the south and west coast of this isle. It grows on the rocks, and is frequently interwoven with the roots of the alga. The red seems to be a good fresh colour when first taken out of the sea, but in a few hours after it becomes pale. Some of the natives take a quantity of the red coral, adding the yolk of an egg roasted to it, for the diarrhoea. Both the red and white coral here is not above five inches long, and about the bigness of a goose quill.

There are many caves to be seen on each quarter of this isle, some of them are believed to be several miles in length. There is a big cave in the village Bornskittag, which is supposed to exceed a mile in length. The natives told me that a piper, who was over-curious, went into the cave with a design to find out the length of it; and after he entered began to play on his pipe, but never returned to give an account of his progress.

There is a cave in the village Rigg, wherein drops of water that issue from the roof petrify into a white limy substance, and hang down from the roof and sides of the cave.

There is a cave in the village Holm, having many petrified twigs hanging from the top; they are hollow from one end to the other, and from five to ten inches in length.

There is a big cave in the rock on the east side of Portree, large enough for eighty persons; there is a well within it, which, together with its situation and narrow entry, renders it an inaccessible fort. One man only can enter it at a time, by the side of a rock, so that with a staff in his hand he is able by the least touch to cast over the rock as many as shall attempt to come into the cave.

On the south side of Loch Portree, there is a large cave, in which many sea-cormorants do build. The natives carry a bundle of straw to the door of the cave in the night-time, and there setting it on fire, the fowls fly with all speed to the light, and so are caught in baskets laid for that purpose. The Golden Cave in Sleat is said to be seven miles in length, from the west to east.

There are many cairns or heaps of stones in this island. Some of the natives say they were erected in the times of heathenism, and that the ancient inhabitants worshipped about them. In popish countries the people still retain the ancient custom of making a tour round them.

Others say these cairns were erected where persons of distinction, killed in battle, had been buried, and that their urns were laid in the ground under the cairns. I had an account of a cairn in Knapdale, in the shire of Argyll, underneath which an urn was found. There are little cairns to be seen in some places on the common road, which were made only where crops happened to rest for some minutes; but they have laid aside the making such cairns now.

There is an erected stone in Kilbride, in Strath, which is ten feet high, and one and a half broad.

There is another of five feet high, placed in the middle of the cairn, on the south side of Loch Uig, and is called the High Stone of Uig.

There are three such stones on the seacoast opposite to Skeriness, each of them three feet high. The natives have a tradition that upon these stones a big cauldron was set, for boiling Fin MacCoul's meat. This gigantic man is reported to have been general of a militia that came from Spain to Ireland, and from thence to lose isles. All his soldiers are called Fienty from *fiun*. He is believed to have arrived in the isles in the reign of King Evan. The natives have many stories of this general and his army, with which I will not trouble the reader. He is mentioned in Bishop Leslie's history.

There are many forts erected on the coast of this isle, and supposed to have been built by the Danes. They are called by the name of *dun*, from *dain*, which in the ancient language signified a fort; they are round in form, and they have a passage all round within the wall; the door of them is low, and many of the stones are of such bulk that no number of the present inhabitants could raise them without an engine.

All these forts stand upon eminences, and are so disposed that there is not one of them which is not in view of some other, and by this means, when a fire is made upon a beacon in any one fort, it is in a few moments after communicated to all the rest; and this hath been always observed upon sight of any number of foreign vessels, or boats approaching the coast.

The forts are commonly named after the place where they are, or the person that built them; as Dun-Skudborg, Dun-Derig, Dun-Skeriness, Dun-David, etc.

There are several little stone houses, built underground, called earth houses, which served to hide a few people and their goods in time of war. The entry to them was on the sea or river side. There is one of them in the village Lachsay, and another in Camstinvag.

There are several little stone houses built above ground, capable only of one person, and round in form. One of them is to be seen in Portree, another at Lincro, and at Culuknock. They are called Teynin-druinich, i.e. 'druid's house'. Druinich signifies a retired person, much devoted to contemplation.

The fuel used here is peats dug out of the heaths. There are cakes of iron found in the ashes of some of them, and at Flodgery village there are peats from which saltpetre sparkles. There is a coal lately discovered at Holm, in Portree, some of which I have seen; there are pieces of coal dug out likewise of the sea-sand in Heldersta of Vaternish, and some found in the village Mogstat.

The cattle produced here are horses, cows, sheep, goats, and hogs. The common workhorses are exposed to the rigour of the season during the winter and spring; and though they have neither corn, hay, or but seldom straw, yet they undergo all the labour that other horses better treated are liable to.

The cows are likewise exposed to the rigour of the coldest seasons, and become mere skeletons in the spring, many of them not being able to rise from the ground without help; but they recover as the season becomes more favourable and the grass grows up: then they acquire new beef, which is both sweet and tender. The fat and lean is not so much separated in them as in other cows, but as it were larded, which renders it very agreeable to the taste. A cow in this isle may be twelve years old, when at the same time its beef is not above four, five, or six months old. When a calf is slain it is a usual custom to cover another calf with its skin, to suck the cow whose calf hath been slain, or else she gives no milk, nor suffers herself to be approached by anybody; and if she discover the cheat, then she grows enraged for some days, and the last remedy used to pacify her is to use the sweetest voice and sing all the time of milking her. When any man is troubled with his neighbour's cows by breaking into his enclosures he brings all to the utmost boundary of his ground, and there drawing a quantity of blood from each cow he leaves them upon the spot, from whence they go away, without ever returning again to trouble him during all that season. The cows often feed upon the *Alga marina*, or sea-ware; and they can exactly distinguish the tide of ebb from the tide of flood, though at the same time they are not within view of the sea; and if one meet them running to the shore at the tide of ebb and offer to turn them again to the hills to graze they will not return. When the tide has ebbed about two hours, so as to uncover the sea-ware, then they steer their course directly to the nearest coast in their usual order – one after another – whatever their number be. There are as many instances of this as there are tides of ebb on the shore. I had occasion to make this observation thirteen times in one week; for though the natives gave me repeated assurances of the truth of it, I did not fully believe it till I saw many instances of it in my travels along the coast. The natives have a remark, that when the cows belonging to one person do of a sudden become very irregular, and run up and down the fields, and make a loud noise without any visible cause, that it is a presage of the master's or mistress's death, of which there were several late instances given me. James Macdonald of Capstil having been killed at the battle of Killicrankie, it was observed that night that his cows gave blood instead of milk. His family and other neighbours concluded this a bad omen. The minister of the place and the mistress of the cows, together with several neighbours, assured me of the truth of this.

There was a calf brought forth in Vaterness without legs. It leaped very far, bellowed louder than any other calf, and drank much more milk. At last the owner killed it. Kenneth, the carpenter, who lives there, told me that he had seen the calf. I was also informed that a cow in Vaternish brought forth five calves at a time, of which three died.

There was a calf at Skeriness, having all its legs double, but the bones had but one skin to cover both. The owner, fancying it to be ominous, killed it, after having lived nine months. Several of the natives thereabouts told me that they had seen it.

There are several calves that have a slit in the top of their ears; and these the natives fancy to be the issue of a wild bull that comes from the sea or fresh lakes; and this calf is by them called *corky-fyre*.

There is plenty of land and waterfowl in this isle – as hawks, eagles of two kinds (the one grey and of a larger size, the other much less and black, but more destructive to young cattle), black cock, heath-hen, plovers, pigeons, wild geese, ptarmigan, and cranes. Of this latter sort I have seen sixty on the shore in a flock together. The sea-fowls are malls of all kinds – coulterneb, guillemot, sea-cormorant, etc. The natives observe that the latter, if perfectly black, makes no good broth, nor is its flesh worth eating, but that a cormorant, which hath any white feathers or down, makes good broth, and the flesh of it is good food, and the broth is usually drunk by nurses to increase their milk.

The natives observe that this fowl flutters with its wings towards the quarter from which the wind is soon after to blow.

The sea-fowl *bunivochil*, or, as some seamen call it, *carara*, and others 'bishop', is as big as a goose, of a brown colour, and the inside of the wings white, the bill is long and broad, and it is footed like a goose, it dives quicker than any other fowl whatever, it is very fat. The case of this fowl being flayed off with the fat, and a little salt laid on to preserve it, and then applied to the thigh bone, where it must lie for some weeks together, is an effectual remedy against the sciatica, of which I saw two instances. It is observed of fire arms that are rubbed over (as the custom is here) with the oil or fat of sea-fowls, that they contract rust much sooner than when done with the fat of land fowl; the fulmar oil from St Kilda only excepted, which preserves iron from contracting rust much longer than any other oil or grease whatsoever. The natives observe that when the sea-pie warbles its notes incessantly, it is a sure presage of fair weather to follow in a few hours after.

The amphibia to be seen in this isle are seals, otters, vipers, frogs, toads, and saps. The otter shuts its eyes when it eats; and this is a considerable disadvantage to it, for then several ravenous fowls lay hold on this opportunity, and rob it of its fish.

The hunters say there is a big otter above the ordinary size, with a white spot on its breast, and this they call the king of otters; it is rarely seen, and very hard to be killed. Seamen ascribe great virtues to the skin; for they say that it is fortunate in battle, and that victory is always on its side. Serpents abound in several parts of this isle; there are three kinds of them, the first black and white spotted, which is the most poisonous, and if a speedy remedy be not made use of after the wound given, the party is in danger. I had an account that a man at Glenmore, a boy at Portree, and a woman at Loch Scahvag, did all die of wounds given by this sort of serpents. Some believe that the serpents wound with the sting only, and not with their teeth; but this opinion is founded upon a bare conjecture, because the sting is exposed to view, but the teeth very rarely seen; they are secured with a hose of flesh, which prevents their being broke; the end of them being hooked and exceeding small, would soon be destroyed, if it had not been for this fence that nature has given them. The longest of the black serpents mentioned above is from two to three, or at most four feet long.

The yellow serpent with brown spots, is not so poisonous, nor so long as the black and white one.

The brown serpent is of all three the last poisonous and smallest and shortest in size.

The remedies used here to extract the poison of serpents are various. The rump of a house-cock stripped of its feathers and applied to the wound, doth powerfully extract poison, if timely applied. The cock is observed after this to swell to a great bulk, far above its former size, and being thrown out into the fields, no ravenous bird of best will ever offer to taste of it.

The forked sting taken out of an adder's tongue, is by the natives steeped in water, with which they wash and cure the wound.

The serpent's head that gives the wound, being applied, is found to be a good remedy.

New cheese applied timely extracts the poison well.

There are two sorts of weasels in the isle, one of which exceeds that of the common size in bigness; the natives say that the breath of it kills calves, and lambs, and that the lesser sort is apt to occasion a decay in such as frequently have them tame about them; especially such as suffer them to suck and lick about their mouths.

VIII

The Inferior Isles about Skye

SOA-BRETTIL lies within a quarter of a mile to the south of the mountain Quillin; it is five miles in circumference, and full of bogs, and fitter for pasturage than cultivation. About a mile on the west side it is covered with wood, and the rest consists of heath and grass, having a mixture of the mertillo all over. The red garden currants grow in this isle, and are supposed to have been carried thither by birds. There has been no venomous creature ever seen in this little isle, until within these two years last that a black and white big serpent was seen by one of the inhabitants, who killed it; they believe it came from the opposite coast of Skye, where there are many big serpents. There is abundance of cod and ling round this isle.

On the south of Sleat lies island Oronsa, which is a peninsula at low water, it is a mile in circumference, and very fruitful in corn and grass. As for the latter, it is said to excel any piece of ground of its extent in those parts.

In the north entry to Kyle-Akin, lie several small isles; the biggest and next to Skye is Ilan Nan Gillin, about half a mile in circumference, covered all over with long heath, and the *Erica baccifera*; there is abundance of seals, and sea-fowls about it.

A league further north lies the isle Pabbay, about two miles in circumference; it excels in pasturage, the cows in it afford near double the milk that they yield in Skye. In the dog-days there is a big fly in this isle which infests the cows, makes them run up and down, discomposes them exceedingly, and hinders their feeding insomuch that they must be brought out of the isle to the isle of Skye. This isle affords abundance of lobsters, limpets, whelks, crabs, and ordinary sea plants.

About half a league further north lies the small isle Gillman, being a quarter of a mile in circumference; the whole is covered with long heath and the *Erica baccifera*. Within a call further north lies the isle Scalpa, very near to Skye, five miles in circumference; it is mountainous from the south end, almost to the north end, it has wood in several parts of it; the south end is most arable, and is fruitful in corn and grass.

About a mile further north is the isle Raasay, being seven miles in length, and three in breadth, sloping on the west and east sides; it has some wood on all the quarters of it, the whole is fitter for pasturage than cultivation, the ground being generally very unequal, but very well watered with rivulets and springs. There is a spring running down the face of a high rock on the east side of the isle; it petrifies into a white substance, of which very fine lime is made, and there is a great quantity of it. There is a quarry of good stone on the same side of the isle; there is abundance of caves on the west side, which serve to lodge several families, who for their convenience in grazing, fishing, etc., resort thither in the summer. On the west side, particularly near to the village Clachan, the shore abounds with smooth stones of different sizes, variegated all over. The same cattle, fowl, and fish are produced here that are found in the isle of Skye. There is a law observed by the natives that all their fishing lines must be of equal length, for the longest is always supposed to have best access to the fish, which would prove a disadvantage to such as might have shorter ones.

There are some forts in this isle, the highest is in the south end; it is a natural strength, and in form like the crown of a hat; it is called Dun-Cann, which the natives will needs have to be from one Canne, cousin to the King of Denmark. The other lies on the side, is an artificial fort, three stories high, and is called Castle Vreokle.

The proprietor of the isle is Mr MacLeod, a cadet of the family of that name; his seat is in the village Clachan. The inhabitants have as great veneration for him as any subjects can have for their king. They preserve the memory of the deceased ladies of the place by erecting a little pyramid of stone for each of them, with the lady's name. These pyramids are by them called crosses; several of them are built of stone and lime, and have three steps of gradual ascent to them. There are eight such crosses about the village, which is adorned with a little tower, and lesser houses, and an orchard with several sorts of berries, pot herbs, etc. The inhabitants are all Protestants, and use the same language, habit, and diet, with the natives of Skye.

About a quarter of a mile further north lies the isle Rona, which is three miles in length; vessels pass through the narrow channel between Raasay and Rona. This little isle is the most unequal rocky piece of ground to be seen anywhere: there is but very few acres fit for digging, the whole is covered with long heath, *Erica baccifera*, mertillus, and some mixture of grass; it is reckoned very fruitful in pasturage: most of the rocks consist of the hectic stone, and a considerable part of them is of a red colour.

There is a bay on the south-west end of the isle, with two entries, the one is on the west side, the other on the south, but the latter is only accessible; it has a rock within the entry, and a good fishing.

About three leagues to the north-west of Rona is the isle Fladda, being almost joined to Skye; it is all plain arable ground, and about a mile in circumference.

About a mile to the north lies the isle Altvig; it has a high rock facing the east, is near two miles in circumference, and is reputed fruitful in corn and grass; there is a little old chapel in it, dedicated to St Turos. There is a rock of about forty yards in length at the north end of the isle, distinguished for its commodiousness in fishing. Herrings are seen about this rock in great numbers all summer, insomuch that the fisher boats are sometimes as it were entangled among the shoals of them.

The isle of Troda lies within half a league to the northern-most point of Skye, called Hunish; it is two miles in circumference, fruitful in corn and grass, and had a chapel dedicated to St Columba. The natives told me that there is a couple of ravens in the isle which suffer none other of their kind to come thither, and when their own young are able to fly they beat them also away from the isle.

Fladda-Chuan, i.e., 'Fladda of the ocean', lies about two leagues distant from the west side of Hunish Point; it is two miles in compass, the ground is boggy, and but indifferent for corn and grass; the isle is much frequented for the plenty of fish of all kinds, on which quarter of it. There are very big whales which pursue the fish on the coast; the natives distinguish one whale for its bigness above all others, and told me that it had many big limpets growing upon its back, and that the eyes of it were of such a prodigious bigness as struck no small terror into the beholders. There is a chapel in the isle dedicated to St Columba, it has an altar in the east end, and there is a blue stone of a round form on it, which is always moist. It is an ordinary custom, when any of the fishermen are detained in the isle by contrary winds, to wash the blue stone with water all round, expecting thereby to procure a favourable wind, which the credulous tenant living in the isle says never fails, especially if a stranger washes the stone: the stone is likewise applied to the sides of people troubled with stitches, and they say it is effectual for that purpose. And so great is the regard they have for this stone that they swear decisive oaths on it.

The monk O'Gorgon is buried near to this chapel, and there is a stone five feet high at each end of his grave. There is abundance of sea-fowl that come to hatch their young in the isle; the coulternebs are very numerous here, it comes in the middle of March, and goes away in the middle of August; it makes a tour round the isle sunways, before it settles on the ground, and another at going away in August; which ceremony is much approved by the tenant of the isle, and is one of the chief arguments he made use of for making the like round, as he sets out to see with his boat.

There is a great flock of plovers that come to this isle from Skye, in the beginning of September, they return again in April, and are said to be near two thousand in all; I told the tenant he might have a couple of these at every meal during the winter and spring, but my motion seemed very disagreeable to him; for he declared that he had never once attempted to take any of them, though he might if he would; and at the same time he told me he wondered how I could imagine that he would be so barbarous as to take the lives of such innocent creatures as came to him only for self-preservation.

There are six or seven rocks within distance of a musket shot, on the south-east side of the isle, the sea running between each of them: that lying more easterly is the fort called Bord Cruin, i.e. a 'round table', from its round form; it is about three hundred paces in circumference, flat in the top, has a deep well within it, the whole is surrounded with a steep rock, and has only one place that is accessible by climbing, and that only by one man at a time: there is a violent current of tide on each side of it, which contributes to render it an impregnable fort, it belongs to Sir Donald MacDonald. One single man above the entry, without being exposed to shot, is able with a staff in his hand, to keep off five hundred attackers; for one only can climb the rock at a time, and that not without difficulty.

There is a high rock on the west side of the fort, which may be secured also by a few hands.

About half a league on the south side the round table lies the rock called Jeskar, i.e. 'fisher', because many fishing boats resort to it; it is not higher than a small vessel under sail. This rock affords a great quantity of scurvy-grass, of an extraordinary size, and very thick; the natives eat it frequently, as well boiled as raw: two of them told me that they happened to be confined there for the space of thirty hours, by a contrary wind; and being without victuals, fell to eating this scurvy-grass, and finding it of a sweet taste, far different from the land scurvy-grass, they ate a large basketful of it, which did abundantly satisfy their appetites until their return home. They told me also that it was not in the least windy, or any other way troublesome to them.

Island Tulm on the west of the wing of Skye, called Trotternes, lies within a musket shot of the castle of the name; it is a hard rock, and clothed with grass; there are two caves on the west side, in which abundance of sea-cormorants build and hatch.

About five leagues to the south-west from Tulm lies the island Ascrib, which is divided into several parts by the sea; it is about two miles in compass, and affords very good pasturage; all kinds of fish abound in the neighbouring sea. On the south-west side of the isle Ascrib, at the distance of two leagues, lie the two small isles of Timan, directly in the mouth of Loch Arnizort; they are only fit for pasturage.

On the west side of Vaterness promontory, within the mouth of Loch Fallart, lies Isa, two miles in compass, being fruitful in corn and grass, and is commodious for fishing of cod and ling.

There are two small isles, called Mingoy, on the north-east side of this isle, which afford good pasturage.

There is a red short kind of dulse growing on the south end of the isle, which occasions a pain in the head when eaten, a property not known in any other dulse whatever.

The two isles Buia and Harlas lie in the mouth of Loch Brackadil; they are both pretty high rocks, each of them about a mile in circumference, they afford good pasturage, and there are redcurrants in these small isles, supposed to have been carried there at first by birds.

The southern parts of Skye, as Sleat and Strath, are a month earlier with their grass than the northern parts; and this is the reason that the cattle and sheep, etc. bring forth their young sooner than in the north side.

The days in summer are both longer here than in the south of England, or Scotland, and the nights shorter, which about the summer solstice is not above an hour and a half in length;

and the further we come south the contrary is to be observed in proportion.

The air here is commonly moist and cold. This disposes the inhabitants to take a larger dose of brandy or other strong liquors than in the south of Scotland, by which they fancy that they qualify the moisture of the air. This is the opinion of all strangers, as well as of the natives, since the one as well as the other drinks at least treble the quantity of brandy in Skye and the adjacent isles that they do in the more southern climate.

The height of the mountains contributes much to the moisture of the place, but more especially the mountain Quillin, which is the husbandman's almanac; for it is commonly observed that if the heavens about that mountain be clear and without clouds in the morning then it is not doubted but the weather will prove fair, and *e contra*, the height of that hill reaching to the clouds breaks them, and then they presently after fall down in great rains according as the wind blows. Thus when the wind blows from the south then all the ground lying to the north of Quillin hills is wet with rains, whereas all the other three quarters are dry.

The south-west winds are observed to carry more rain with them than any other, and blow much higher in the most northern point of Skye than they do two miles further south; for which I could perceive no visible cause, unless it be the height of the hill about two miles south from that point; for after we come to the south side of it the wind is not perceived to be so high as on the north side by half.

It is observed of the east wind that though it blow but very gentle in the isle of Skye and on the west side of it for the space of about three or four leagues towards the west, wet, as we advance more westerly, it is sensibly higher, and when we come near to the coast of the more western isles of Uist, Harris, etc., it is observed to blow very fresh, though at the same time it is almost calm on the west side of the isle Skye. The wind is attended with fair weather, both in this and other western isles.

The sea in time of a calm is observed to have a rising motion before the north wind blows, which it has not before the approaching of any other wind.

The north wind is still colder, and more destructive to corn, cattle, etc., than any other.

Women observe that their breasts contract to a lesser bulk when the wind blows from the north, and that then they yield less milk than when it blows from any other quarter, and they make the like observation in other creatures that give milk.

They observe that when the sea yields a kind of pleasant and sweet scent it is a sure presage of fair weather to ensue.

The wind in summer blows stronger by land than by sea, and the contrary in winter.

In the summer the wind is sometimes observed to blow from different quarters at the same time. I have seen two boats sail quite contrary ways, until they came within less than a league of each other, and then one of them was becalmed, and the other continued to sail forward.

The tide of ebb here runs southerly, and the tide of flood northerly, where no head lands or promontories are in the way to interpose; for in such cases the tides are observed to hold a course quite contrary to the ordinary motion in these isles and the opposite mainland. This is observed between the east side of Skye and the opposite continent, where the tide of ebb runs northerly, and the tide of flood southerly, as far as Killach-stone, on the south-east of Skye, both tides running directly contrary to what is to be seen in all the western isles and opposite continent. The natives at Kylakin told me that they had seen three different ebbings successively on that part of Skye.

The tide of ebb is always greater with north winds than when it blows from any other quarter, and the tide of flood is always higher with south winds than any other.

The two chief springtides are on the tenth of September and on the tenth or twentieth of March.

The natives are very much disposed to observe the influence of the moon on human bodies, and for that cause they never dig their peats but in the decrease: for they observe that if they are cut in the increase they continue still moist and never burn clear, nor are they without smoke, but the contrary is daily observed of peats cut in the decrease.

They make up their earthen dykes in the decrease only, for such as are made at the increase are still observed to fall.

They fell their timber, and cut their rushes in time of the decrease.

IX

The Diseases Known and not Known in Skye—Of the Various Effects of Fishes on Several Constitutions in These Islands—Yeast, How Preserved by Natives—Effects of Eating Hemlock Root—Graddan—Their Habit—Way of Fighting

⟐

THE gout, corns in the feet, convulsions, madness, fits of the mother, vapours, palsy, lethargy, rheumatisms, wens, ganglions, king's evil, ague, surfeits, and consumptions are not frequent, and barrenness and abortion very rare.

The diseases that prevail here are fevers, stitches, colic, headache, migraine, jaundice, sciatica, stone, smallpox, measles, rickets, scurvy, worms, fluxes, toothache, cough, and squinance.

The ordinary remedies used by the natives, are taken from plants, roots, stones, animals, etc.

To cure a pleurisy the letting of blood plentifully is an ordinary remedy.

Whey, in which violets have been boiled, is used as a cooling and refreshing drink for such as are ill of fevers. When the patient has not a sweat duly, their shirt is boiled in water, and afterwards put on them; which causes a speedy sweat. When the patient is very costive, and without passage by stool or urine, or passes the ordinary time of sweating in fevers, two or three handfuls of the sea plant called dulse, boiled in a little water, and some fresh butter with it, and the infusion drunk procures passage both ways, and sweat shortly after: the dulse growing on stone, not that on the sea-ware, is only proper in this case.

To procure sleep after a fever, the feet, knees, and ankles of the patient are washed in warm water, into which a good quantity of chickweed is put, and afterwards some of the plant is applied warm to the neck, and between the shoulders, as the patient goes to bed.

The tops of nettles, chopped small, and mixed with a few whites of raw eggs, applied to the forehead and temples, by way of a frontel, is used to procure sleep.

Foxglove, applied warm plasterwise to the part affected, removes pains that follow after fevers.

The sea plant linarich, is used to procure sleep, as is mentioned among its virtues.

Erica baccifera, boiled a little in water, and applied warm to the crown of the head and temples, is used likewise as a remedy to procure sleep.

To remove stitches, when letting blood does not prevail, the part affected is rubbed with an ointment made of camomile and fresh butter, or of brandy with fresh butter, and others apply a quantity of raw scurvy-grass chopped small.

The scarlet fever, which appeared in this isle only within these two years last, is ordinarily cured by drinking now and then a glass of brandy. If an infant happen to be taken with it, the nurse drinks some brandy, which qualifies the milk, and proves a successful remedy.

The common alga, or sea-ware, is yearly used with success to manure the fruit trees in Sir Donald Macdonald's orchard at Armidill: several affirm, that if a quantity of sea-ware be used about the roots of fruit trees whose growth is hindered by the sea air, this will make them grow and produce fruit.

Headache is removed by taking raw dulse and linarich applied cold by way of a plaster to the temples. This likewise is used as a remedy to remove the migraine.

The jaundice is cured by the vulgar, as follows: the patient being stripped naked behind to the middle of the back, he who acts the surgeon's part marks the eleventh bone from the rump on the back with a black stroke in order to touch it with his tongs, as mentioned already.

Sciatica is cured by applying the case with the fat of the carara-fowl to the thigh bone; and it must not be removed from thence till the cure is performed.

Flamula Jovis, or spirewort, being cut small, and a limpet shell filled with it, and applied to the thigh bone, causes a blister to rise about the bigness of an egg; which being cut, a quantity of watery matter issues from it: the blister rises three times, and being emptied as often, the cure is performed. The sea plant *linarich* is applied to the place, to cure and dry the wound.

Crowfoot of the moor is more effectual for raising a blister, and curing the sciatica, than *Flamula Jovis*: for that sometimes fails of breaking, or raising the skin, but the crowfoot seldom fails.

Several of the common people have the boldness to venture upon the *Flamula Jovis*, instead of a purge. They take a little of the infusion, and drink it in melted fresh butter as the properest vehicle: and this preserves the throat from being excoriated.

For the stone they drink water-gruel without salt. They likewise eat allium or wild garlic, and drink the infusion of it boiled in water, which they find effectual both ways. The infusion of the sea plant dulse boiled is also good against the stone; as is likewise the broth of whelks and limpets. And against the colic, costiveness, and stitches a quantity of scurvy-grass, boiled in water, with some fresh butter added, and eaten for some days, is an effectual remedy.

To kill worms, the infusion of tansy in whey, or aqua vitae, taken fasting, is an ordinary medicine with the islanders.

Caryophylata Alpina Chamedress fol. It grows on marble in divers parts, about Christ Church in Strath; never observed before in Britain, and but once in Ireland, by Mr Hiaton. [*Morison's Hist. Ray Synopsis*, 137.]

Carmel, alias knaphard, by Mr James Sutherland called *Argatilis sylvaticus*. It has a blue flower in July. The plant itself is not used, but the root is eaten to expel wind; and they say it prevents drunkenness by frequent chewing of it; and being so used, gives a good relish to all liquors, milk only excepted. It is aromatic, and the natives prefer it to spice for brewing aqua vitae. The root will keep for many years; some say that it is cordial, and allays hunger.

Shunnis is a plant highly valued by the natives, who eat it raw, and also boiled with fish, flesh, and milk. It is used as a sovereign remedy to cure the sheep of the cough. The root taken fasting expels wind. It was not known in Britain except in the northwest isles, and some parts of the opposite continent. Mr James Sutherland sent it to France some years ago.

A quantity of wild sage, chewed between one's teeth, and put into the ears of cows or sheep that become blind, cures them, and perfectly restores their sight, of which there are many fresh instances both in Skye and Harris, by persons of great integrity.

A quantity of wild sage chopped small, and eaten by horses mixed with their corn, kills worms. The horse must not drink for ten hours after eating it.

The infusion of wild sage after the same manner produces the like effect.

Wild sage cut small, and mixed among oats given to a horse fasting, and kept without drink for seven or eight hours after, kills worms.

Fluxes are cured by taking now and then a spoonful of the syrup of blue berries that grow on the mertillus.

Plantain boiled in water, and the hectic stone hearted red hot quenched in the same, is successfully used for fluxes.

Some cure the toothache by applying a little of the *Flamula Jovis* in a limpet shell to the temples.

A green turf heated among embers, as hot as can be endured, and by the patient applied to the side of the head affected, is likewise used for the toothache.

For coughs and colds, water-gruel with a little butter is the ordinary cure.

For coughs and hoarseness they used to bathe the feet in warm water, for the space of a quarter of an hour at least; and then rub a little quantity of deer's grease (the older the better) to the soles of their feet by the fire. The deer's grease alone is sufficient in the morning; and this method must be continued until the cure is performed. And it may be used by young or old, except women with child, for the first four months, and such as are troubled with vapours.

Hart's tongue and maidenhair boiled in wort and the ale drunk is used for coughs and consumptions.

Milk or water, wherein the hectic stone hath been boiled or quenched red hot, and being taken for ordinary drink, is also efficacious against a consumption.

The hands and feet often washed in water, in which the hectic stone has been boiled, is esteemed restorative.

Yarrow, with the hectic stone boiled in milk, and frequently drunk, is used for consumptions.

Water-gruel is also found by experience to be good for consumptions. It purifies the blood, and procures appetite, when drunk without salt.

There is a smith in the parish of Kilmartin, who is reckoned a doctor for curing faintness of the spirits. This he performs in the following manner:

The patient being laid on the anvil with his face uppermost, the smith takes a big hammer in both his hands, and making his face all grimace, he approaches his patient; and then drawing his hammer from the ground, as if he designed to hit him with his full strength on the forehead, he ends in a faint, else he would be sure to cure the patient of all diseases; but the smith being accustomed to the performance, has a dexterity of managing his hammer with discretion; though at the same time he must do it so as to strike terror in the patient; and this, they say, has always the designed effect.

The smith is famous for his pedigree; for it has been observed of a long time that there has been but one only child born in the family, and that always a son, and when he arrived to man's estate, the father died presently after: the present smith makes up the thirteenth generation of that race of people who are bred to be smiths, and all of them pretend to this cure.

Ilica passio, or twisting of the guts, has been several times cured by drinking a draught of cold water, with a little oatmeal in it, and then hanging the patient by the heels for some time. The last instance in Skye was by John Morison, in the village of Talisker, who by this remedy alone cured a boy of fourteen years of age. Dr Pitcairn told me that the like cure had been performed in the shire of Fife for the same disease. A cataplasm of hot dulse, with its juice, applied several times to the lower part of the belly, cured the iliac passion.

The sea plant dulse is used, as is said above, to remove colics; and to remove that distemper and costiveness, a little quantity of fresh butter, and some scurvy-grass boiled and eaten with its infusion, is a usual and effectual remedy.

A large handful of the sea plant dulse, growing upon stone, being applied outwardly, as is mentioned above, against the *ilica passio,*takes away the afterbirth with great ease and safety; this remedy is to be repeated until it produce the desired effect, though some hours may be intermitted: the fresher the dulse is, the operation is the stronger: for if it is above two or three days old, little is to be expected from it in this case. This plant seldom or never fails of success, though the patient had been delivered several days before; and of this I have lately seen an extraordinary instance at Edinburgh in Scotland, when the patient was given over as dead.

Dulse, being eaten raw or boiled, is by daily experience found to be an excellent antiscorbutic; it is better raw in this case, and must be first washed in cold water.

For a fracture, the first thing they apply to a broken bone is the white of an egg, and some barley-meal; and then they tie splinters round it, and keep it so tied for some days. When the splinters are untied, they make use of the following ointment, viz. a like quantity of *Betonica Pauli,* St John's wort, golden rod, all cut and bruised in sheep's grease, or fresh butter, to a consistence; some of this they spread on a cloth, and lay on the wound, which continues untied for a few days.

Giben of St Kilda, i.e. the fat of sea-fowls made into a pudding in the stomach of the fowl, is also an approved vulnerary for man or beast.

The vulgar makes purges of the infusion of scurvy-grass, and some fresh butter, and this they continue to take for the space of a week or two, because it is mild in its operation.

They use the infusion of the sea plant dulse after the same manner, instead of a purge.

Eyes that are bloodshot or become blind for some days are cured here by applying some blades of the plant fern, and the yellow is by them reckoned best; this they mix with the white of an egg, and lay it on some coarse flax – and the egg next to the face and brows, and the patient is ordered to lie on his back.

To open a tumour or boil they cut female jacobea small, mix it with some fresh butter on a hot stone, and apply it warm; and this ripens and draws the tumour quickly, and without pain; the same remedy is used for women's breasts that are hard or swelled.

For taking the syroms out of the hands they use ashes of burnt sea-ware, mixed with salt water, and washing their hands in it, without drying them, it kills the worms.

Burnt ashes of sea-ware preserve cheese, instead of salt; which is frequently practised in this isle. Ashes of burnt sea-ware scour flaxen thread better, and make it whiter than anything else.

When their feet are swelled and benumbed with cold, they scarify their heels with a lancet.

They make blisters of the plant mercury, and some of the vulgar use it as a purge, for which it serves both ways.

They make blisters also of the roots of flags, water, and salt butter.

They have found out a strange remedy for such as could never ease nature at sea by stool or urine. There were three such men in the parish of St Mary's, in Trotterness. Two of them I knew, to wit, John Macphade and Finlay Macphade; they lived on the coast, and went often a fishing, and after they had spent some nine or ten hours at sea, their bellies would swell; for after all their endeavours to get passage either ways, it was impracticable until they came to land, and then they found no difficulty in the thing. This was a great inconvenience to any boat's crew in which either of these three men had been fishing, for it obliged them often to forbear when the fishing was most plentiful, and to row to the shore with any of these men that happened to become sick; for landing was the only remedy. At length one of their companions thought of an experiment to remove this inconvenience; he considered that when any of these men had got their feet on dry ground they could then ease nature with as much freedom as easy as any other person; and therefore he carried a large green turf of earth to the boat, and placed the green side uppermost, without telling the reason. One of these men who was subject to the infirmity above-mentioned, perceiving an earthen turf in the boat, was surprised at the sight of it, and enquired for what purpose it was brought thither? He that laid it there answered that he had done it to serve him, and that when he was disposed to ease nature he might find himself on land though he was at sea. The other took this as an affront, so that from words they came to blows; their fellows with much ado did separate them, and blamed him that brought the turf into the boat, since such a fancy could produce no other effect than a quarrel. All of them employed their time eagerly in fishing, until some hours after that the angry man, who before was so much affronted at the turf, was so ill of the swelling of his belly as usual, that he begged of the crew to row to the shore, but this was very disobliging to them all. He that intended to try the experiment with the turf, bid the sick man stand on it, and he might expect to have success by it; but he refused, and still resented the affront which he thought was intended upon him; but at last all the boat's crew urged him to try what the turf might produce, since it could not make him worse than he was. The man being in great pain was by their repeated importunities prevailed upon to stand with his feet on the turf; and it had the wished effect, for nature became obedient both ways; and then the angry man changed his note, for he thanked his doctor whom he had some hours before beat. And from that time none of these three men ever went to sea without a green turf in their boat, which proved effectual. This is matter of fact, sufficiently known and attested by the better part of the parishioners still living upon the place.

The ancient way the islanders used to procure sweat was thus: A part of an earthen floor was covered with fire, and when it was sufficiently heated the fire was taken away, and the ground covered with a heap of straw; upon this straw a quantity of water was poured, and the patient lying on the straw, the heat of it put his whole body into a sweat.

To cause any particular part of the body to sweat, they dig a hole in an earthen floor and fill it with hazel sticks and dry rushes; above these they put a hectic stone, red hot, and pouring some water into the hole, the patient holds the part affected over it, and this procures a speedy sweat.

Their common way of procuring sweat is by drinking a large draught of water-gruel with some butter as they go to bed.

Of the Various Effects of Fishes on Several Constitutions in These Islands

Dongal MacEwan became feverish always after eating fish of any kind, except thornback and dogfish.

A ling fish, having brown spots on the skin, causes such as eat of its liver to cast their skin from head to foot. This happened to three children in the hamlet of Talisker, after eating the liver of a brown spotted ling.

Finlay Ross and his family, in the parish of Uig, having eaten a fresh ling fish, with brown spots on its skin, he and they became indisposed and feverish for some few days, and in a little time after they were blistered all over. They say that when the fresh ling is salted a few days, it has no such effect.

There was a horse in the village Bretill which had the erection backward, contrary to all other of its kind.

A weaver in Portree has a faculty of erecting and letting fall his ears at pleasure, and opens and shuts his mouth on such occasions.

A boy in the castle of Duntulm, called 'Mister' to a by-name, hath a pain and swelling in his great toe at every change of the moon, and it continues only for the space of one day, or two at most.

Allan Macleod, being about ten years of age, was taken ill of a pain which moved from one part of his body to another, and where it was felt the skin appeared blue; it came to his toe, thigh, testicles, arms, and head; when the boy was bathed in warm water he found most ease. The hinder part of his head, which was last affected, had a little swelling; and a woman endeavouring to squeeze the humour out of it, by bruising it on each side with her nails, she forced out at the same time a little animal near an inch in length, having a white head sharp pointed, the rest of its body of a red colour, and full of small feet on each side. Animals of this sort have been seen in the head and legs of several persons in the isles, and are distinguished by the name of *fillan*.

Yeast, How Preserved by Natives

A rod of oak, of four, five, six, or eight inches about, twisted round like a with, boiled in wort, well dried, and kept in a little bundle of barley-straw, and being steeped again in wort, causeth it to ferment, and procures yeast: the rod is cut before the middle of May, and is frequently used to furnish yeast; and being preserved and used this manner, it serves for many years together. I have seen the experiment tried, and was shown a piece of a thick with, which hath been preserved for making ale with, for about twenty or thirty years.

Effects of Eating Hemlock Root

Fergus Caird, an empiric, living in the village Talisker, having by a mistake eaten hemlock root, instead of the white wild carrot, his eyes did presently roll about, his countenance became very pale, his sight had almost failed him, the frame of his body was all in a strange convulsion, and his pudenda retired so inwardly, that there was no discerning whether he had then been male or female. All the remedy given him in this state was a draught of hot milk, and a little aqua vitae added to it; which he no sooner drank, but he vomited presently after, yet the root still remained in his stomach. They continued to administer the same remedy for the space of four or five hours together, but in vain; and about an hour after they ceased to give him anything, he voided the root by stool, and then was restored to his former state of health: he is still living, for anything I know, and is of a strong healthful constitution.

Some few years ago, all the flax in the barony of Trotterness was overrun with a great quantity of green worms, which in a few days would have destroyed it, had not a flock of ravens made a tour round the ground where the flax grew, for the space of fourteen miles, and eat up the worms in a very short time.

The inhabitants of this isle are generally well proportioned, and their complexion is for the most part black. They are not obliged to art in forming their bodies, for nature never fails to act her part bountifully to them; and perhaps there is no part of the habitable globe where so few bodily imperfections are to be seen, nor any children that go more early. I have observed several of them walk alone before they were ten months old; they are bathed all over every morning and evening, some in cold, some in warm water, but the latter is most commonly used, and they wear nothing straight about them. The mother generally suckles the child, failing of which a nurse is provided, for they seldom bring up any by hand; they give new-born infants fresh butter to take away the miconium, and this they do for several days; they taste neither sugar, nor cinnamon, nor have they any daily allowance of sack bestowed on them, as the custom is elsewhere, nor is the nurse allowed to taste ale.

The generality wear neither shoes nor stockings before they are seven, eight, or ten years old; and many among them wear no nightcaps before they are sixteen years old, and upwards; some use none all their lifetime, and these are not so liable to head-aches, as others who keep their heads warm.

They use nothing by way of prevention of sickness, observing it as a rule to do little or nothing of that nature. The abstemiousness of the mothers is no small advantage to the children: they are a very prolific people, so that many of their numerous issue must seek their fortune on the continent, and not a few in foreign countries, for want of employment at home. When they are any way fatigued by travel, or otherwise, they fail not to bathe their feet in warm water, wherein red moss has been boiled, and rub them with it going to bed.

The ancient custom of rubbing the body by a warm hand opposite to the fire, is now laid aside, except from the lower part of the thigh downwards to the ankle; this they rub before and behind, in cold weather, and at going to bed. Their simple diet contributes much to their state of health, and long life; several among them of my acquaintance arrived at the age of eighty, ninety, and upwards; but the Lady Macleod lived to the age of

103 years: she had then a comely head of hair, and a case of good teeth, and always enjoyed the free use of her understanding until the week in which she died.

The inhabitants of this and all the Western Isles do wear their shoes after Mr Locke's mode, in his book of education; and among other great advantages by it, they reckon these two – that they are never troubled with the gout, or corns in their feet.

They lie for the most part on beds of straw, and some on beds of heath; which latter being made after their way, with the tops uppermost, are almost as soft as a feather bed, and yield a pleasant scent after lying on them once. The natives by experience have found it to be effectual for drying superfluous humours, and strengthening the nerves. It is very refreshing after a fatigue of any kind. The Picts are said to have had an art of brewing curious ale with the tops of heath, but they refused to communicate it to the Scots, and so it is quite lost.

A native of this isle requires treble the dose of physic that will serve one living in the south of Scotland for a purge; yet an insider is easier purged in the south than at home. Those of the best rank are easier wrought on by purging medicines, than the vulgar.

The inhabitants are of all people easiest cured of green wounds; they are not so liable to fevers as others on such occasions; and therefore they never cut off arm or leg, though never so ill broke, and take the freedom to venture on all kinds of meat and drink, contrary to all rule in such cases, and yet commonly recover of their wounds.

Many of the natives, upon occasion of sickness, are disposed to try experiments, in which they succeed so well that I could not hear of the least inconvenience attending their practice. I shall only bring one instance more of this, and that is of the illiterate empiric Neil Beaton in Skye; who of late is so well known in the isles and continent, for his great success in curing several dangerous distempers, though he never appeared in the quality of a physician until he arrived at the age of forty years, and then also without the advantage of education. He pretends to judge of the various qualities of plants and roots by their different tastes; he has likewise a nice observation of the colours of their flowers, from which he learns their astringent and loosening qualities; he extracts the juice of plants and roots after a chemical way, peculiar to himself, and with little or no charge.

He considers his patient's constitution before any medicine is administered to them: and he has formed such a system for curing diseases as serves for a rule to him upon all occasions of this nature.

He treats Riverius's *Lilium Medicinae*, and some other practical pieces that he has heard of, with contempt; since in several instances it appears that their method of curing has failed, where his had good success.

Some of the diseases cured by him are as follows: running sores in legs and arms, grievous headaches; he had the boldness to cut a piece of a woman's skull broader than half a crown, and by this restored her to perfect health. A gentlewoman of my acquaintance having contracted a dangerous pain in her belly some days after her delivery of a child, and several medicines being used, she was thought past recovery, if she continued in that condition a few hours longer, at last this doctor happened to come there, and being employed, applied a simple plant to the part affected, and restored the patient in a quarter of an hour after the application.

One of his patients told me that he sent him a cap interlined with some seeds, etc., to wear for the cough, which it removed in little time; and it had the like effect upon his brother.

The success attending this man's cures was so extraordinary that several people thought his performances to have proceeded rather from a compact with the devil, than from the virtue of simples. To obviate this, Mr Beaton pretends to have had some education from his father, though he died when he himself was but a boy. I have discoursed him seriously at different times, and am fully satisfied that he uses no unlawful means for obtaining an end.

His discourse of the several constitutions, the qualities of plants, etc., was more solid than could be expected from one of his education. Several sick people from remote isles came to him, and some from the shire of Ross, at seventy miles distant, sent for his advice. I left him very successful, but can give no further account of him since that time.

They are generally a very sagacious people, quick of apprehension, and even the vulgar exceed all those of their rank and education I ever yet saw in any other country. They have a great genius for music and mechanics. I have observed several of their children that before they could speak were capable to distinguish and make choice of one tune before another upon the violin; for they appeared always uneasy until the tune which they fancied was played, and then they expressed their satisfaction by the motions of their head and hands.

There are several of them who invent tunes very taking in the south of Scotland and elsewhere. Some musicians have endeavoured to pass for first inventors of them by changing their name, but this has been impracticable; for whatever language gives the modern name, the tune still continues to speak its true original; and of this I have been showed several instances.

Some of the natives are very dexterous in engraving trees, birds, deer, dogs, etc., upon bone and horn, or wood, without any other tool than a sharp-pointed knife.

Several of both sexes have a quick vein of poesy, and in their language (which is very emphatic) they compose rhyme and verse, both which powerfully affect the fancy. And in my judgment (which is not singular in this matter) with as great force as that of any ancient or modern poet I ever yet read. They have generally very retentive memories; they see things at a great distance. The unhappiness of their education, and their want of converse with foreign nations, deprives them of the opportunity to cultivate and beautify their genius, which seems to have been formed by nature for great attainments. And on the other hand, their retiredness may be rather thought an advantage, at least to their better part;

according to that of the historian: '*Plus valuit apud hos ignorantia vitiorum, quam apud Graecos omnia praecepta philosophorum*': 'The ignorance of vices is more powerful among those than all the precepts of philosophy are among the Greeks.'

For they are to this day happily ignorant of many vices that are practised in the learned and polite world. I could mention several, for which they have not as yet got a name, or so much as a notion of them.

The diet generally used by the natives consists of fresh food, for they seldom taste any that is salted, except butter. The generality eat but little flesh, and only persons of distinction eat it every day and make three meals, for all the rest eat only two, and they eat more boiled than roasted. Their ordinary diet is butter, cheese, milk, potatoes, colworts, *brochan*, i.e., oatmeal and water boiled. The latter taken with some bread is the constant food of several thousands of both sexes in this and other isles, during the winter and spring; yet they undergo many fatigues both by sea and land, and are very healthful. This verifies what the poet saith, '*Populis sat est lymphaque ceresque*': 'Nature is satisfied with bread and water.'

There is no place so well stored with such great quantity of good beef and mutton, where so little of both is consumed by eating. They generally use no fine sauces to entice a false appetite, nor brandy or tea for digestion; the purest water serves them in such cases. This, together with their ordinary exercise, and the free air, preserves their bodies and minds in regular frame, free from the various convulsions that ordinarily attend luxury. There is not one of them too corpulent, nor too meagre.

The men servants have always double the quantity of bread, etc., that is given to women servants, at which the latter are no ways offended, in regard of the many fatigues by sea and land which the former undergo.

Oon, which in English signifies froth, is a dish used by several of the islanders, and some on the opposite mainland, in time of scarcity, when they want bread. It is made in the following manner: A quantity of milk or whey is boiled in a pot, and then it is wrought up to the mouth of the pot with a long stick of wood, having a cross at the lower end. It is turned about like the stick for making chocolate; and being thus made, it is supped with spoons. It is made up five or six times in the same manner, and the last is always reckoned best and the first two or three frothings the worst. The milk or whey that is in the bottom of the pot is reckoned much better in all respects than simple milk. It may be thought that such as feed after this rate are not fit for action of any kind; but I have seen several that lived upon this sort of food, made of whey only, for some months together, and yet they were able to undergo the ordinary fatigue of their employments, whether by sea or land; and I have seen them travel to the tops of high mountains as briskly as any I ever saw.

Some who live plentifully make these dishes above said of goats' milk, which is said to be nourishing. The milk is thickened, and tastes much better after so much working. Some add a little butter and nutmeg to it. I was treated with this dish in several places; and being asked whether this said dish or chocolate was best, I told them that if we judged by the effects this dish was preferable to chocolate; for such as drink often of the former enjoy a better state of health than those who use the latter.

Graddan

The ancient way of dressing corn, which is yet used in several isles, is called *graddan*, from the Irish word *grad*, which signifies quick: A woman sitting down takes a handful of corn, holding it by the stalks in her left hand, and then sets fire to the ears, which are presently in a flame. She has a stick in her right hand, which she manages very dexterously, beating off the grain at the very instant when the husk is quite burnt; for if she miss of that she must use the kiln, but experience has taught them this art to perfection. The corn may be so dressed, winnowed, ground, and baked within an hour after reaping from the ground. The oat bread dressed as above is loosening, and that dressed in the kiln astringent, and of greater strength for labourers: but they love the *graddan*, as being more agreeable to their taste. Skye, saw two women at this employment, and wondering to see so much flame and smoke he came near and finding that it was corn they burnt, he ran away in great haste telling the natives that he had seen two mad women very busy burning corn. The people came to see what the matter was, and laughed at the captain's mistake, though he was not a little surprised at the strangeness of a custom that he had never seen or heard of before.

There are two fairs of late held yearly at Portree, on the east side of Skye. The convenience of the harbour, which is in the middle of the isle, made them choose this for the fittest place. The first holds about the middle of June, the second about the beginning of September. The various products of this and the adjacent isles and continent are sold here – viz. horses, cows, sheep, goats, hides, skins, butter cheese, fish, wool, etc.

All the horses and cows sold at the fair swim to the mainland over one of the ferries or sounds called *kyles* – one of which is on the east, the other on the south side of Skye. That on the east is about a mile broad, and the other on the south is half a mile. They begin when it is near low water and fasten a twisted with about the lower jaw of each cow. The other end of the with is fastened to another cow's tail; and the number so tied together is commonly five. A boat with four oars rows off, and a man sitting in the stern holds the with in his hand to keep up the foremost cow's head; and thus all the five cows swim as fast as the boat rows; and in this manner above a hundred may be ferried over in one day. These cows are sometimes drove about 400 miles further south. They soon grow fat, and prove sweet and tender beef.

Their Habit

The first habit wore by persons of distinction in the islands was the *leni-croich*, from the Irish word *leni*, which signifies a shirt, and *croach*, 'saffron' because their shirt was dyed with that herb. The ordinary number of ells used to make this robe was twenty-four. It was the upper garb, reaching below the knees, and was tied with a belt round the middle; but the islanders have laid it aside about a hundred years ago.

They now generally use coat, waistcoat, and breeches, as elsewhere, and on their heads wear bonnets made of thick cloth – some blue, some black, and some grey.

Many of the people wear trews. Some have them very fine woven like stockings of those made of cloth. Some are coloured, and others striped. The latter are as well shaped as the former, lying close to the body from the middle downwards, and tied round with a belt about the haunches. There is a square piece of cloth which hangs down before. The measure for shaping the trews is a stick of wood, whose length is a cubit, and that divided into the length of a finger and a half a finger, so that it requires more skill to make it than the ordinary habit.

The shoes anciently wore were a piece of the hide of a deer, cow, or horse, with the hair on, being tied behind and before with a point of leather. The generality now wear shoes, having one thin sole only, and shaped after the right and left foot so that what is for one foot will not serve the other.

But persons of distinction wear the garb in fashion in the south of Scotland.

The plaid wore only by the men is made of fine wool, the thread as fine as can be made of that kind. It consists of divers colours; and there is a great deal of ingenuity required in sorting the colours so as to be agreeable to the nicest fancy. For this reason the women are at great pains, first to give an exact pattern of the plaid upon a piece of wood, having the number of every thread of the stripe on it. The length of it is commonly seven double ells. The one end hangs by the middle over the left arm, the other going round the body, hangs by the end over the left arm also – the right hand above it is to be at liberty to do anything upon occasion. Every isle differs from each other in their fancy of making plaids as to the stripes in breadth and colours. This humour is as different through the mainland of the Highlands, in so far that they who have seen those places are able at first view of a man's plaid to guess the place of his residence.

When they travel on foot the plaid is tied on the breast with a bodkin of bone or wood (just as the spina wore by the Germans, according to the description of C. Tacitus). The plaid is tied round the middle with a leather belt. It is plaited from the belt to the knee very nicely. This dress for footmen is found much easier and lighter than breeches or trews.

The ancient dress wore by the women, and which is yet wore by some of the vulgar called *arisad*, is a white plaid, having a few small stripes of black, blue, and red. It reached from the neck to the heels, and was tied before on the breast with a buckle of silver or brass, according to the quality of the person. I have seen some of the former of a hundred marks value. It was broad as any ordinary pewter plate, the whole curiously engraven with various animals, etc. There was a lesser buckle which was wore in the middle of the larger, and above two ounces weight. It had in the centre a large piece of crystal, or some finer stone, and this was set all round with several finer stones of a lesser size.

The plaid being plaited all round, was tied with a belt below the breast. The belt was of leather and several pieces of silver intermixed with the leather like a chain. The lower end of the belt has a piece of plate about eight inches long and three in breadth, curiously engraven, the end of which was adorned with fine stones or pieces of red coral. They wore sleeves of scarlet cloth, closed at the end as men's vests, with gold lace round them, having plate buttons set with fine stones. The head dress was a fine kerchief of linen straight about the head, hanging down the back taper-wise. A large lock of hair hangs down their cheeks above their breast, the lower end tied with a knot of ribbands.

The islanders have a great respect for their chiefs and heads of tribes, and they conclude grace after every meal with a petition to God for their welfare and prosperity. Neither will they, as far as in them lies, suffer them to sink under my misfortune; but in case of a decay of estate, make a voluntary contribution on their behalf, as a common duty to support the credit of their families.

Way of Fighting

The ancient way of fighting was by set battles; and for arms some had broad two-handed swords and head pieces, and others bows and arrows. When all their arrows were spent they attacked one another with sword in hand. Since the invention of guns they are very early accustomed to use them, and carry their pieces with them wherever they go. They likewise learn to handle the broadsword and target. The chief of each tribe advances with his followers within shot of the enemy, having first laid aside their upper garments; and after one general discharge they attack them with sword in hand, having their target on their left hand (as they did at Killiecrankie), which soon brings the matter to an issue, and verifies the observation made of them by our historians: '*Aut mors cito, aut victoria laeta.*'

This isle is divided into three parts, which are possessed by different proprietors. The southern part called Sleat is the property and title of Sir Donald Macdonald, knight and baronet. His family is always distinguished from all the tribes of his name by the Irish as well as English, and called Macdonald absolutely, and by way of excellence; he being reckoned by genealogists and all others the first for antiquity among all the ancient tribes, both in the isles and continent. He is lineally descended from Somerled, who, according to Buchanan, was Thane of Argyll. He got the Isles into his possession by virtue of his wife's right. His son was called Donald, and from him all the families of the name Macdonald are descended. He was the first of that name who had the title of King of the Isles. One of that name subscribing a charter granted by the king of Scots to the family of Roxburgh, writes as follows: 'Donald, King of the Isles, witness.' He would not pay homage to the king for the Isles, but only for the lands which he held of him on the continent.

One of Donald's successors married a daughter of King Robert II, the first of the name of Stuart, by whom he acquired several lands in the Highlands. The earldom of Ross came to this family by marrying the heiress of the house of Lesly. One of the earls of Ross, called John, being of an easy temper, and too liberal to the Church, and to his vassals and friends, his son Aeheas (by Buchanan called Donald) was so opposite to his father's conduct that he gathered together an army to oblige him from giving away any more of his estate. The father raised an army against his son, and fought him at sea on the coast of Mull. The place is since called the Bloody Bay. The son, however, had the victory. This disposed the father to go straight to the king, and make over the right of all his estate to him. The son kept possession some time after. However, this occasioned the fall of that great family, though there are yet extant several ancient tribes of the name, both in the isles and continent. Thus far the genealogists Macvurich and Hugh Macdonald, in their manuscripts.

The next adjacent part to Slait, and joining it on the north side, is Strath. It is the property of the Laird of Mackinnon, head of an ancient tribe.

On the north-west side of Strath lies that part of Skye called Macleod's Country, possessed by Macleod. Genealogists say he is lineally descended from Leod, son to the Black Prince of Man. He is head of an ancient tribe.

The barony of Trotterness, on the north side Skye, belongs to Sir Donald Macdonald. The proprietors and all the inhabitants are Protestants, except twelve, who are Roman Catholics. The former observe the festivals of Christmas, Easter, Good Friday, and that of St Michael's. Upon the latter they have a cavalcade in each parish, and several families bake the cake called St Michael's bannock.

X

Bute—Arran—Ailsa—Gigha

⟶➤●◀⟵

THE isle of Bute, being ten miles in length, lies on the west side of Cowal, from which it is separated by a narrow channel, in several parts not a mile broad. The north end of this isle is mountainous and heathy, being more designed for pasturage than cultivation. The mould is brown or black, and in some parts clayey. The ground yields a good produce of oats, barley, and pease. There is but little wood growing there, yet there is a coppice at the side of Loch Fad. The ground is arable from the middle to the southward; the hectic stone is to be had in many parts of this isle, and there is a quarry of red stone near the town of Rosa, by which the fort there, and the chapel on its north side, have been built. Rothesay, the head town of the shire of Bute and Arran, lies on the east coast of Bute, and is one of the titles of the Prince of Scotland. King Robert III created his son Duke of Rothesay and Steward of Scotland; and afterwards Queen Mary created the Lord Darnley Duke of Rothesay before her marriage with him. This town is a very ancient royal borough, but thinly peopled, there not being above a hundred families in it, and they have no foreign trade. On the north side of Rothesay there is a very ancient ruinous fort, round in form, having a thick wall, and about three stories high, and passages round within the wall. It is surrounded with a wet ditch; it has a gate on the south and a double gate on the east, and a bastion on each side the gate, and without these there is a drawbridge, and the sea flows within forty yards of it. The fort is large enough for exercising a battalion of men; it has a chapel and several little houses within, and a large house of four stories high fronting the eastern gate. The people here have a tradition that this fort was built by King Rosa, who is said to have come to this isle before King Fergus I. The other forts are Dun-Owle and Dun-Allin, both on the west side.

The churches here are as follows: Kilmichael, Kilblain, and Kil-Chattan, in the South Parish; and Lady Kirk in Rothesay is the most northerly parish. All the inhabitants are Protestants.

The natives here are not troubled with any epidemical disease. The smallpox visits them commonly once every sixth or seventh year. The oldest man now living in this isle is one Fleming, a weaver in Rothesay. His neighbours told me that he could never ease nature at sea, who is ninety years of age. The inhabitants generally speaking the English and Irish tongue, and wear the same habit with those of the other islands. They are very industrious fishers, especially for herring, for which use they are furnished with about eighty large boats. The tenants pay their rent with the profit of herrings, if they are to be had anywhere on the western coast.

The principal heritors here are Stuart of Bute, who is the hereditary sheriff of this shire, and hath his seat in Rosa; Ballantine of Kames, whose seat is at the head of the bay of that name, and has an orchard by it; Stuart of Estick, whose seat has a park and orchard. And about a mile to the south of Rothesay, next lies two isles called Cumbrae the greater, and the lesser, the former is within a league of Bute. This island has a chapel and a well, which the natives esteem a catholicism for all diseases. This isle is a mile in length, but the other isle is much less in compass. Both isles are the property of Montgomery of Skelmorlie.

Arran

The name of this isle is by some derived from Arran, which in the Irish language signifies bread. Others think it comes more probably from Arin or Arfyn, which in their language is as much as the place of the giant Fin MacCoul's slaughter or execution; for *aar* signifies slaughter, and so they will have Arin only the contraction of Arrin or Fin. The received tradition of the great giant Fin MacCoul's military valour, which he exercised upon the ancient natives here, seems to favour this conjecture; this, they say, is evident from the many stones set up in divers places of the isle, as monuments upon the graves of persons of note that were killed in battle. The isle is twenty-four miles from south to north, and seven miles from east to west. It lies between the isle of Bute and Kintyre, in the opposite mainland. The isle is high and mountainous, but slopes on each side round the coast, and the glen is only made use of for tillage. The mountains near Brodick Bay are of a considerable height; all the hills generally afford a good pasturage, though a great part of them be covered only with heath.

The mould here is of divers colours, being black and brown near the hills and clayey and sandy upon the coast.

The natives told me that some places of the isle afford fuller's earth. The coast on the east side is rocky near the shore. The stones on the coast, for some miles beneath Brodick, are all of a colour, and of these the castle of Brodick is built. The natives say that the mountains near the castle of Brodick afford crystal, and that the Duchess of Hamilton put so great a value on it as to be at the charge of cutting a necklace of it, which the inhabitants take as a great honour done them, because they have a great veneration for her grace. There is no considerable woods here, but a few coppices, yet that in the glen towards the west is above a mile in length. There are capacious fields of arable ground on each side Brodick Bay, as also on the opposite western coast. The largest and best field for pasturage is that on the south-west side.

Several rivers on each side this isle afford salmon, particularly the two rivers on the west called Machir side, and the two in Kirkmichael and Brodick Bay.

The air here is temperately cold and moist, which is in some measure qualified by the fresh breezes that blow from the hills, but the natives think a dram of strong waters is a good corrective.

There are several caves on the coast of this isle. Those on the west are pretty large, particularly that in Druim-cruey. A hundred men may sit or lie in it; it is contracted gradually from the floor upwards to the roof. In the upper end there is a large piece of rock formed like a pillar. There is engraven on it a deer, and underneath it a two-handed sword. There is a void space on each side this pillar.

The south side of the cave has a horseshoe engraven on it. On each side the door there is a hole cut out, and that, they say, was for holding big trees on which the caldrons hang for boiling their beef and venison. The natives say that this was the cave in which Fin MacCoul lodged during the time of his residence in this isle, and that his guards lay in the lesser caves which are near this big one. There is a little cave joining to the largest, and this they call the cellar.

There is a cave some miles more southerly on the same coast, and they told me that the minister preached in it sometimes, in regard of it being more centrical than the parish church.

Several erected stones are to be seen on each side this isle. Four of these are near Brodick Bay, about the distance of seventy yards from the river, and are seven feet high each. The highest of these stones that fell under my observation was on the south side of Kirkmichael River, and is above fifteen feet high. There is a stone coffin near it, which has been filled with human bones, until of late that the river washed away the earth and the bones that were in the coffin. MacLouis, who had seen them, says they were of no larger size than those of our own time. On the west side there are some stones erected in Baelliminich, and a fourth at some distance from these, about six feet high each. In the moor on the east side Druim-cruey, there is a circle of stones; the area is about thirty paces. There is a stone of the same shape and kind about forty paces to the west of the circle. The natives say that this circle was made by the giant Fin MacCoul, and that to the single stone, Bran, Fin MacCoul's hunting dog, was usually tied. About half a mile to the north side of Baelliminich there are two stones erected, each of them eight feet high.

There is a circle of big stones a little to the south of Druim-cruey, the area of which is about twelve paces. There is a broad thin stone in the middle of this circle, supported by three lesser stones. The ancient inhabitants are reported to have burnt their sacrifices on the broad stone in time of heathenism.

There is a thin broad stone tapering towards the top erected within a quarter of a mile of the sea, near Machir river, and is nine feet high; and at some little distance from the river there is a large cavern of stones.

There is an eminence of about a thousand paces in compass on the sea coast in Druim-cruey village, and it is fenced about with a stone wall. Of old it was a sanctuary, and whatever number of men or cattle could get within it were secured from the assaults of their enemies, the place being privileged by universal consent.

The only good harbour in this isle is Lamlash, which is in the south-east end of the isle of that name.

There is a great fishing of cod and whiting in and about this bay.

The whole isle is designed by nature more for pasturage than cultivation. The hills are generally covered all over with heath, and produce a mixture of the *Erica baccifera,* catsail, and juniper, all which are very agreeable to the eye in summer. The highest hills of this island are seen at a considerable distance from several parts of the continent and north-west isles, and they serve instead of a forest to maintain the deer, which are about four hundred in number, and they are carefully kept by a forester to give sport to the Duke of Hamilton, or any of his family that go a hunting there. For if any of the natives happen to kill a deer without licence, which is not often granted, he is liable to a fine of £20 Scots for each deer. And when they grow too numerous, the forester grants licences for killing a certain number of them, on condition they bring the skins to himself.

The cattle here are horses and cows of a middle size, and they have also sheep and goats. This isle affords the common sea and land fowls that are to be had in the Western Isles. The black cock is not allowed to be killed here without a licence; the transgressors are liable to a fine.

The castle of Brodick, on the north side of the bay of that name, stands on a plain, from which there is about 400 paces of a gradual descent towards the sea.

This castle is built in a long form. From south to north there is a wall of two stories high that encompasses the castle and tower. The space within the wall on the south side the castle is capable of mustering a battalion of men.

The castle is four storeys high, and has a tower of great height joined to the north side, and that has a bastion close to it, to which a lower bastion is added. The south and west sides are surrounded with a broad wet ditch, but the east and north sides have a descent which will not admit of a wet ditch. The gate looks to the east. This castle is the Duke of Hamilton's seat when his Grace or any of the family make their summer visit to this island. The bailiff or steward has his residence in this castle, and he has a deputation to act with full power to levy the rents, give leases of the lands, and hold courts of justice.

There is another castle belonging to the duke in the north side of the isle, at the head of Loch Kenistil, in which there is a harbour for barks and boats. The isle of Arran is the Duke of Hamilton's property (a very small part excepted). It lies in the sheriffdom of Bute, and made part of the diocese of Argyll.

The inhabitants of this island are composed of several tribes. The most ancient family among them is by the natives reckoned to be MacLouis, which in the ancient language signifies the son of Lewis. They own themselves to be descended of French parentage. Their surname in English is Fullerton, and their title Kirk-Mitchell, the place of their residence. If tradition be true, this little family is said to be of 700 years standing. The present possessor obliged me with the sight of his old and new charters, by which he is one of the king's coroners within this island, and as such he hath a halbert peculiar to his office. He has his right of late from the family of Hamilton, wherein his title and perquisites of coroner are confirmed to him and his heirs. He is obliged to have three men to attend him upon all public emergencies, and he is bound by his office to pursue all malefactors and to deliver them to the steward, or in his absence to the next judge. And if any of the inhabitants refuse to pay their rents at the usual term, the coroner is bound to take him personally or to seize his goods. And if it should happen that the coroner with his retinue of three men is not sufficient to put his office in execution, then he summons all the inhabitants to concur with him; and immediately they rendezvous to the place, where he fixes his coroner's staff. The perquisites due to the coroner are a firelet or bushel of oats and a lamb from every village in the isle, both which are punctually paid him at the ordinary terms.

The inhabitants of this isle are well proportioned, generally brown, and some of a black complexion. They enjoy a good state of health, and have a genius for all callings or employments, though they have but few mechanics. They wear the same habit with those of the nearest isles, and are very civil. They all speak the Irish language, yet the English tongue prevails on the east side, and ordinarily the ministers preach in it, and in Irish on the west side. Their ordinary asseveration is 'By Nale!', for I did not hear any oath in the island. The churches in this isle are: Kilbride in the southeast, Kilmore in the south, Cabel-Vual a chapel, Kilmichael in the village of that name, St James's Church at the north end.

The natives are all Protestants. They observe the festivals of Christmas, Good Friday, and Easter. I had like to have forgot a valuable curiosity in this isle which they call Baul Muluy, i.e. 'Molingus, his stone globe'. This saint was chaplain to Macdonald of the Isles. His name is celebrated here on the account of this globe, so much esteemed by the inhabitants. This stone for its intrinsic value has been carefully transmitted to posterity for several ages. It is a green stone, much like a globe in figure, about the bigness of a goose egg.

The virtue of it is to remove stitches from the sides of sick persons, by laying it close to the place affected; and if the patient does not outlive the distemper, they say the stone removes out of the bed of its own accord, and *e contra*. The natives use this stone for swearing decisive oaths upon it.

They ascribe another extraordinary virtue to it, and it is this: The credulous vulgar firmly believe that if this stone is cast among the front of an enemy they will all run away; and that as often as the enemy rallies, if this stone is cast among them, they still lose courage, and retired. They say that Macdonald of the Isles carried this stone about him, and that victory was always on his side when he threw it among the enemy. The custody of this globe is the peculiar privilege of a little family called clan Chattons, alias Macintosh. They were ancient followers of Macdonald of the Isles. This stone is now in the custody of Margaret Miller, alias Macintosh. She lives in Baelliminich, and preserves the globe with abundance of care. It is wrapped up in fair linen cloth, and about that there is a piece of woollen cloth; and she keeps it still locked up in her chest, when it is not given out to exert its qualities.

Ailsa

Is a big rock, about six leagues to the south-west of Arran; it rises in form of a sugar loaf, but the top is plain, and large enough for drawing up a thousand men in ranks; there is a freshwater lake in the middle of the plain, the whole isle is covered with long grass, and is inaccessible, except on the south-west side, by a stair cut out in the rock; in the middle of it there is a small tower of three storeys high with the top. There is a fresh water spring issuing out of the side of this great rock; below the entry there is a place where the fishers take up their residence during their stay about this rock in quest of cod and ling; and there is a good anchorage for their vessels very near their tents.

This rock in the summertime abounds with variety of sea-fowl, that build and hatch in it. The solan geese and coulterneb are most numerous here; the latter are by the fishers called *albanich*, which in the ancient Irish language signifies Scotsmen.

The isle has a chapel on the top called Fiunnay, and an ancient pavement or causeway.

Ailsa is the Earl of Cassillis' property, the tenant who farms it pays him one hundred marks Scots yearly; the product of the isle is hogs, fowl, down and fish. The isle Avon, above a mile in circumference, lies to the south of Kintyre Mull; it hath a harbour for barks on the north.

Gigha

The isle Gigha lies about a league from Lergy on the west side of Kintyre; it is four miles in length, and one in breadth, was formerly in the diocese, and is still part of the sheriffdom of Argyll. This isle is for the most part arable, but rocky in other parts; the mould is brown and clayey, inclining to red; it is good for pasturage and cultivation. The corn growing here is oats and barley. The cattle bred here are cows, horses, and sheep. There is a church in this island called Kilchattan, it has an altar in the east end, and upon it a font of stone which is very large, and hath a small hole in the middle which goes quite through it. There are several tombstones in and about this church; the family of the Macneils, the principal possessors of this isle, are buried under the tombstones on the east side the church, where there is a plot of ground set apart for them. Most of all the tombs have a two-handed sword engraven on them, and there is one that has the representation of a man upon it.

Near the west side the church there is a stone of about sixteen feet high, and four broad, erected upon the eminence. About sixty yards distance from the chapel there is a square stone erected about ten feet high; at this the ancient inhabitants bowed, because it was there where they had the first view of the church.

There is a cross four feet high at a little distance, and a cavern of stone on each side of it.

This isle affords no wood of any kind, but a few bushes of juniper on the little hills. The stones upon which the scur corkir grows, which dyes a crimson colour, are found here; as also those that produce the crottil, which dyes a philamot colour. Some of the natives told me that they used to chew nettles, and hold them to their nostrils to staunch bleeding at the nose; and that nettles being applied to the place would also stop bleeding at a vein, or otherwise.

There is a well in the north end of this isle called Tobermore, i.e. a 'great well', because of its effects, for which it is famous among the islanders; who, together with the inhabitants, use it as a catholicon for diseases. It is covered with stone and clay, because the natives fancy that the stream that flows from it might overflow the isle; and it is always opened by a *diroch*, i.e. an 'inmate', else they think it would not exert its virtues. They ascribe one very extraordinary effect to it, and it is this: that when any foreign boats are wind-bound here (which often happens) the master of the boat ordinarily gives the native that lets the water run a piece of money; and they say that immediately afterwards the wind changes in favour of those that are thus detained by contrary winds. Every stranger that goes to drink of the water of this well, is accustomed to leave on its stone cover a piece of money, a needle, pin or one of the prettiest variegated stones they can find.

The inhabitants are all Protestants, and speak the Irish tongue generally, there being but few that speak English; they are grave and reserved in their conversation; they are accustomed not to bury on Friday; they are fair or brown in complexion, and use the same habit, diet, etc. that is made use of in the adjacent continent and isles. There is only one inn in this isle.

The isle Caray lies a quarter of a mile south from Gigha; it is about a mile in compass, affords good pasturage, and abounds with coneys. There is a harbour for barks on the north-east end of it. This island is the property of MacAlister of Lergy, a family of the Macdonalds.

XI

Jura—Colonsay—Mull—Iona

———◆———

THE isle of Jura is by a narrow channel of about half a mile broad separated from Islay. The natives say that Jura is so called from Dih and Rah, two brethren, who are believed to have been Danes, the names Dih and Rah signifying as much as without grace or prosperity. Tradition says that these two brethren fought and killed one another in the village Knock-Cronm, where there are two stones erected of seven feet high each, and under them, they say, there are urns, with the ashes of the two brothers; the distance between them is about sixty yards. The isle is mountainous along the middle, where there are four hills of a considerable height. The two highest are well known to seafaring men by the name of the Paps of Jura. They are very conspicuous from all quarters of sea and land in those parts.

This isle is twenty-four miles long, and in some places six or seven miles in breadth. It is the Duke of Argyll's property, and part of the sheriffdom of Argyll.

The mould is brown and greyish on the coast, and black in the hills, which are covered with heath and some grass that proves good pasturage for their cattle, which are horses, cows, sheep, and goats. There is a variety of land and waterfowl here. The hills ordinarily have about three hundred deer grazing on them, which are not to be hunted by any without the steward's licence. This isle is perhaps the wholesomest plot of ground either in the isles or continent of Scotland, as appears by the long life of the natives and their state of health, to which the height of the hills is believed to contribute in a large measure, by the fresh breezes of wind that come from them to purify the air, whereas Islay and Gigha, on each side this isle, are much lower, and are not so wholesome by far, being liable to several diseases that are not here. The inhabitants observe that the air of this place is perfectly pure, from the middle of March till the end or middle of September. There is no epidemical disease that prevails here. Fevers are but seldom observed by the natives, and any kind of flux is rare. The gout and agues are not so much as known by them, neither are they liable to sciatica. Convulsions, vapours, palsies, surfeits, lethargies, migraines, consumptions, rickets, pains of the stomach, or coughs, are not frequent here, and none of them are at any time observed to become mad. I was told by several of the natives that there was not one woman died of childbearing there these thirty-four years past. Blood-letting and purging are not used here.

If any contract a cough, they use brochan only to remove it. If after a fever one chances to be taken ill of a stitch, they take a quantity of ladywrack, and half as much of red fog, and boil them in water. The patients sit upon the vessel, and receive the fume, which by experience they find effectual against this distemper. Fevers and the diarrhoea are found here only when the air is foggy and warm, in winter or summer.

The inhabitants for their diet make use of beef and mutton in the winter and spring, so also of fish, butter, cheese, and milk. The vulgar take *brochan* frequently for their diet during the winter and spring; and *brochan* and bread used for the space of two days restores lost appetite.

The women of all ranks eat a lesser quantity of food than the men. This and their not wearing anything straight about them is believed to contribute much to the health of both the mothers and children.

There are several fountains of excellent water in this isle. The most celebrated of them is that of the mountain Beinbrek in the

Tarbat, called Toubir ni Lechkin, that is, 'the well in a stony descent'. It runs easterly, and they commonly reckon it to be lighter by one half than any other water in this isle; for though one drink a great quantity of it at a time, the belly is not swelled, or any ways burdened by it. Natives and strangers find it efficacious against nauseousness of the stomach and the stone. The River Nissa receives all the water that issues from this well, and this is the reason they give why salmon here are in goodness and taste far above those of any other river whatever. The river of Crockbreck affords salmon also, but they are not esteemed so good as those of the River Nissa.

Several of the natives have lived to a great age. I was told that one of them, called Gillouir MacCrain, lived to have kept 180 Christmases in his own house. He died about fifty years ago, and there are several of his acquaintances living to this day, from whom I had this account.

Bailiff Campbell lived to the age of 106 years; he died three years ago; he passed the thirty-three last years before his death in this isle. Donald MacNamill, who lives in the village of Killearn at present, is arrived at the age of ninety years.

A woman of the isle of Scarba, near the north end of this isle, lived seven score years, and enjoyed the free use of her senses and understanding all her days; it is now two years since she died.

There is a cave, called King's Cave on the west side of the Tarbat, near the sea; there is a well at the entry which renders it the more convenient for such as may have occasion to lodge in it.

About two miles further from the Tarbat, there is a cave at Corpich which hath an altar in it; there are many small pieces of petrified substance hanging from the roof of this cave.

There is a place where vessels used to anchor on the west side of this island, called Whitfarlan, about 100 yards north from the porter's house.

About four leagues south from the north end of this isle, lies the bay Da'l Yaul, which is about half a mile in length; there is a rock on the north side of the entry, which they say is five fathom deep, and but three fathom within.

About a league further to the south, on the same coast, lies the small isles of Jura, within which there is a good anchoring place; the south entry is the best: island Nin Gowir must be kept on the left hand; it is easily distinguished by its bigness from the rest of the isles. Conney Isle lies to the north of this island. There are black and white spotted serpents in this isle; their head being applied to the wound, is by the natives used as the best remedy for their poison. Within a mile of the Tarbat there is a stone erected about eight feet high. Loch Tarbat on the west side runs easterly for about five miles, but is not a harbour for vessels, or lesser boats, for it is altogether rocky.

The shore on the west side affords coral and coralline. There is a sort of dulse growing on this coast, of a white colour.

Between the north end of Jura, and the isle Scarba, lies the famous and dangerous gulf, called Cory Vrekan, about a mile in breadth; it yields an impetuous current, not to be matched anywhere about the isle of Britain. The sea begins to boil and ferment with the tide of flood, and resembles the boiling of a pot; and then increases gradually, until it appears in many whirl-pools, which form themselves in sort of pyramids, and immediately after spout up as high as the mast of a little vessel, and at the same time make a loud report. These white waves run two leagues with the wind before they break; the sea continues to re-peat these various motions from the beginning of the die of flood, until it is more then half-flood, and then it decreases gradually until it hath ebbed about half an hour, and continues to boil till it is within an hour of low water. This boiling of the sea is not above a pistol-shot distant from the coast of Scarba Isle, where the white waves meet and spout up: they call it the Kaillach, i.e. 'an old hag'; and they say that when she puts on her kerchief, i.e. the whitest wave, it is then reckoned fatal to approach her. Not-withstanding this great ferment of the sea, which brings up the least shell from the ground, the smallest fisher boat may venture to cross this gulf at the last hour of the tide of flood, and at the last hour of the tide of ebb.

This gulf hath its name from Brekan, said to be son to the King of Denmark, who has drowned here, cast ashore in the north of Jura, and buried in a cave, as appears from the stone, tomb, and altar there.

The natives told me that about three years ago an English vessel happened inadvertently to pass through this gulf at the time when the sea began to boil; the whiteness of the waves, and their spouting up, was like the breaking of the sea upon a rock; they found themselves attracted irresistibly to the white rock, as they then supposed it to be: this quickly obliged them to consult their safety, and so they betook themselves to the small boat with all speed, and thought it no small happiness to land safe in Jura, committing the vessel under all her sails to the uncertain conduct of tide and wind. She was driven to the opposite continent of Knapdale, where she was no sooner arrived than the tide and wind became contrary to one another, and so the vessel was cast into a creek, where she was safe; and then the master and crew were, by the natives of this isle, conducted to her, where they found her as safe as they left her, though all her sails were still hoisted.

The natives gave me an account, that some years ago a vessel had brought some rats hither, which increased so much that they became very uneasy to the people, but on a sudden they all vanished; and now there is not one of them in the isle.

There is a church here called Killearn, the inhabitants are all Protestants, and observe the festivals of Christmas, Easter, and Michaelmas; they do not open a grave on Friday, and bury none on that day, except the grave has been opened before.

The natives here are very well proportioned, being generally black of complexion and free from bodily imperfections. They speak the Irish language, and wear the plaid, bonnet, etc., as other islanders.

The isle of Islay lies to the west of Jura, from which it is separated by a narrow channel; it is twenty-four miles in length from south to north, and eighteen from east to west; there are some little mountains about the middle on the east side. The coast is for the most part heathy and uneven, and by consequence not proper for tillage; the north end is also full of heaths and hills. The south-west and west is pretty well cultivated, and there is six miles between Kilrow on the west, and Port Escock in the east, which is arable and well inhabited. There is about one thousand little hills on this road, and all abound with limestone; among which there is lately discovered a lead mine in three different places, but it has not turned to any account as yet. The corn growing here is barley and oats.

There is only one harbour in this isle, called Loch Dale; it lies near the north end, and is of a great length and breadth; but the depth being in the middle, few vessels come within half a league of the land side.

There are several rivers in this isle affording salmon. The freshwater lakes are well stocked with trouts, eels, and some with salmons: as Loch Guirm, which is four miles in circumference, and hath several forts built on an island that lies in it.

Loch Finlagan, about three miles in circumference, affords salmon, trouts, and eels: this lake lies in the centre of the isle. The isle Finlagan, from which this lake hath its name, is in it. It is famous for being once the court in which the great Macdonald, King of the Isles, had his residence; his houses, chapel, etc., are now ruinous. His *guards de corps,* called *lucht-taeh,* kept guard on the lake side nearest to the isle; the walls of their houses are still to be seen there.

The High Court of Judicature, consisting of fourteen, sat always here; and there was an appeal to them from all the courts in the isles: the eleventh share of the sum in debate was due to the principal judge. There was a big stone of seven feet square, in which there was a deep impression made to receive the feet of Macdonald; for he was crowned King of the Isles standing in this stone, and swore that he would continue his vassals in the possession of their lands, and do exact justice to all his subjects: and then his father's sword was put into his hand. The Bishop of Argyll and seven priests anointed him king, in presence of all heads of the tribes in the isles and continent, and were his vassals; at which time the orator rehearsed a catalogue of his ancestors, etc.

There are several forts built in the isles that are in freshwater lakes, as in Ilan Loch Guirm, and Ilan Viceain, there is a fort called Dunnivag in the south-west side of the isle, and there are several caves in different places of it. The largest that I saw was in the north end, and is called Vah Vernag; it will contain 200 men to stand or sit in it. There is a kill for drying corn made on the east side of it; and on the other side there is a wall built close to the side of the cave, which was used for a bedchamber, it had a fire on the floor, and some chairs about it, and the bed stood close to the wall. There is a stone without the cave door, about which the common people make a tour sunways.

A mile on the south-west side of the cave is the celebrated well called Toubir in Knahar, which in the ancient language is as much as to say, 'the well that sallied from one place to another': for it is a received tradition among the vulgar inhabitants of this isle, and the opposite isle of Colonsay, that this well was first in Colonsay, until an imprudent woman happened to wash her hands in it, and that immediately after, the well being thus abused, came in an instant to Islay, where it is like to continue, and is ever since esteemed a catholicon for diseases by the natives and adjacent islanders; and the great resort to it is commonly every quarter-day.

It is common with sick people to make a vow to come to the well, and after drinking, they make a tour sunways round it, and then leave an offering of some small token, such as a pin, needle, farthing, or the like, on the stone cover which is above the well. But if the patient is not like to recover, they send a proxy to the well, who acts as above-mentioned, and carries home some of the water to be drank by the sick person.

There is a little chapel beside this well, to which such had found the benefit of the water, came back and returned thanks to God for their recovery.

There are several rivers on each side of this isle that afford salmon. I was told by the natives that the Brion of Islay, a famous judge, is according to his own desire, buried standing on the brink of the River Laggan, having in his right hand a spear, such as they use to dart at the salmon.

There are some isles on the coast of this island, as island Texa on the south-west, about a mile in circumference; and island Ouirsa, a mile likewise in circumference, with the small isle called Nave. The names of the churches in this isle are as follows: Kil-Chollim Kill, St Columbus his church near Port Escock, Kil-Chovan in Rins, on the west side Nerbols in the Rins, St Columbus his church in Laggan, a chapel in island Nave, and Kilhan Alen, north-west of Wilrow. There is a cross standing near St Columbus's or Port Escock side, which is ten feet high. There are two stones set up at the east side of Loch Finlagan, and they are six feet high. All the inhabitants are Protestants; some among them observe the festivals of Christmas and Good Friday. They are well proportioned and indifferently healthful. The air here is not near so good as that of Jura, from which it is but a short mile distant; but Islay is lower and more marshy, which makes it liable to several diseases that do not trouble those of Jura. They generally speak the Irish tongue; all those of the best rank speak English; they use the same habit and diet with those of Jura. This isle is annexed to the crown of Scotland. Sir Hugh Campbell of Caddell is the king's steward there, and has one half of the island. This isle is reckoned the furthest west of all the isles in Britain. There is a village on the west coast of it called Cul, i.e. 'the back part'; and the natives say it was so called because the ancients thought it the back of the world, as being the remotest part of that side of it. The natives of Islay, Colonsay, and Jura say that there is an island lying to the south-west of these isles, about the distance of a day's sailing, for which they have only a bare tradition. Mr MacSwen, present minister in the isle Jura, gave me the following account of it, which he had from the master of an English vessel that happened to anchor at that little isle, and came afterwards to Jura, which is thus:

> As I was sailing some thirty leagues to the south-west of Islay, I was becalmed near a little isle, where I dropped anchor and went ashore. I found it covered all over with long grass. There was abundance of seals lying on the rocks and on the shore; there is likewise a multitude of sea-fowls in it; there is a river in the middle, and on each side of it I found great heaps of fish bones of many sorts; there are many planks and boards cast up upon the coast of the isle, and it being all plain, and almost level with the sea, I caused my men (being then idle) to erect a heap of the wood about two stories high; and that with a design to make the island more conspicuous to seafaring men.

This isle is four English miles in length, and one in breadth. I was about thirteen hours sailing between this isle and Jura. Mr John MacSwen, above mentioned, having gone to the isle of Colonsay some few days after, was told by the inhabitants that from an eminence near the monastery in a fair day they saw it were the top of a little mountain in the south-west sea, and that they doubted not but it was land, though they never observed it before. Mr MacSwen was confirmed in this opinion by the account above mentioned; but when the summer was over, they never saw this little hill, as they called it, any more; the reason which is supposed to be this, that the high winds in all probability had cast down the pile of wood that forty seamen had erected the preceding year in that island, which, by reason of the description above recited, we may aptly enough call the Green Island.

The Isle of Colonsay

About two leagues to the north of Islay lies the isle Oronsay. It is separated from Colonsay only at the tide of flood. This peninsula is four miles in circumference, being for the most part a plain arable, dry, sandy soil, and is fruitful in corn and grass; it is likewise adorned with a church, chapel, and monastery. They were built by the famous St Columbus, to whom the church is dedicated. There is an altar in this church, and there has been a modern crucifix on it, in which several precious stones were fixed; the most valuable of these is now in the custody of MacDuffie, in black Raimused village, and it is used as a catholicon for diseases. There are several burying-places here, and the tombstones for the most part have a two-handed sword engraved on them. On the south side of the church within lie the tombs of MacDuffie and of the cadets of his family; there is a ship under sail and a two-handed sword engraven on the principal tombstone, and this inscription, *Hic jacit Malcolumbus MacDuffie de Collonsay*; his coat of arms and colour-staff is fixed in a stone, through which a hole is made to hold it. There is a cross at the east and west sides of this church, which are now broken; their height was about twelve feet each; there is a large cross on the west side of the church, of an entire stone very hard; there is a pedestal of three steps, by which they ascend to it, it is sixteen feet high, and a foot and a half broad; there is a large crucifix on the west side of this cross, it has an inscription underneath, but not legible, being almost worn off by the injury of time; the other side has three engraven on it.

About a quarter of a mile on the south side of the church there is a cairn, in which there is a stone cross fixed, called MacDuffie's Cross; for when any of the heads of this family were to be interred, their corpse was laid on this cross for some moments, in their way toward the church.

On the north side of the church there is a square stone wall, about two stories high; the area of it is about fourscore paces, and it is joined to the church wall: within this square there is a lesser square of one storey high, and about sixty paces wide, three sides of it are built of small pillars, consisting of two thin stones each, and each pillar vaulted above with two thin stones tapering upwards. There are inscriptions on two of the pillars, but few of the letters are perfect. There are several houses without the square which the monks lived in. There is a garden at twenty yards distance on the north side the houses.

The natives of Colonsay are accustomed, after their arrival on Oronsay Isle, to make a tour sunways about the church, before they enter upon any kind of business. My landlord having one of his family sick of a fever asked for my book, as a singular favour, for a few moments. I was not a little surprised at the honest man's request, he being illiterate; and when he told me the reason of it I was no less amazed, for it was to fan the patient's face with the leaves of the book, and this he did at night. He sought the book next morning, and again in the evening, and then thanked me for so great a favour, and he told me the sick person was much better by it, and thus I understood that they had an ancient custom of fanning the face of the sick with the leaves of the Bible.

The isle Colonsay is four miles in length from east to west, and sandy on the coast, and affords but a very small product, though they plough their ground three times; the middle is rocky and heathy, which in most places is prettily mingled with thick evergreens of *Erica baccifera,* juniper, and cat's tail.

The cattle bred here are cows, horses, and sheep, all of a low size. The inhabitants are generally well proportioned, and of a black complexion; they speak only the Irish tongue, and use the habit, diet, etc. that is used in the Western Isles: they are all Protestants, and observe the festivals of Christmas, Easter, and Good Friday; but the women only observe the festival of the nativity of the Blessed Virgin. Kilouran is the principal church in this isle, and the village in which this church is, hath its name from it. There are two ruinous chapels in the south side of this isle. There are two stone chests found lately in Kilouran sands, which were composed of five stones each, and had human bones in them. There are some freshwater lakes abounding with trouts in this isle. There are likewise several forts here, one of which is called Duncoll; it is near the middle of the isle, it hath large stones in it, and the wall is seven feet broad.

The other fort is called Dun-Evan: the natives have a tradition among them, of a very little generation of people, that lived here, called Lusbirdan, the same with pigmies. This isle is the Duke of Argyll's property.

Mull

The Isle of Mull lies on the west coast opposite to Lochaber, Swoonard, and Moydart. It is divided from these by a narrow channel, not exceeding half a league in breadth; the isle is twenty-four miles long, from south to north, and as many in breadth from east to west. A south-east moon causes high tide here. This isle is in the sheriffdom of Argyll; the air here is temperately cold and moist; the fresh breezes that blow from the mountains do in some measure qualify it: the natives are accustomed to take a large dose of aqua vitae as a corrective, when the season is very moist, and then they are very careful to chew a piece of charmel root, finding it to be aromatic; especially when they intend to have a drinking bout, for they say this in some measure prevents drunkenness.

The mould is generally black, and brown, both in the hills and valleys, and in some parts a clay of different colours. The heaths afford abundance of turf and peats, which serve the natives for good fuel. There is a great ridge of mountains about the middle of the isle, one of them very high, and therefore called Bein Vore, i.e. a 'great mountain'. It is to be seen from all the Western Isles, and a considerable part of the continent. Both mountains and valleys afford good pasturage for all sorts of cattle, as sheep, goats, and deer, which herd among the hills and bushes. The horses are but of a low size, yet very sprightly; their black cattle are likewise low in size, but their flesh is very delicious and fine. There is abundance of wildfowl in the hills and valleys; and among them the black cock, heath hen, ptarmigan, and very fine hawks; the seacoast affords all such fowl as are to be had in the Western Isles. The corn growing here is only barley and oats. There is great variety of plants in the hills and valleys, but there is no wood here, except a few coppices on the coast. There are some bays, and places for anchorage about the isle. The Bay of Duart on the east side, and to the north of the castle of that name, is reckoned a safe anchoring place, and frequented by strangers. Lochbuy on the opposite west side, is but an indifferent harbour, yet vessels go into it for herring.

The coast on the west abounds with rocks for two leagues west and south-west. The Bloody Bay is over against the north end of island Columkil, and only fit for vessels of about a hundred ton.

Some few miles further to the north-east is Loch Leven, the entry lies to the westward, and goes twelve miles easterly; there are herrings to be had in it sometimes and it abounds with oysters, cockles, mussels, clams, etc.

Loch Lay lies on the south side of Loch Leven; it is proper only for small vessels; herring are to be had in it sometimes, and it abounds with variety of shellfish: the small isles, called the White Isle, and Isle of Kids, are within this bay. To the north of Loch Leven lies Loch Scafford; it enters south-west, and runs north-east: within it lies the isles Eorsae and Inchkenneth, both of which are reputed very fruitful in cattle and corn.

There is a little chapel in this isle, in which many of the inhabitants of all ranks are buried. Upon the north side of Loch Scafford lies the isle of Ulva; it is three miles in circumference, and encompassed with rocks and shelves, but fruitful in corn, grass, etc.

To the west of Ulva, lies the isle of Gometra, a mile in circumference, and fruitful in proportion to the other isles.

About four miles further lie the small isles called Kernburg-More and Kernburg-Beg; they are naturally very strong, faced all round with a rock, having a narrow entry, and a violent current of a tide on each side, so that they are almost impregnable. A very few men are able to defend these two forts against a thousand. There is a small garrison of the standing forces in them at present.

To the south of these forts lie the small isles of Fladday, Lungay, Back, and the Call of the Back; cod and ling are to be had plentifully about all these islands.

Near to the north-east end of Mull lies the isle Calve; it is above two miles in compass, has a coppice, and affords good pasturage for all kind of cattle. Between this isle and the isle of Mull, there is a capacious and excellent bay, called Toubir Mory, i.e., 'the Virgin Mary's well'; because the water of a well of that name, which is said to be medicinal, runs into the bay.

One of the ships of the Spanish Armada, called the *Florida*, perished in this bay, having been blown up by one Smallet, of Dunbarton, in the year 1588. There was a great sum of gold and money on board the ship, which disposed the Earl of Argyll, and some Englishmen, to attempt the recovery of it; but how far the latter succeeded in this enterprise is not generally well known; only that some pieces of gold and money, and a golden chain was taken out of her. I have seen some fine brass cannon, some pieces of eight, teeth, beads, and pins that had been taken out of that ship. Several of the inhabitants of Mull told me that they had conversed with their relations that were living at the harbour when this ship was blown up; and they gave an account of an admirable providence that appeared in the preservation of one Dr Beaton (the famous physician of Mull), who was on board the ship when she blew up, and was then sitting on the upper deck, which was blown up entire, and thrown a good way off; yet the doctor was saved; and lived several years after.

The black and white Indian nuts are found on the west side of this isle; the natives pulverise the black kernel or the black nut, and drink it in boiled milk for curing the diarrhoea.

There are several rivers in the isle that afford salmon, and some rivers abound with the black mussel that breeds pearl. There are also some freshwater lakes that have trouts and eels. The whole isle is very well watered with many springs and fountains. They told me of a spring in the south side of the mountain Bein Vore, that has a yellow coloured stone at the bottom, which doth not burn, or become hot, though it should be kept in the fire for a whole day together.

The amphibia in this isle are seals, otters, vipers, of the same kind as those described in the isle of Skye, and the natives use the same cures for the biting of vipers. Foxes abound in this isle, and do much hurt among the lambs and kids.

There are three castles in the isle, to wit, the castle of Duart, situated on the east, built upon a rock; the east side is surrounded by the sea. This was the seat of Sir John Maclean, head of the ancient family of the Macleans; and is now, together with the estate, which was the major part of the island, become the Duke of Argyll's property, by the forfeiture of Sir John.

Some miles further on the west coast stands the Castle of Moy, at the head of Lochbuy, and is the seat of Maclean of Lochbuy.

There is an old castle at Aros in the middle of the island, now in ruins. There are some old forts here called *duns*, supposed to have been built by the Danes. There are two parish churches in the isle, viz., Killinchen-Benorth, Loch Leven, and a little chapel called Kilwichk-Ewin, at the lake above Loch Lay; each parish hath a minister. The inhabitants are all Protestants, except two or three, who are Roman Catholics; they observe the festivals of Christmas, Easter, Good Friday, and St Michael's. They speak the Irish language generally, but those of the best rank speak English; they wear the same habit as the rest of the islanders.

Iona

This isle in the Irish language is called I Colmkil, i.e. 'the isthmus of Columbus the clergyman'. Colum was his proper name, and the addition of *kil*, which signifies a church, was added by the islanders by way of excellence; for there were few churches then in the remote and lesser isles.

The natives have a tradition among them that one of the clergymen who accompanied Columbus in his voyage thither, having at a good distance espied the isle, and cried joyfully to Columbus in the Irish language, '*Chi mi i*', 'I see her' – meaning thereby the country of which they had been in quest – that Columbus then answered, 'It shall be from henceforth called Y.'

The isle is two miles long from south to north, and one in breadth, from east to west. The east side is all arable and plain, fruitful in corn and grass; the west side is high and rocky.

This isle was anciently a seminary of learning, famous for the severe discipline and sanctity of Columbus. He built two church-es and two monasteries in it, one for men, the other for women, which were endowed by the kings of Scotland and of the Isles; so that the revenues of the church then amounted to 4,000 merks per annum. Iona was the Bishop of the Isles' cathedral, after the Scots lost the Isle of Man, in which King Gratilinch erected a church to the honour of our Saviour, called *Fanum Sodorense*. Hence it was that the Bishop of the Isles was styled *Episcopus Sodorensis*. The vicar of Iona was parson of Soroby in Tiree and Dean of the Isles. St Mary's Church here is built in form of a cross, the choir twenty yards long, the cupola twenty-one feet square, the body of the church of equal length with the choir, and the two cross aisles half that length. There are two chapels on each side of the choir, and entry to them opens with large pillars neatly carved in *basso relievo*. The steeple is pretty large; the doors, windows, etc. are curiously carved; the altar is large and of as fine marble as any I ever saw. There are several abbots buried within the church. MacIlikenich's statue is done in black marble, as big as the life, in an episcopal habit, with a mitre, crozier, ring, and stones along the breast, etc. The rest of the abbots are done after the same manner. The inscription on the tomb is as follows:

Hic jacet Joannes MacFingone, Abbas de Oui, qui obiit anno Domini milesimo quingentesimo.

Bishop Knox and several persons of distinction, as MacLeod of Harris, have also been buried here.

There are the ruins of a cloister behind the church, as also of a library, and under it a large room; the natives say it was a place for public disputations.

There is a heap of stones without the church, under which Mackean of Ardminurchin lies buried. There is an empty piece of ground between the church and the gardens, in which murderers and children that died before baptism were buried. Near to the west end of the church in a little cell lies Columbus' tomb, but without inscription. This gave me occasion to cite the distich, asserting that Columbus was buried in Ireland, at which the natives of Iona seemed very much displeased, and affirmed that the Irish who said so were impudent liars; that Columbus was once buried in this place, and that none ever came from Ireland since to carry away this corpse, which, had they attempted, would have proved equally vain and presumptuous.

Near St Columba's tomb is St Martin's cross, an entire stone of eight feet high; it is a very hard and red stone, with a mixture of grey in it. On the west side of the cross is engraven a large crucifix, and on the east a tree; it stands on a pedestal of the same kind of stone. At a little further distance is Dun Ni Manich, i.e. 'Monk's fort', built of stone and lime, in form of a bastion, pretty high. From this eminence the monks had a view of all the families in the isle, and at the same time enjoyed the free air. A little further to the west lie the black stones, which are so called, not from their colour, for that is grey, but from the effects that tradition say ensued upon perjury, if any one became guilty of it after swearing on these stones in the usual manner, for an oath made on them was decisive in all controversies.

Macdonald, King of the Isles, delivered the rights of their lands to his vassals in the isles and continent, with uplifted hands and bended knees, on the black stones; and in this posture, before many witnesses, he solemnly swore that he would never recall those rights which he then granted: and this was instead of his great seal. Hence it is that when one was certain of what he affirmed, he said positively, I have freedom to swear this matter upon the black stones.

On the south side the gate, without the church, is the tailors' house, for they only wrought in it. The natives say that in the time of a plague the outer gate was quite shut up, and that all provisions were thrown in through a hole in the gate for that purpose.

At some distance south from St Mary's is St Ouran's Church, commonly called Reliqui Ouran; the saint of that name is buried within it.

The laird of Mackinnon has a tomb within this church, which is the stateliest tomb in the isle. On the wall above the tomb there is a crucifix engraven, having the arms of the family underneath – viz. a boar's head, with a couple of sheep's bones in its jaws. The tombstone has a statue as big as life, all in armour, and upon it a ship under sail, a lion at the head, and another at the feet. The inscription on the tomb is thus:

Hic est Abbas Lachlani, Macfingone, and ejus Filius Abbatis de I. tatis in Dno M° ccc Ann.

There are other persons of distinction in the church, all done in armour.

On the south side of the church, mentioned above, is the burial place in which the kings and chiefs of tribes are buried, and over them a shrine: there was an inscription, giving an account of each particular tomb, but time has worn them off. The middlemost had written on it, 'The Tombs of the Kings of Scotland': of which forty-eight lie there.

Upon that on the right hand was written, 'The Tombs of the Kings of Ireland'; of which four were buried here.

And upon that on the left hand was written, 'The Kings of Norway'; of which eight were buried here.

On the right hand, within the entry to the churchyard, there is a tombstone now overgrown with earth, and upon it there is written, '*Hic jacet Joannes Turnbull, quondam Episcopus Canterburiensis*'. This I deliver upon the authority of Mr Jo. MacSwen, minister of Jura, who says he read it.

Next to the king's is the tombstone of Macdonald of Ila; the arms, a ship with hoisted sailes, a standard, four lions, and a tree; the inscription, '*Hic jacet Corpus Angusii Macdonuill de Ile*'.

In the west end are tombs of Gilbrid and Paul Sporran, ancient tribes of the Macdonalds.

The families of Maclean, of Duart, Lochbuy, and Coll, lie next, all in armour as big as the life.

Macallister, a tribe of the Macdonalds, Macouery of Ulvay, are both done as above.

There is a heap of stones on which they used to lay the corpse while they dug the grave. There is a stone likewise erected here, concerning which the credulous natives say that whosoever reaches out his arm along the stone three times, in the name of the Father, Son, and Holy Ghost, will never err in steering the helm of a vessel.

One tomb hath a clergyman, with this inscription upon it, '*Sancta*', etc.

About a quarter of a mile further south is the Church Ronald, in which several prioresses are buried. One of the inscriptions is:

Hic jacet Dna. Anna Terleti, filiam quandam prioriss de Iona, quae obiit Anno M° Christi, Animam Abrahamo commendamus.

Another inscription is: '*Behag nijn Sorle vic Il vrid priorissa*', i.e. 'Bathia, daughter to Somerled, son of Gilbert, prioress'.

Without the nunnery there is such another square as that beside the monastery for men. The two pavements, which are of a hard red stone, are yet entire. In the middle of the longest pavement there is a large cross like to that mentioned above, and is called MacLean's cross. There are nine places on the east side the isle, called ports for landing.

The dock which was dug out of Port Churich is on the shore, to preserve Columbus' boat called *curich*, which was made of ribs of wood, and the outside covered with hides; the boat was long and sharp-pointed at both ends. Columbus is said to have transported eighteen clergymen in this boat to Iona.

There are many pretty variegated stones on the shore below the dock; they ripen to a green colour, and are then proper for carving. The natives say these stones are fortunate, but only for some particular thing, which the person thinks fit to name, in exclusion of everything else.

There was a tribe here called Clan Vic n'Oster, from Ostiarii; for they are said to have been porters. The tradition of these is that before Columbus died thirty of his family lived then in Iona, and that upon some provocation Columbus entailed a curse upon them, which was that they might all perish to the number of five, and that they might never exceed that number, to which they were accordingly reduced; and ever since, when any woman of the family was in labour, both she and the other four were afraid of death; for if the child that was to be then born did not die, they say one of the five was sure to die; and this they affirm to have been verified on every such occasion successively to this day. I found one only of this tribe living in the isle, and both he and the natives of this and of all the Western Isles unanimously declare that this observation never failed; and all this little family is now extinct, except this one poor man.

The life of Columbus, written in the Irish character, is in the custody of John MacNeil, in the isle of Barra; another copy of it is kept by MacDonald of Benbecula.

The inhabitants have a tradition that Columbus suffered no women to stay in the isle except the nuns; and that all the tradesmen who wrought in it were obliged to keep their wives and daughters in the opposite little isle, called on that account Women's Isle. They say likewise that it was to keep women out of the isle that he would not suffer cows, sheep, or goats to be brought to it.

Beda, in this *Ecclesiastical History*, Lib. 3, Cap. 4, gives this account of him:

In the year of our Lord 565 (at the time that Justin the Younger succeeded Justinian in the government of the

Roman empire) the famous Columba, a presbyter and abbot, but in habit and life a monk, came from Ireland to Britain to preach the Word of God, to the northern provinces of the Picts, that is to those who by high and rugged mountains are separated from the southern provinces. For the southern Picts, who have their habitation on this side the same hills, had, as they affirm themselves, renounced idolatry, and received the faith a long time before, by the preaching of Ninian the Bishop, a most reverend and holy man, of the country of the Britons, who was regularly educated at Rome in the mysteries of truth.

In the ninth year of Meilochen, son to Pridius, King of Picts, a most powerful king, Columbus, by his preaching and example, converted that nation to the faith of Christ. Upon this account, they gave him the isle above mentioned (which he calls Hii, Book 3, Chap. 3) to erect a monastery in, which his successors possess to this day, and where he himself was buried in the seventy-seventh year of his age, and the thirty-second after his going to Britain to preach the gospel. He built a noble monastery in Ireland before his coming to Britain, from both which monasteries he and his disciples founded several other monasteries in Britain and Ireland, among all which the monastery of the island in which his body is interred has the preeminence. The isle has a rector, who is always a presbyter-abbot, to whose jurisdiction the whole province and the bishops themselves ought to be subject, though the thing be unusual, according to the example of that first doctor, who was not a bishop, but a presbyter and monk, and of whose life and doctrine some things are said to be wrote by his disciples. But whatever he was, this is certain, that he left successors eminent for their great chastity, divine love, and regular institution.

This monastery furnished bishops to several dioceses of England and Scotland, and amongst others Aidanus, who was sent from thence, and was Bishop of Lindisfarne, now Holy Island.

XII

Tiree—Coll—Rum—Muck—
Cannay—Egg

THIS isle lies about eight leagues to the west of Iona, or I
Colmkil.

The land is low and moorish, but there are two little hills on the
south-west side; the mould is generally brown, and for the most
part sandy. The western side is rocky for about three leagues; the
isle affords no convenient harbour for ships, but has been always
valued for its extraordinary fruitfulness in corn, yet being tilled
every year, it is become less fruitful than formerly. There is a
plain piece of ground about six miles in compass on the east coast
called the Rive; the grass is seldom suffered to grow the length of
half an inch, being only kept as a common, yet is believed to excel
any parcel of land of its extent in the isles, or opposite continent;
there are small channels in it, through which the tide of flood
comes in, and it sometimes overflows the whole.

The isle is four miles in length from the south-east to the north-
west; the natives for the most part live on barley-bread, butter,
milk, cheese, fish, and some eat the roots of silverweed; there are
but few that eat any flesh, and the servants use water-gruel often
with their bread. In plentiful years the natives drink ale generally. There are three alehouses in the isle; the brewers preserve
their ale in large earthen vessels, and say they are much better for

this purpose than those of wood; some of them contain twelve English gallons. Their measure for drink is a third part larger than any I could observe in any other part of Scotland. The ale that I had in the inn being too weak, I told my host of it, who promised to make it better, for this end he took a hectic stone, and having made it red hot in the fire, he quenched it in the ale. The company and I were satisfied that the drink was a little more brisk, and I told him that if he could add some more life to our ale he would extremely oblige the company. This he frankly undertook, and to effect it toasted a barley cake, and having broken it in pieces he put it into the dish with the ale, and this experiment we found as effectual as the first. I enquired of him if he had any more art to revive our ale and then he would make it pretty good; he answered that he knew of nothing else but a malt cake, which he had not then ready, and so we were obliged to content ourselves with what pains had been already used to revive our drink. The natives preserve their yeast by an oaken with which they twist and put into it; and for future use, keep it in barley-straw. The cows and horses are of a very low size in this isle, being in the winter and springtime often reduced to eat sea-ware. The cows give plenty of milk; when they have enough of fresh sea-ware to feed on it fattens them; the horses pace naturally, and are very sprightly though little. The ground abounds with flint stone; the natives tell me they find pieces of sulphur in several places. The west winds drive the ordinary Indian nuts to the shore of this isle, and the natives use them, as above, for removing the diarrhoea; and the water of the well called Toubir in Donich is by the natives drunk as a catholicon for diseases.

Some years ago, about one hundred and sixty little whales, the biggest not exceeding twenty feet long, ran themselves ashore in this isle, very seasonably, in time of scarcity, for the natives did eat them all, and told me that the seapork, i.e. the whale, is both wholesome and very nourishing meat. There is a freshwater lake in the middle of the isle, on the east side of which there is an old castle now in ruins. The isle being low and moorish is unwholesome, and makes the natives subject to the ague. The inhabitants living in the south-east parts are for the most part bald, and have but very thin hair on their heads. There is a cave in the south-west which the natives are accustomed to watch in the night, and then take many cormorants on it. There are several forts in the isle; one in the middle of it, and Dun-Taelk in Baelly Petris: they are in form the same with those in the northern isles. There are several great and small circles of stones in this isle. The inhabitants are all Protestants; they observe the festivals of Christmas, Good Friday, Easter, and St Michael's Day. Upon the latter there is a general cavalcade, at which all the inhabitants rendezvous. They speak the Irish tongue, and wear the Highland dress. This isle is the Duke of Argyll's property, it being one of the isles lately possessed by the laird of Maclean; the parish church in the isle is called Soroby, and is a parsonage.

The Isle of Coll

This lies about half a league to the east and north-east of Tiree, from which it hath been severed by the sea. It is ten miles in length, and three in breadth; it is generally composed of little rocky hills covered with heath. The north side is much plainer, and arable ground, affording barley and oats; the inhabitants always feed on the latter, and those of Tiree on the former. The isle of Coll produces more boys than girls; as if nature intended both these isles for mutual alliances, without being at the trouble of going to the adjacent isles or continent to be matched. The parish book, in which the number of the baptised is to be seen, confirms this observation.

There are several rivers in this isle that afford salmon. There is a freshwater lake in the south-east side, which hath trouts and eels. Within a quarter of a mile lies a little castle, the seat of Maclean of Coll, the proprietor of the isle; he and all the inhabitants are Protestants; they observe the festivals of Christmas, Good Friday, Easter, and St Michael: at the latter they have a general cavalcade. All the inhabitants speak the Irish tongue (a few excepted), and wear the habit used by the rest of the islanders. This isle is much wholesomer than that of Tiree. I saw a gentleman of Maclean of Coll's family here, aged eighty-five, who walked up and down the fields daily.

Cod and ling abound on the coast of this isle, and are of a larger size here than in the adjacent isles or continent.

On the south-east coast of this isle lie the train of rocks called the Carn of Coll; they reach about half a league from the shore, and are remarkable for their fatality to seafaring men, of which there are several late instances. There is no venomous creature in this island or that of Tiree.

Rum

This isle lies about four leagues south from Skye; it is mountainous and healthy, but the coast is arable and fruitful. The isle is five miles long from south to north, and three from east to west; the north end produces some wood. The rivers on each side afford salmon. There is plenty of land and sea-fowl; some of the latter, especially the puffin, build in the hills as much as in the rocks on the coast, in which there are abundance of caves: the rock facing the west side is red, and that on the east side grey. The mountains have some hundred of deer grazing in them. The natives gave me an account of a strange observation, which they say proves fatal to the posterity of Lachlin, a cadet of Maclean of Coll's family; that if any of them shoot at a deer on the mountain Finchra, he dies suddenly, or contracts some violent distemper, which soon puts a period to his life. They told me some instances to this purpose: whatever may be in it, there is none of the tribe above-named will ever offer to shoot the deer in that mountain.

The bay Loch Scresord on the east side is not fit for anchoring, except without the entry.

There is a chapel in this isle; the natives are Protestants; Maclean of Coll is proprietor, and the language and habit the same with the northern isles.

Isle Muck

It lies a little to the south-west of Rum, being four miles in circumference, all surrounded with a rock; it is fruitful in corn and grass; the hawks in the rocks here are reputed to be very good. The cattle, fowls, and amphibia of this island are the same as in other isles; the natives speak the Irish tongue only, and use the habit worn by their neighbours.

Isle Cannay

This isle lies about half a mile off Rum; it is two miles from south to north, and one from east to west. It is for the most part surrounded with a high rock, and the whole fruitful in corn and grass: the south end hath plenty of cod and ling.

There is a high hill in the north end, which disorders the needle in the compass: I laid the compass on the stony ground near it, and the needle went often round with great swiftness, and instead of settling towards the north, as usual, it settled here due east. The stones in the surface of the earth are black, and the rock below facing the sea is red; some affirm that the needle of a ship's compass, failing by the hill, is disordered by the force of the magnet in this rock: but of this I have no certainty.

The natives call this isle by the name Tarsin at sea; the rock Heisker on the south end abounds with wild geese in August, and then they cast their quills. The church in this isle is dedicated to St Columbus. All the natives are Roman Catholics; they use the language and habit of the other isles. Allan Macdonald is proprietor. There is good anchorage on the north-east of this isle.

A Description of the Isle of Egg

This isle lies to the south of Skye about four leagues; it is three miles in length, a mile and a half in breadth, and about nine in circumference; it is all rocky and mountainous from the middle towards the west; the east side is plainer, and more arable: the whole is indifferent good for pasturage and cultivation. There is a mountain in the south end, and on the top of it there is a high rock called Skur Egg, about a hundred and fifty paces in circumference, and has a freshwater lake in the middle of it; there is no access to this rock but by one passage, which makes it a natural fort. There is a harbour on the south-east side of this isle which may be entered into by either side the small isle without it. There is a very big cave on the south-west side of this isle, capable of containing several hundreds of people. The coast guarding the north-west is a soft quarry of white stone, having some caves in it. There is a well in the village called Fivepennies, reputed efficacious against several distempers: the natives told me that it never fails to cure any person of their first disease, only by drinking a quantity of it for the space of two or three days; and that if a stranger lie at this well in the night-time, it will procure a deformity in some part of his body, but has no such effect on a native; and this they say hath been frequently experimented.

There is a heap of stones here, called Martin Dessil, i.e. a place consecrated to the saint of that name, about which the natives oblige themselves to make a tour round sunways.

There is another heap of stones, which they say was consecrated to the Virgin Mary.

In the village on the south coast of this isle there is a well, called St Katherine's Well; the natives have it in great esteem, and believe it to be a catholicon for diseases. They told me that it had been such ever since it was consecrated by one Father Hugh, a popish priest, in the following manner: he obliged all the inhabitants to come to this well, and then employed them to bring together a great heap of stones at the head of the spring, by way of penance. This being done, he said mass at the well, and then consecrated it; he gave each of the inhabitants a piece of wax candle, which they lighted, and all of them made the *dessil*, of going round the well sunways, the priest leading them: and from that time it was accounted unlawful to boil any meat with the water of this well.

The natives observe St Katherine's anniversary; all of them come to the well, and having drank a draught of it, they make the *dessil* round it sunways; this is always performed on the 15th day of April. The inhabitants of this isle are well proportioned; they speak the Irish tongue only, and wear the habit of the islanders; they are all Roman Catholics except one woman, that is a Protestant.

There is a church here on the east side the isle, dedicated to St Donnan, whose anniversary they observe.

About thirty yards from the church there is a sepulchral urn under ground; it is a big stone hewn to the bottom, about four feet deep, and the diameter of it is about the same breadth; I caused them to dig the ground above it, and we found a flat thin stone covering the urn: it was almost full of human bones, but no head among them, and they were fair and dry. I inquired of the natives what was become of the heads, and they could not tell; but one of them said, perhaps their heads had been cut off with a two-handed sword, and taken away by the enemy. Some few paces to the north of the urn there is a narrow stone passage under ground, but how far it reaches they could give me no account.

The natives dare not call this isle by its ordinary name of Egg when they are at sea, but island Nim-ban-More, i.e. 'the isle of big women'. St Donnan's Well, which is in the south-west end, is in great esteem by the natives, for St Donnan is the celebrated tutelar of this isle. The natives do not allow Protestants to come to their burial.

The proprietors of the isle are Allan MacDonald of Moydart, and Allan MacDonald of Moron.

XIII

St Kilda, or Hirt

—⟫●⟪—

THE first of these names is taken from one Kilder, who lived here; and from him the large well Toubir-Kilda has also its name. Hirta is taken from the *ier*, which in that language signifies west: this isle lies directly opposite to the isles of North Uist, Harris, etc. It is reckoned eighteen leagues from the former, and twenty from Harries. This isle is by Peter Goas, in a map he made of it at Rotterdam, called St Kilder, it is the remotest of all the Scots north-west isles. It is about two miles in length, and one in breadth; it is faced all round with a steep rock, except the bay on the south-east, which is not a harbour fit for any vessel, though in the time of a calm one may land upon the rock, and get up into the island with a little combing. The land rises pretty high in the middle, and there is one mountain higher than any other part of the island. There are several fountains of good water on each side this isle. The corn produced here is oats and barley, the latter is the largest in the Western Isles.

The horses and cows here are of a lower size than in the adjacent isles, but the sheep differ only in the bigness of their horns, which are very long.

There is an ancient fort on the south end of the bay called Dunfir-Volg, i.e. 'the fort of the Volscii'. This is the sense put upon the word by the antiquaries of the opposite isles of Uist.

The isle of Soa is nearly half a mile distant from the west side of St Kilda; it is a mile in circumference, very high and steep all round. Borera lies above two leagues north of St Kilda; it is near a mile in circumference, the most of it surrounded with a high rock. The largest and the two lesser isles are good for pasturage, and abound with a prodigious number of sea-fowl from March till September; the solan geese are very numerous here, insomuch that the inhabitants commonly keep yearly above twenty thousand young and old in their little stone houses, of which there are some hundreds for preserving their fowls, eggs, etc. They use no salt for preserving their fowl; the eggs of the sea wildfowl are preserved some months in the ashes of peats, and are astringent to such as be not accustomed to eat them.

The solan goose is in size somewhat less than a land goose, and of a white colour except the tips of the wings which are black, and the top of their head which is yellow; their bill is long, small pointed, and very hard, and pierces an inch deep into wood, in their descent after a fish laid on a board, as some use to catch them. When they sleep they put their head under their wings, but one of them keeps watch, and if that be surprised by the fowler (which often happens) all the rest are then easily caught up the neck, one after another, but if the sentinel gives warning, by crying loud, then all the flock make their escape. When this fowl fishes for herring it flies about sixty yards high, and then descends perpendicularly into the sea, but after all other fish it descends a-squint; the reason for this manner of pursuing the herrings is, because they are in greater shoals than any other fish whatsoever.

There is a barren tribe of solan geese that keep always together and never mix among the rest that build and hatch. The solan geese come to those islands in March, taking the advantage of a south-west wind; before their coming they send a few of their number as harbingers before them, and when they have made a tour round the isles they return immediately to their company, and in a few days after the whole flock comes together and stays till September. The native make a pudding of the fat of this fowl in the stomach of it, and boil it in their water-gruel, which they call *brochan*; they drink it likewise for removing the cough. It is by daily experience found to be an excellent vulnerary.

The inhabitants eat the solan goose egg raw, and by experience find it to be a good pectoral. The solan geese are daily making up their nests from March till September, they make them in the shelves of high rocks; they fish, hatch, and make their nests by turns, and they amass for this end a great heap of grass, and such other things as they catch floating on the water. The steward of St Kilda told me that they had found a red coat in a nest, a brass sundial, and an arrow, and some Molucca beans in another nest. This solan goose is believed to be the sharpest sighted of all sea-fowls; it preserves five or six herrings in its gorget entire, and carries them to the nest, where it spews them out to serve as food to the young ones. They are observed to go a-fishing to several isles that lie about thirty leagues distant, and carry the fish in their gorget all that way; and this is confirmed by the English hooks, which are found sticking to the fish bones in their nests, for the natives have no such hooks among them.

They have another bird here called *fulmar*. It is a grey fowl, about the size of a moorhen; it has a strong bill, with wide nostrils; as often as it goes to sea, it is certain a sign of a western wind, for it sits always on the rock when the wind is to blow from any other quarter. This fowl, the natives say, picks its food out of live whales, and that it eats sorrel, for both sorts of food are found in its nest. When any one approaches the fulmar it spouts out at its bill about a quart of pure oil. The natives surprise the fowl, and preserve the oil, and burn it in their lamps. It is good against rheumatic pains and aches in the bones; the inhabitants of the adjacent isles value it as a catholicon for diseases; some take it for a vomit, others for a purge. It has been successfully used against rheumatic pains in Edinburgh and London; in the latter it has been lately used to assuage the swelling of a sprained foot, a cheek swelled with the toothache, and for discussing a hard boil; and proved successful in all the three cases.

There is plenty of cod and ling of a great size round this isle, the improvement of which might be of great advantage.

The inhabitants are about two hundred in number, and are well proportioned; they speak the Irish language only; their habit is much like that used in the adjacent isles, but coarser. They are not subject to many diseases; they contract a cough as often as any strangers land and stay for any time among them, and it continues for some eight or ten days; they say the very infants on the breast are infected by it. The men are stronger than the inhabitants of the opposite Western Isles; they feed much on fowl, especially the solan geese, puffin, and fulmar, eating no salt with them. This is believed to be the cause of a leprosy that is broken out among them of late. One of them that was become corpulent, and had his throat almost shut up, being advised by me to take salt with his meat, to exercise himself more in the fields than he had done of late, to forbear eating of fat fowl, and the fat pudding called *giben*, and to eat sorrel, was very much concerned because all this was very disagreeable; and my advising him to eat sorrel was perfectly a surprise to him; but when I bid him consider how the fat fulmar eat this plant he was at last disposed to take my advice; and by this means alone in few days after, his voice was much clearer, his appetite recovered, and he was in a fair way of recovery. Twelve of these lepers died the year after of this distemper, and were in the same condition with this man.

Both sexes have a genius for poesy, and compose entertaining verses and songs in their own language, which is very emphatical. Some years ago about twenty of their number happened to be confined on the rock Stack N'armin for several days together, without any kind of food. The season then not favouring their endeavours to return home, one of their number plucked all their knives out of the hafts, wrought a hook out of each, and then beat them out to their former length. He had a stone for an anvil, and a dagger for a hammer and file; and with these rude hooks and a few sorry fishing lines they purchased fish for their maintenance during their confinement for several days in the rock. All the men in the isle having gone to the isle Boreray for purchase, the rope that fastened their boat happened to break, and by this unlucky accident the boat was quite lost, and the poor people confined in the isle from the middle of March till the latter end of May, without so much as a crust of bread; but they had sheep, fowl, and fish in abundance. They were at a loss how to acquaint their wives and friends that all of them were alive; but to effect this, they kindled as many fires on the top of an eminence as there were men in number, this was no sooner seen, and the fires counted, than the women understood the signal, and were so overjoyed at this unexpected news that they fell to labour the ground with the footspade, a fatigue they had never been accustomed to; and that year's product of corn was the most plentiful that they had for many years before. After the steward's arrival in the isle, about the end of May, he sent his galley to bring home all the men confined in the isle, about the end of May, he sent his galley to bring home all the men confined in the isle to their so much longed for St Kilda, where the mutual joy between them and their wives and other relations was extraordinary.

The inhabitants are of the reformed religion; they assemble in the churchyard on the Lord's day, and in the morning they say the Lord's prayer, creed and ten commandments. They work at no employment till Monday, neither will they allow a stranger to work sooner. The officer, or steward's deputy commonly, and sometimes any of their neighbours, baptise their children soon after they are born, and in the following form: *A.I.* 'I baptise you to your father and mother, in the name of the Father, Son and Holy Ghost.' They marry early and publicly, all the natives of both sexes being present. The officer who performs the marriage tenders a crucifix to the married couple, who lay their right hands on it, and then the marriage is ratified.

They observe the festivals of Christmas, Easter, Good Friday, and that of All Saints. Upon the latter they bake a large cake, in form of a triangle, furrowed round, and it must be all eaten that night. They are hospitable, and charitable to strangers, as well as the poor belonging to themselves, for whom all the families contribute a proportion monthly, and at every festival each family sends them a piece of mutton or beef.

They swear decisive oaths by the crucifix, and this puts an end to any controversy; for there is not one instance, or the least suspicion of perjury among them. The crucifix is of brass, and about nine inches in length; it lies upon the altar but they pay no religious worship to it. One of the inhabitants was so sincere, that (rather than forswear himself on the crucifix) he confessed a capital crime before the minister and myself. They never swear or steal, neither do they take God's name in vain at any time; they are free from whoredom and adultery, and of those other immoralities that abound so much everywhere else.

One of the inhabitants called Roderick, a fellow that could not read, obtruded a false religion upon the credulous people, which he pretended to have received from St John the Baptist. It is remarkable that in his rhapsodies, which he called prayers, he had the word Eli; and to this purpose, Eli is our Preserver. There is a little hill, upon which he says John the Baptist delivered sermons and prayers to him; this is called John's Bush, and made the people believe it was so sacred, that if either cow or sheep did taste of its grass, they were to be killed immediately after, and the owners were to eat them, but never without the company of the impostor. He made them likewise believe that each of them had a tutelar saint in heaven to intercede for them, and the anniversary of every one of those was to be necessarily observed, by having a splendid treat, at which the impostor was always the principal person. He taught the women a devout hymn, which he said he had from the Virgin Mary; he made them believe that it secured any woman from miscarriage that could repeat it by heart, and each of them paid the impostor a sheep for it.

Upon Mr Campbell's arrival and mine in St Kilda, Roderick made a public recantation of his imposture; and being then by us brought to the isle of Harris, and afterwards to the isle of Skye, he has made public confession in several churches of his converse with the devil, and not John the Baptist, as he pretended, and seems to be very penitent. He is now in Skye isle, from whence he is never to return to his native country. His neighbours are heartily glad to be rid of such a villain, and are now happily delivered from the errors he imposed upon them. The isle is the Laird of MacLeod's property; he is head of one of the most ancient tribes in the isles; he bestows the isle upon a cadet of his name, whose fortune is low, to maintain his family, and he is called steward of it; he visits the isle once every summer, to demand the rents, viz. down, wool, butter, cheese, cows, horses, fowl, oil, and barley. The steward's deputy is one of the natives, and stays always upon the place; he has free lands, and an omer of barley from each family; and has the honour of being the first and last in their boat, as they go and come to the lesser isles or rocks. The ancient measure of omer and cubit continues to be used in this isle. They have neither gold nor silver, but barter among themselves and the steward's men for what they want. Some years ago the steward determined to exact a sheep from every family in the isle, the number amounting to twenty-seven; and for this he put them in mind of a late precedent, of their having given the like number to his predecessor. But they answered that what they gave then was voluntary, and upon an extraordinary occasion of his being wind-bound to the isle, and that this was not be a custom afterwards. However, the steward sent his brother, and with him a competent number of men, to take the sheep from them by force; but the natives, arming themselves with their daggers and fishing rods, attacked the steward's brother, giving him some blows on the head, and forced him and his party to retire, and told them that they would pay no new taxes; and by this stout resistance they preserved their freedom from such imposition.

The inhabitants live contentedly together in a little village on the side St Kilda, which they commonly call the country; and the isle Boreray, which is little more than two leagues distant from them, they call the northern country. The distance between their houses is by them called the High Street; their houses are low built, of stone, and cement of dry earth; they have couples and ribs of wood covered large baskets all full of eggs. The least of the baskets contained four hundred big eggs, and the rest eight hundred and above of lesser eggs. They had with them at the same time about two thousand sea-fowl, and some fish, together with some limpets, called patella, the biggest I ever saw. They catch many fowls likewise, by laying their gins, which are made of horsehair, having a noose at the distance of two feet each; the ends of the rope at which the noose hangs are secured by stone.

The natives gave me an account of a very extraordinary risk which one of them ran as laying his gins, which was thus: As he was walking barefoot along the rock where he had fixed his gin, he happened to put his toe in a noose, and immediately fell down the rock, but hung by the toe, the gin being strong enough to hold him, and the stones that secured it on each end being heavy. The poor man continued hanging thus for the space of a night, on a rock twenty fathoms height above the sea, until one of his neighbours, hearing him cry, came to his rescue, drew him up by the feet, and so saved him.

These poor people do sometimes fall down as they climb the rocks, and perish. Their wives on such occasions make doleful songs, which they call lamentations. The chief topics are their courage, their dexterity in climbing, and their great affection which they showed to their wives and children.

It is ordinary with a fowler, after he has got his purchase of fowls, to pluck the fattest, and carry it home to his wife as a mark of his affection; and this is called the rock-fowl.

The bachelors do in like manner carry this rock-fowl to their sweethearts, and it is the greatest present they can make, considering the danger they run in acquiring it.

The richest man in the isle has not above eight cows, eighty sheep, and two or three horses. If a native here have but a few cattle he will marry a woman, though she have no other portion from her friends but a pound of horse hair to make a gin to catch fowls.

The horses here are very low of stature, and employed only to carry home their peats and turf, which is their fuel. The inhabitants ride their horses (which were but eighteen in all) at the anniversary cavalcade of All Saints; this they never fail to observe. They begin at the shore, and ride as far as the houses; they use no saddles of any kind, nor bridle, except a rope of straw which manages the horse's head; and when they have all taken the horses by turns, the show is over for that time.

This isle produces the finest hawks in the Western Isles, for they go many leagues for their prey, there being no hand fowl in St Kilda proper for them to eat, except pigeons and plovers.

One of the inhabitants of St Kilda, being some time ago wind-bound in the isle of Harris, was prevailed on by some of them that traded to Glasgow to go thither with them. He was astonished at the length of the voyage, and of the great kingdoms, as he thought them, that is isles, by which they sailed; the largest in his way did not exceed twenty-four miles in length, but he considered how much they exceeded his own little native country.

Upon his arrival at Glasgow, he was like one that had dropped from the clouds into a new world, whose language, habit, etc., were in all respects new to him; he never imagined that such big houses of stone were made with hands; and for the pavements of the streets, he thought it must needs be altogether natural, for he could not believe that men would be at the pains to beat stones into the ground to walk upon. He stood dumb at the door of his lodging with the greatest admiration; and when he saw a coach and two horses, he thought it to be a little house they were drawing at their tail, with men in it; but he condemned the coachman for a fool to sit so uneasy, for he thought it safer to sit on the horse's back. The mechanism of the coach wheel, and its running about, was the greatest of all his wonders.

When he went through the streets, he desired to have one to lead him by the hand. Thomas Ross, a merchant, and others, that took the diversion to carry him through the town, asked his opinion of the High Church. He answered that it was a large rock, yet there were some in St Kilda much higher, but that these were the best caves he ever saw; for that was the idea which he conceived of the pillars and arches upon which the church stands. When they carried him into the church, he was yet more surprised, and held up his hands with admiration, wondering how it was possible for men to build such a prodigious fabric, which he supposed to be the largest in the universe. He could not imagine what the pews were designed for, and he fancied the people that wore masks (not knowing whether they were men or women) had been guilty of some ill thing, for which they dared not show their faces. He was amazed at women wearing patches, and fancied them to have been blisters. Pendants seemed to him the most ridiculous of all things; he condemned periwigs mightily, and much more the powder used in them; in fine, he condemned all things as superfluous he saw not in his own country. He looked with amazement on every thing that was new to him. When he heard the church bells ring he was under a mighty consternation, as if the fabric of the world had been in great disorder. He did not think there had been so many people in the world as in the city of Glasgow; and it was a great mystery to him to think what they could all design by living so many in one place. He wondered how they could all be furnished with provision; and when he saw big loaves, he could not tell whether they were bread, stone, or wood. He was amazed to think how they could be provided with ale, for he never saw any there that drank water. He wondered how they made them fine clothes, and to see stockings made without being first cut, and afterwards sewn, was no small wonder to him. He thought it foolish in women to wear thin silks, as being a very improper habit for such as pretended to any sort of employment. When he saw the women's feet, he judged them to be of another shape than those of the men, because of the different shape of their shoes. He did not approve of the heels of shoes worn by men or women; and when the observed horses with shoes on their feet, and fastened with iron nails, he could not forbear laughing, and thought it the most ridiculous thing that ever fell under his observation. He longed to see his native country again, and passionately wished it were blessed with ale, brandy, tobacco and iron, as Glasgow was.

There is a couple of large eagles who have their nest on the north end of the isle: the inhabitants told me that they commonly make their purchase in the adjacent isles and continent, and never take so much as a lamb or hen from the place of their abode, where they propagate their kind. I forgot to give an account of a singular providence that happened to a native in the isle of Skye, called Neil, who when an infant was left by his mother in the field, not far from the houses on the north side of Loch Portree, an eagle came in the meantime, and carried him away in its talons as far as the south side of the loch, and there laying him on the ground, some people that were herding sheep there perceived it, and hearing the infant cry, ran immediately to its rescue, and by good providence found him untouched by the eagle, and carried him home to his mother. He is still living in that parish, and by reason of this accident, is distinguished among his neighbours by the surname of Eagle.

XIV

An Account of the Second Sight, in Irish Called *Taish*

THE second sight is a singular faculty of seeing an otherwise invisible object, without any previous means used by the person that sees it for that end; the vision makes such a lively impression upon the seers, that they neither see nor think of anything else, except the vision, as long as it continues: and then they appear pensive or jovial, according to the object which was represented to them.

At the sight of a vision, the eyelids of the person are erected, and the eyes continue staring until the object vanishes. This is obvious to others who are by, when the persons happen to see a vision, and occurred more than once to my own observation, and to others that were with me.

There is one in Skye, of whom his acquaintance observed, that when he sees a vision, the inner part of his eyelids turn so far upwards, that after the object disappears, he must draw them down with his fingers, and sometimes employs others to draw them down, which he finds to be much the easier way.

This faculty of the second sight does not lineally descend in a family, as some imagine, for I know several parents who are endowed with it, but their children not, and vice versa. Neither is it acquired by any previous compact. And after a strict enquiry, I could never learn from any among them, that this factually was communicable any way whatsoever. The seer knows neither the object, time, nor place of a vision, before it appears; and the same object is often seen by different persons, living at a considerable distance from one another. The true way of judging as to the time and circumstance of an object, is by observation; for several persons of judgment, without this faculty, are more capable to judge of the design of a vision, than a novice that is a seer. If an object appear in the day or night, it will come to pass sooner or later accordingly.

If an object is seen early in the morning (which is not frequent) it will be accomplished in a few hours afterwards. If at noon, it will commonly be accomplished that very day. If in the evening, perhaps that night; if after candles be lighted, it will be accomplished that night: the latter always in accomplishment by weeks, months, and sometimes years, according to the time of night the vision is seen.

When a shroud is perceived about one, it is a sure prognostic of death. The time is judged according to the height of it about the person; for if it is not seen above the middle, death is not to be expected for the space of a year, and perhaps some months longer, and as it is frequently seen to ascend higher towards the head, death is concluded to be at hand within a few days, if not hours, as daily experience confirms. Examples of this kind were shown me, when the persons of whom the observations then made enjoyed perfect health.

One instance was lately foretold by a seer that was a novice, concerning the death of one of my acquaintance; this was communicated to a few only, and with great confidence; I being one of the number, did not in the least regard it, until the death of the person about the time foretold, did confirm me of the certainty of the prediction. The novice mentioned above, is now a skilful seer, as appears from many late instances; he lives in the parish of St Mary's, the most northern in Skye.

If a woman is seen standing at a man's left hand, it is a presage that she will be his wife, whether they be married to others, or unmarried at the time of the apparition.

If two or three women are seen at once standing near a man's left hand, she that is next him will undoubtedly be his wife first, and so on, whether all three, or the man be single or married at the time of the vision or not; of which there are several late instances among those of my acquaintance. It is an ordinary thing for them to see a man that is to come to the house shortly after, and if he is not of the seer's acquaintance, yet he gives such a lively description of his stature, complexion, habit, etc. that upon his arrival he answers the character given him in all respects.

If the person so appearing be one of the seer's acquaintance, he will tell his name, as well as other particulars; and he can tell by his countenance whether he comes in a good or bad humour.

I have been seen thus myself by seers of both sexes at some hundred miles distance; some that saw me in this manner had never seen me personally, and it happened according to their visions, without any previous design of mine to go to those places, my coming there being purely accidental.

It is ordinary with them to see houses, gardens, and trees, in places void of all three; and this in process of time used to be accomplished: as at Mogstot, in the isle of Skye, where there were but a few sorry cow-houses thatched with straw, yet in a few years after, the vision which appeared often was accomplished, by the building of several good houses on the very spot represented to the seers, and by the planting of orchards there.

To see a spark of fire fall upon one's arm or breast is a fore-runner of a dead child to be seen in the arms of those persons; of which there are several fresh instances.

To see a seat empty at the time of one's sitting in it, is a presage of that person's death quickly after.

When a novice, or one that has lately obtained the second sight, sees a vision in the night-time without doors, and comes near a fire, he presently falls into a swoon.

Some find themselves as it were in a crowd of people, having a corpse which they carry along with them; and after such visions the seers come in sweating, and describe the people that appeared: if there be any of their acquaintance among them, they give an account of their names, as also of the bearers, but they know nothing concerning the corpse.

All those who have the second sight do not always see these visions at once, though they be together at the time. But if one who has this faculty designedly touch his fellow seer at the instant of a vision's appearing, then the second sees it as well as the first; and this is sometimes discerned by those that are near them on such occasions.

There is a way of foretelling death by a cry that they call *taisk*, which some call a *wraith* in the Lowlands.

They hear a loud cry without doors, exactly resembling the voice of some particular person, whose death is foretold by it. The last instance given me of this kind was in the village Rigg, in the isle of Skye.

Five women were sitting together in the same room, and all of them heard a loud cry passing by the window; they thought it plainly to be the voice of a maid who was one of the number, she blushed at the time, though not sensible of her so doing, contracted a fever next day, and died that week.

Things also are foretold by smelling, sometimes as follows. Fish or flesh is frequently smelled in a fire, when at the same time neither of the two are in the house, or in any probability like to be had in it for some weeks or months; for they seldom eat flesh, and though the sea be near them, yet they catch fish but seldom in the winter and spring. This smell several persons have, who are not endued with the second sight, and it is always accomplished soon after.

Children, horses, and cows see the second sight, as well as men and women advanced in years.

That children see it is plain from their crying aloud at the very instant that a corpse or any other vision appears to an ordinary seer. I was present in a house where a child cried out of a sudden, and being asked the reason of it, he answered that he had seen a great white thing lying on the board which was in the corner: but he was not believed, until a seer who was present told them that the child was in right; for, said he, I saw a corpse and the shroud about it, and the board will be used as part of a coffin, or some way employed about a corpse; and accordingly it was made into a coffin for one who was in perfect health at the time of the vision.

That horses see it is likewise plain from their violent and sudden starting, when the rider or seer in company with him sees a vision of any kind, night or day. It is observable of the horse, that he will not go forward that way, until he be led about at some distance from the common road, and then he is in a sweat.

A horse fastened by the common road on the side of Loch Skeriness in Skye, did break his rope at noonday, and ran up and down without the least visible cause. But two of the neighbourhood that happened to be at a little distance and in view of the horse, did at the same time see a considerable number of men about a corpse directing their course to the church of Snizort; and this was accomplished within a few days after by the death of a gentlewoman who lived thirteen miles from that church and came from another parish from whence very few came to Snizort to be buried.

That cows see the second sight appears from this; that when a woman is milking a cow and then happens to see the second sight the cow runs away in a great fright at the same time, and will not be pacified for some time after.

Before I mention more particulars discovered by the second sight, it may not be amiss to answer the objections that have lately been made against the reality of it.

Object. 1. These seers are visionary and melancholy people, and fancy they see things that do not appear to them or anybody else.

Answer. The people of these isles, and particularly the seers, are very temperate, and their diet is simple and moderate in quantity and quality, so that their brains are not in all probability disordered by undigested fumes of meat or drink. Both sexes are free from hysteric fits, convulsions, and several other distempers of that sort; there's no madmen among them, nor any instance of self-murder. It is observed among them that a man drunk never sees the second sight; and that he is a visionary, would discover himself in other things as well as in that; and such as see it are not judged to be visionaries by any of their friends or acquaintance.

Object. 2. There is none among the learned able to oblige the world with a satisfying account of those visions, therefore it is not to be believed.

Answer. If everything for which the learned are not able to give a satisfying account be condemned as impossible we may find many other things generally believed that must be rejected as false by this rule. For instance, yawning and its influence, and that the loadstone attracts iron; and yet these are true as well as harmless, though we can give no satisfying account of their causes, how much less can we pretend to things that are supernatural?

Object. 3. The seers are impostors, and the people who believe them are credulous, and easily imposed upon.

Answer. The seers are generally illiterate and well-meaning people, and altogether void of design, nor could I ever learn that any of them made the least gain by it, neither is it reputable among them to have that faculty; besides the people of the isles are not so credulous as to believe implicitly before the thing foretold is accomplished; but when it actually comes to pass afterwards it is not in their power to deny it without offering violence to their senses and reason. Besides, if the seers were deceivers, can it be reasonable to imagine that all the islanders who have not the second sight should combine together and offer violence to their understandings and senses, to force themselves to believe a lie from age to age. There are several persons among them whose birth and education raise them above the suspicion of concurring with an imposture merely to gratify an illiterate and contemptible sort of persons; nor can a reasonable man believe that children, horses, and cows could be pre-engaged in a combination to per-suade the world of the reality of the second sight.

Such as deny those visions give their assent to several strange passages in history upon the authority aforesaid of historians that lived several centuries before our time, and yet they deny the people of this generation the liberty to believe their intimate friends and acquaintance, men of probity and unquestionable reputation, and of whose veracity they have greater certainty than we can have of any ancient historian.

Every vision that is seen comes exactly to pass according to the true rules of observation, though novices and heedless persons do not always judge by those rules. I remember the seers returned me this answer to my objection and gave several instances to that purpose, whereof the following is one.

A boy of my acquaintance was often surprised at the sight of a coffin close by his shoulder, which put him into a fright and made him to believe it was a forerunner of his own death, and this his neighbours also judged to be the meaning of that vision; but a seer that lived in the village Knockow, where the boy was then a servant, told them that they were under a great mistake, and desired the boy to lay hold of the first opportunity that offered; and when he went to a burial to remember to act as a bearer for some moments: and this he did accordingly, within a few days after, when one of his acquaintance died; and from that time for-ward he was never troubled with seeing a coffin at his shoulder, though he has seen many at a distance, that concerned others. He is now reckoned one of the exactest seers in the parish of St Mary's in Skye, where he lives.

There is another instance of a woman in Skye, who frequently saw a vision representing a woman having a shroud about her up to the middle, but always appeared with her back towards her, and the habit in which it seemed to be dressed resembled her own: this was a mystery for some time, until the woman tried an experiment to satisfy her curiosity, which was, to dress herself contrary to the usual way; that is, she put that part of her clothes behind, which was always before, fancying that the vision at the next appearing would be easier distinguished: and it fell out accordingly, for the vision soon after presented itself with its face and dress looking towards the woman, and it proved to resemble herself in all points, and she died in a little time after.

There are visions seen by several persons, in whose days they are not accomplished; and this is one of the reasons why some things have been seen that are said to never come to pass, and there are also several visions seen which are not understood until they be accomplished.

The second sight is not a late discovery seen by one or two in a corner, or a remote isle, but it is seen by many persons of both sexes, in several isles, separated above forty or fifty leagues from one another: the inhabitants of many of these isles never had the least converse by word or writing; and this faculty of seeing visions, having continued, as we are informed by tradition, ever since the plantation of these isles, without being disproved by the nicest sceptic, after the strictest inquiry, seems to be a clear proof of its reality.

It is observable that it was much more common twenty years ago than at present; for one in ten do not see it now, that saw it then.

The second sight is not confined to the Western Isles alone, for I have an account that it is likewise seen in several parts of Holland, but particularly in Bommel, by a woman, for which she is courted by some, and dressed by others. She sees a smoke about one's face, which is a forerunner of the death of a person so seen, and she did actually foretell the death of several that lived there: she was living in that town this last winter.

The corpse-candles, or 'dead men's lights' in Wales, which are certain prognostics of death, are well known and attested.

The second sight is likewise seen in the Isle of Man, as appears by this instance: Captain Leaths, the chief magistrate of Belfast, in his voyage 1690, lost thirteen men by a violent storm, and upon his landing upon the Isle of Man, an ancient man, clerk to a parish there, told him immediately that he had lost thirteen men: the captain inquiring how he came to knowledge of that, he answered, that it was by thirteen lights which he had seen come into the churchyard; as Mr Sacheverel tells us, in his late description of the Isle of Man.

It were ridiculous to suppose a combination between the people of the Western Isles of Scotland, Holland, Wales, and the Isle of Man, since they are separated by long seas, and are people of different languages, governments, and interests: they have no correspondence between them, and it is probable that those inhabiting the north-west isles have ever yet heard that any such visions are seen in Holland, Wales, or the Isle of Man.

Four men of the village Flodgery in Skye being at supper, one of them did suddenly let fall his knife on the table, and looked with an angry countenance; the company observing it inquired this reason, but he returned them no answer until they had supped, and then he told them that when he let fall his knife, he saw a corpse, with the shroud about it, laid on the table which surprised him, and that a little time would accomplish the vision. It fell out accordingly, for in a few days after one of the family died, and happened to be laid out on that very table. This was told me by the master of the family.

Daniel Stewart, an inhabitant of Hole in the north parish of St Mary's in the isle of Skye, saw at noonday five men on horseback riding northward; he ran to meet them, and when he came to the road he could see none of them, which was very surprising to him, and he told it to his neighbours: the very next day he saw the same number of men and horse coming along the road, but was not so ready to meet them as before, until he heard them speak, and then he found them to be those that he had seen the day before in a vision; this was the only vision of the kind he had ever seen in his life. The company he saw was Sir Donald MacDonald and his retinue, who at the time of the vision was at Armadale, near forty miles south from the place where the man lived.

A woman of Stornvay, in Lewis, had a maid who saw visions, and often fell into a swoon; her mistress was very much concerned about her, but could not find out any means to prevent her seeing those things; at last she resolved to pour some of the water used in baptism on her maid's face, believing this would prevent her seeing any more sights of this kind. And accordingly she carried her maid with her next Lord's day, and both of them sat near the basin in which the water stood, and after baptism, before the minister had concluded the last prayer, she put her hand in the basin, took up as much water as she could, and threw it on the maid's face; at which strange action the minister and the congregation were equally surprised. After prayer the minister enquired of the woman the meaning of such an unbecoming and distracted action; she told him it was to prevent her maid's seeing visions; and it fell out accordingly, for from that time she never once more saw a vision of any kind. This account was given me by Mr Morison, minister of the place, before several of his parishioners who knew the truth of it. I submit the matter of fact to the censure of the learned; but for my own part I think it to have been one of Satan's devices to make credulous people have an esteem for holy water.

John Morison, of Bragir, in Lewis, a person of unquestionable sincerity and reputation, told me that within a mile of his house a girl of twelve years old was troubled at the frequent sight of a vision, resembling herself in stature, complexion, dress, etc., and seemed to stand or sit, and to be always employed as the girl was; this proved a great trouble to her: her parents, being much concerned about it, consulted the said John Morison, who enquired if the girl was instructed in the principles of her religion, and finding she was not he bid them teach her the Creed, Ten Commandments, and the Lord's Prayer, and that she should say the latter daily after her prayers. Mr Morison and his family joined in prayer in the girl's behalf, begging that God of his goodness would be pleased to deliver her from the trouble of such a vision: after which, and the girl's complying with the advice as above, she never saw it any more.

A man living three miles to the north of the said John Morison is much haunted by a spirit, appearing in all points like to himself; and he asks many impertinent questions of the man when in the fields, but speaks not a word to him at home, though he seldom misses to appear to him every night in the house, but to no other person. He told this to one of his neighbours, who advised him to cast a live coal at the face of the vision the next time he appeared; the man did so next night, and all the family saw the action; but the following day the same spirit appeared to him in the fields, and beat him severely, so as to oblige him to keep his bed for the space of fourteen days after. Mr Morison, minister of the parish, and several of his friends came to see the man, and joined in prayer that he might be freed from this trouble, but he was still haunted by that spirit a year after I left Lewis.

A man in Knockow, in the parish of St Mary's, the northern-most in Skye, being in perfect health, and sitting with his fellow servants at night, was on a sudden taken ill, and dropped from his seat backward, and then fell a-vomiting; at which all the family were much concerned, he having never been subject to the like before: but he came to himself soon after, and had no sort of pain about him. One of the family, who was accustomed to see the second sight, told them that the man's illness proceeded from a very strange cause, which was thus: An ill-natured woman (naming her by her name), who lives in the next adjacent village of Bornskittag, came before him in a very furious and angry manner, her countenance full of passion, and her mouth full of reproaches, and threatened him with her head and hands, until he fell over as you have seen him. This woman had a fancy for the man, but was like to meet with a disappointment as to his marrying her. This instance was told me by the master of the family, and others who were present when it happened.

One that lived in St Mary's, on the west side of the isle of Skye, told Mr MacPherson, the minister, and others, that he saw a vision of a corpse coming towards the church, not by the common road, but by a more rugged way, which rendered the thing incredible, and occasioned his neighbours to call him a fool; but he bid them have patience and they would see the truth of what he asserted in a short time: and it fell out accordingly, for one of the neighbourhood died, and his corpse was carried along the same unaccustomed way, the common road being at that time filled with a deep snow. This account was given me by the minister and others living there.

Mr Macpherson's servant foretold that a kiln should take fire, and being some time after reproved by his master for talking so foolishly of the second sight, he answered that he could not help his seeing such things as presented themselves to his views in very lively manner, adding further, I have just now seen that boy sitting by the fire with his face red, as if the blood had been running down his forehead, and I could not avoid seeing this: and as for the accomplishment of it within forty-eight hours, there is no doubt, says he, it having appeared in the daytime. The minister became very angry at his man, and charged him never to speak one word more of the second sight, or if he could not hold his tongue, to provide himself another master, telling him he was an unhappy fellow, who studied to abuse credulous people with false predictions. There was no more said on this subject until the next day, that the boy of whom the seer spoke, came in, having his face all covered with blood; which happened by his falling on a heap of stones. This account was given me by the minister and others of his family.

Daniel Dow, alias Black, an inhabitant of Bornskittag, was frequently troubled at the sight of a man, threatening to give him a blow; he knew no man resembling this vision; but the stature, complexion and habit were so impressed on his mind, that he said he could distinguish him from any other, if he should happen to see him. About a year after the vision appeared first to him, his master sent him to Kyle-Raes, about thirty miles further southeast, where he was no sooner arrived, than he distinguished the man who had so often appeared to him at home; and within a few hours after, they happened to quarrel, and came to blows, so as one of them (I forgot which) was wounded in the head. This was told me by the seer's master, and others who live in the place. The man himself has his residence there, and is one of the precisest seers in the isles.

Sir Norman MacLeod, and some others playing at tables, at a game called in Irish *falmermore*, wherein there are three of a side, and each of them threw the dice by turns; there happened to be one difficult point in the disposing of one of the tablemen: this obliged the gamester to deliberate before he was to change his man, since upon the disposing of it the winning or losing of the game depended. At last the butler who stood behind, advised the player where to place his man; with which he complied, and won the game. This being thought extraordinary, and Sir Norman hearing one whisper him in the ear, asked who advised him so skilfully. He answered it was the butler, but this seemed more strange for he could not play at tables. Upon this, Sir Norman asked him how long it was since he had learnt to play, and the fellow owned that he never played in his life, but that he saw the spirit Browny reaching his arm over the player's head, and touched the part with his finger on the point where the tableman was to be placed. This was told me by Sir Norman and others, who happened to be present at the time.

Daniel Dow, above named, foretold the death of a young woman in Minginis, within less than twenty-four hours before the time; and accordingly she died suddenly in the fields, though at the time of the prediction she was in perfect health; but the shroud appearing close about her head, was the ground of his confidence, that her death was at hand.

The same Daniel Dow foretold the death of a child in his master's arms, by seeing a spark of fire fall on his left arm; and this was likewise accomplished soon after the prediction.

Some of the inhabitants of Harris sailing round the isle of Skye, with a design to go to the opposite mainland, were strangely surprised with an apparition of two men hanging down by the ropes that secured the mast, but could not conjecture what it meant. They pursued the voyage, but the wind turned contrary, and so forced them into Broadford in the isle of Skye, where they found Sir Donald MacDonald keeping a sheriff's court, and two criminals receiving sentence of death there: the ropes and mast of that very boat were made use of to hang those criminals. This was told me by several who had this instance from the boat's crew.

Several persons living in a certain family, told me that they had frequently seen two men standing at a young gentlewoman's left hand, who was their master's daughter: they told the men's names; and being her equals, it was not doubted but she would be married to one of them: and perhaps to the other, after the death of the first. Some time after a third man appeared, and he seemed always to stand nearest to her of the three, but the seers did not know him, though they could describe him exactly. And within some months after, this man, who was seen last, did actually come to the house, and fulfilled the description given of him by those who never saw him but in a vision; and he married the woman shortly after. They live in the isle of Skye; both they and others confirmed the truth of this instance when I saw them.

Macleod's porter passing by a galley that lay in the dock, saw her filled with men, having a corpse, and near to it he saw several of Macleod's relations: this did in a manner persuade him that his master was to die soon after, and that he was to be the corpse which was to be transported in the galley. Some months after the vision was seen, Macleod, with several of his relations and others, went to the isle of Mull; where, some days after, Maclean of Torlosk happened to die, and his corpse was transported in the galley to his burial place, and Macleod's relations were on board to attend the funeral, while Macleod stayed ashore, and went along with the corpse after their landing.

Mr Dougal Macpherson, minister of St Mary's, on the west side of Skye, having his servants in the kiln drying of corn, the kiln happened to take fire, but was soon extinguished. And within a few months after one of the minister's servants told him that the kiln would be on fire again shortly, at which he grew very angry with his man, threatening to beat him if he should presume to prophesy mischief by that lying way of the second sight. Notwithstanding this, the man asserted positively and with great assurance that the kiln would certainly take fire, let them use all the precautions they could. Upon this, Mr Macpherson had the curiosity to enquire of his man if he could guess within what space of time the kiln would take fire. He told him before Hallowtide. Upon which, Mr Macpherson called for the key of the kiln, and told his man that he would take care of the kiln until the limited day was expired, for none shall enter it sooner and by this means I shall make the devil, if he is the author of such lies, and you both liars. For this end he kept the key of the kiln in his press until the time was over, and then delivered the key to the servants, concluding his man to be a fool and a cheat. Then the servants went to dry corn in the kiln, and were charged to have a special care of the fire; yet in a little time after the kiln took fire; and it was all in a flame, according to the prediction, though the man mistook the time. He told his master that within a few moments after the fire of the kiln had been first extinguished, he saw it all in a flame again! And this appearing to him in the daytime, it would come to pass the sooner.

John Macnormand and Daniel MacEwin, travelling along the road, two miles to the north of Snizort church, saw a body of men coming from the north, as if they had a corpse with them to be buried in Snizort; this determined them to advance towards the river, which was then a little before them, and having waited at the ford, thinking to meet those that they expected with the funeral, were altogether disappointed, for after taking a view of the ground all round them, they discovered that it was only a vision. This was very surprising to them both, for they never saw anything by way of the second sight before or after that time. This they told their neighbours when they came home, and it happened that about two or three weeks after a corpse came along that road from another parish, from which few or none are brought to Snizort, except persons of distinction, so that this vision was exactly accomplished.

A gentleman, who is a native of Skye did, when a boy, dislodge a seer in the isle of Raasay, and upbraid him for his ugliness, as being black by name and nature. At last the seer told him very angrily, 'My child, if I am black, you'll be red ere long.' The master of the family chid him for this, and bid him give over his foolish predictions, since nobody believed them; but next morning the boy being at play near the houses, fell on a stone, and wounded himself in the forehead, so deep, that to this day there is a hollow scar in that part of it.

James Beaton, surgeon in the isle of North Uist, told me that, being in the isle of Mull, a seer told him confidently that he was shortly to have a bloody forehead; but he disregarded it, and called by some of the Macleans to go along with them to attack a vessel belonging to the Earl of Argyll, who was then coming to possess Mull by force; they attacked the vessel, and one of the Macleans being wounded, the said James, while dressing the wound, happened to rub his forehead, and then some of his patient's blood stuck to his face, which accomplished the vision.

My Lord Viscount Tarbat, one of her majesty's secretaries of state in Scotland, travelling in the shire of Ross, in the north of Scotland, came into a house, and sat down in an armed chair. One of his retinue, who had the faculty of seeing the second sight, spoke to some of my lord's company, desiring them to persuade him to leave the house, 'For,' said he, 'there is a great misfortune will attend somebody in it, and that within a few hours.' This was told my lord, but he did not regard it. The seer did soon after renew his entreaty with much eagerness, begging that my lord might remove out of that unhappy chair, but had no other answer than to be exposed for a fool. Some hours after my lord removed, and pursued his journey; but was not gone many hours when a trooper riding upon the ice, near the house whence my lord removed, fell and broke his thigh, and being afterwards brought into that house, was laid in the armed chair, where his wound was dressed, which accomplished the vision. I heard this instance from several hands, and had it since confirmed by my lord himself.

A man in the parish of St Mary's, in the barony of Trotterness, in Skye, called Lachlin, lay sick for the space of some months, decaying daily, insomuch that all his relations and acquaintances despaired of his recovery. One of the parishioners, called Archibald Macdonald, being reputed famous for his skill in foretelling things to come by the second sight, asserted positively that the sick man would never die in the house where he then lay. This being thought very improbable all the neighbours condemned Archibald as a foolish prophet; upon which he passionately affirmed that if ever that sick man dies in the house where he now lies, I shall from henceforth renounce my part of heaven; adding withal, the sick man was to be carried alive out of the house in which he then lay, but that he would never return to it alive; and then he named the persons that should carry out the sick man alive. The man having lived some weeks longer than his friends imagined, and proving uneasy and troublesome to all the family, they considered that Archibald had reason for his peremptory assertion, and therefore they resolved to carry him to a house joining to that in which he then lay; but the poor man would by no means give his consent to be moved from a place where he believed he should never die, so much did he rely on the words of Archibald, of whose skill he had seen many demonstrations. But at last his friends being fatigued day and night with the sick man's uneasiness they carried him against his inclination to another little house which was only separated by an entry from that in which he lay, and their feet were scarce within the threshold when the sick man gave up the ghost; and it was remarkable that the two neighbours which Archibald named would carry him out were actually the persons that did so. At the time of the prediction, Archibald saw him carried out as above, and when he was within the door of the other house he saw him all white, and the shroud being about him occasioned his confidence as above mentioned. This is matter of fact which

Mr Daniel Nicholson, minister of the parish, and a considerable number of the parishioners are able to vouch for, and ready to attest, if occasion requires.

The same Archibald Macdonald happened to be in the village Knockow one night, and before supper told the family that he had just seen the strangest thing he ever saw in his life, to wit, a man with an ugly long cap, always shaking his head; but that the strangest of all was a little kind of a harp which he had, with four strings only, and that it had two hart's horns fixed in the front of it. All that heard this odd vision fell a-laughing at Archibald, telling him that he was dreaming or had not his wits about him, since he pretended to see a thing that had no being, and was not so much as heard of in any part of the world. All this could not alter Archibald's opinion, who told them that they must excuse him if he laughed at them after the accomplishment of the vision. Archibald returned to his own house, and within three or four days after a man with the cap, harp, etc. came to the house, and the harp, strings, horns, and cap answered the description of them at first view; he shook his head when he played, for he had two bells fixed to his cap. This harper was a poor man and made himself a buffoon for his bread, and was never before seen in those parts; for at the time of the prediction he was in the isle of Barra, which is above twenty leagues distant from that part of Skye. This story is vouched by Mr Daniel Martin, and all his family and such as were then present, and live in the village where this happened.

Mr Daniel Nicholson, minister of St Mary's in Skye, the parish in which Archibald Macdonald lived, told me that one Sunday after sermon at the chapel Uig, he took occasion to inquire of Archibald if he still retained that unhappy faculty of seeing the second sight, and he wished him to lay it aside if possible; 'For,' said he, 'it is no true character of a good man.' Archibald was highly displeased, and answered that he hoped he was no more unhappy than his neighbours, for seeing what they could not perceive; adding, 'I had,' says he, 'as serious thoughts as my neighbours in time of hearing a sermon today, and even then I saw a corpse laid on the ground close to the pulpit, and I assure you it will be accomplished shortly for it was in the daytime.' Mr Nicholson and several parishioners then present endeavoured to dissuade Archibald from this discourse, but he still asserted that it would quickly come to pass, and that all his other predictions of this kind had ever been accomplished. There was none in the parish then sick, and few are buried at that little chapel, may sometimes not one in a year is buried there; yet when Mr Nicholson returned to preach in the said chapel two or three weeks after, he found one buried in the very spot named by Archibald. This story is vouched by Mr Nicholson, and several of the parishioners still living.

Mr Daniel Nicholson, above mentioned, being a widower at the age of forty-four, this Archibald saw in a vision a young gentlewoman in a good dress frequently standing at Mr Nicholson's right hand, and this he often told the parishioners positively, and gave an account of her complexion, stature, habit, and that she would in time be Mr Nicholson's wife; this being told the minister by several of them, he desired them to have no regard to what that foolish dreamer had said; 'For,' said he, 'it is twenty to one if ever I marry again.' Archibald happened to see Mr Nicholson soon after this slighting expression, however he persisted still in his opinion, and said confidently that Mr Nicholson would certainly marry, and that the woman would in all points make up the character he gave of her, for he saw her as often as he saw Mr Nicholson. This story was told me above a year before the accomplishment of it; and Mr Nicholson, some two or three years after Archibald's prediction, went to a synod in Bute, where he had the first opportunity of seeing one Mrs Morison, and from that moment fancied her and afterwards married her. She was no sooner seen in the isle of Skye than the natives, who had never seen her before, were satisfied that she did completely answer the character given of her, etc. by Archibald.

One who had been accustomed to see the second sight, in the isle of Egg, which lies about three or four leagues to the south-west part of the isle of Skye, told his neighbours that he had frequently seen an apparition of a man in a red coat lined with blue, and having on his head a strange sort of blue cap, with a very high cock on the fore part of it, and that the man who there appeared was kissing a comely maid in the village where the seer dwelt; and therefore declared that a man in such a dress would certainly debauch or marry such a young woman. This unusual vision did much expose the seer for all the inhabitants treated him as a fool, though he had on several other occasions foretold things that afterwards were accomplished; this they thought one of the most unlikely things to be accomplished, that could have entered into any man's head. This story was then discoursed of in the isle of Skye, and all that heard it, laughed at it; it being a rarity to see any foreigner in Egg, and the young woman had no thoughts of going anywhere else. This story was told me at Edinburgh, by Norman Macleod of Grabam, in September, 1688, he being just then come from the isle of Skye; and there were present, the Laird of Macleod, and Mr Alexander Macleod, advocate, and others.

About a year and a half after the late revolution, Major Ferguson, now colonel of one of her majesty's regiments of foot, was then sent by the government with 600 men, and some frigates to reduce the islanders that had appeared for King James, and perhaps the small isle of Egg had never been regarded, though some of the inhabitants had been at the battle of Killiecrankie, but by a mere accident which determined Major Ferguson to go to the isle of Egg, which was this: a boat's crew of the isle of Egg happened to be in the isle of Skye, and killed one of Major Ferguson's soldiers there; upon notice of which, the major directed his course to the isle of Egg, where he was sufficiently revenged of the natives: and at the same time, the maid above-mentioned being very handsome, was then forcibly carried on board one of the vessels by some of the soldiers, where she was kept above twenty-four hours, and ravished, and brutishly robbed at the same time of her fine head of hair. She is since married in the isle, and in good reputation; her misfortune being pitied, and not reckoned her crime.

Sir Norman Macleod, who has his residence in the isle of Bernera, which lies between the isles of North Uist and Harris, went to the isle of Skye about business, without appointing any time for his return; his servants, in his absence, being all together in the large hall at night, one of them who had been accustomed to see the second sight told the rest they must remove, for they would have abundance of other company in the hall that night. One of his fellow servants answered that there was very little appearance of that, and if he had seen any vision of company, it was not like to be accomplished this night. But the seer insisted upon it, that it was. They continued to argue the improbability of it, because of the darkness of the night, and the danger of coming through the rocks that lie round the isle; but within an hour after, one of Sir Norman's men came to the house, bidding them provide lights, etc. for his master had newly landed; and thus the prediction was immediately accomplished.

Sir Norman, hearing of it called for the seer, and examined him about it; he answered that he had seen the spirit called Browny in human shape come several times, and make a showing of carrying an old woman that sat by the fire to the door, and at last seemed to carry her out by neck and heels, which made him laugh heartily, and gave occasion to the rest to conclude he was mad to laugh so without reason. This instance was told me by Sir Norman himself.

Four men from the isles of Skye and Harris having gone to Barbados, stayed there for fourteen years; and though they were wont to see the second sight in their native country, they never saw it in Barbados; but upon their return to England, the first night after their landing they saw the second sight, as was told me by several of their acquaintance.

John Morison, who lives in Bernera of Harris, wears the plant called *Fuga daemonum* sewed in the neck of his coat, to prevent his seeing of visions, and says he never saw any since he first carried that plant about him. He suffered me to feel the plant in the neck of his coat, but would by no means let me open the seam, though I offered him a reward to let me do it.

A spirit, by the country people called Browny, was frequently seen in all the most considerable families in the isles and north of Scotland, in the shape of a tall man; but within these twenty or thirty years past he is seen but rarely.

There were spirits also that appeared in the shape of women, horses, swine, cats, and some like fiery balls, which would follow men in the fields; but there has been but few instances of these for forty years past.

These spirits used also to form sounds in the air, resembling those of a harp, pipe, crowing of a cock, and of the grinding of querns: and sometimes they have heard voices in the air by night, singing Irish songs; the words of which songs some of my acquaintance still retain. One of them resembled the voice of a woman who had died some time before, and the song related to her state in the other world. These accounts I had from persons of as great integrity as any are in the world.

XV

A Brief Account of the Advantages the Isles Afford by Sea and Land, and Particularly for a Fishing Trade

THE north-west isles are of all others most capable of improvement by sea and land; yet by reason of their distance from trading towns, and because of their language, which is Irish, the inhabitants have never had any opportunity to trade at home or abroad, or to acquire mechanical arts and other sciences: so that they are still left to act by the force of their natural genius, and what they could learn by observation. They have not yet arrived to a competent knowledge in agriculture, for which cause many tracts of rich ground lie neglected, or at least but meanly improved in proportion to what they might be. This is the more to be regretted, because the people are as capable to acquire arts or sciences as any other in Europe. If two or more persons skilled in agriculture were sent from the lowlands, to each parish in the isles, they would soon enable the natives to furnish themselves with such plenty of corn as would maintain all their poor and idle people; many of which, for want of subsistence at home, are forced to seek their livelihood in foreign countries, to the great loss, as well as dishonour of the nation. This would enable them also to furnish the opposite barren parts of the continent with bread; and so much the more that in plentiful years they afford them good quantities of corn in this infant state of their agriculture. They have many large parcels of ground never yet manured, which if cultivated would maintain double the number of the present inhabitants, and increase and preserve their cattle; many of which, for want of hay or straw, die in the winter and spring: so that I have known particular persons lose above one hundred cows at a time, merely by want of fodder.

This is so much the more inexcusable because the ground in the Western Isles is naturally richer in many respects than in many other parts of the continent, as appears from several instances, particularly in Skye, and the opposite Western Isles, in which there are many valleys, etc. capable of good improvement, and of which divers experiments have been already made; and besides most of those places have the convenience of freshwater lakes and rivers, as well as of the sea, near at hand, to furnish the inhabitants with fish of many sorts, and *Alga marina* for manuring the ground.

In many places the soil is proper for wheat; and that their grass is good is evident from the great product of their cattle: so that if the natives were taught and encouraged to take pains to improve their corn and hay, to plant, enclose, and manure their ground, drain lakes, sow wheat and peas, and plant orchards and kitchen gardens, etc. they might have as great plenty of all things for the sustenance of mankind as any other people in Europe.

I have known a hundred families, or four or five persons apiece at least, maintained their own little farms, for which they paid not above five shillings sterling, one sheep, and some pecks of corn per annum each; which is enough to show that, by a better improvement, that country would maintain many more inhabitants than live now in the isles.

If any man be disposed to live a solitary, retired life, and to withdraw from the noise of the world, he may have a place of retreat there in a small island, or in the corner of a large one, where he may enjoy himself, and live at a very cheap rate.

If any family, reduced to low circumstances, had a mind to retire to any of these isles, there is no part of the known world where they may have the products of sea and land cheaper, live more securely, or among a more tractable and mild people. And that the country in general is healthful, appears from the good state of health enjoyed by the inhabitants.

I shall not offer to assert that there are mines of gold or silver in the Western Isles, from any resemblance they may bear to other parts that afford mines, but the natives affirm that gold dust has been found, at Griminis on the western coast of the isle of North Uist, and at Copveaul in Harris; in which, as well as in other parts of the isles, the teeth of the sheep which feed there are dyed yellow.

There is a good lead mine, having a mixture of silver in it, on the west end of the isle of Islay, near Port Escock; and Buchanan and others say, that the isle Lismore affords lead: and Sleat and Strath, on the south-west of Skye, are in stone, ground, grass, etc. exactly the same with that part of Islay, where there is a lead mine. And if search were made in the isles and hills of the opposite main, it is not improbable that some good mines might be discovered in some of them.

I was told by a gentleman of Lochaber, that an Englishman had found some gold dust in a mountain near the River Lochy, but could never find out the place again after his return from England. That there have been gold mines in Scotland, is clear, from the manuscripts mentioned by Dr Nicholson, now Bishop of Carlisle, in his late *Scots His. Library*.

The situation of these isles for promoting trade in general, appears advantageous enough; but more particularly for a trade with Denmark, Sweden, Hamburg, Holland, Britain, and Ireland. France and Spain seem remote, yet they do not exceed a week's sailing, with a favourable wind.

The general opinion of the advantage that might be reaped from the improvement of the fish trade in these isles, prevailed among considering people in former times to attempt it.

The first that I know of, was by King Charles I, in conjunction with a company of merchants; but it miscarried because of the civil wars, which unhappily broke out at that time.

The next attempt was by King Charles II who also joined with some merchants; and this succeeded well for a time. I am assured by such as saw the fish catched by that company, that they were reputed the best in Europe of their kind, and accordingly, were sold for a greater price; but this design was ruined thus: the king having occasion for money, was advised to withdraw that which was employed in the fishery; at which the merchants being displeased, and disagreeing likewise among themselves, they also withdrew their money, and the attempt has never been renewed since that time.

The settling of a fishery in those parts would prove of great advantage to the government, and be an effectual means to advance the revenue, by the customs in exports and imports, etc.

It would also be a nursery of stout and able seamen in a very short time, to serve the government on all occasions. The inhabitants of the isles and opposite mainland being very prolific already, the country would beyond all peradventure become very populous in a little time, if a fishery were once settled among them. The inhabitants are not contemptible for their number at present, nor are they to learn the use of the oar, for all of them are generally very dexterous at it: so that those places need not to be planted with a new colony, but only furnished with proper materials, and a few expert hands, to join with the natives to set on foot and advance a fishery.

The people inhabiting the Western Isles of Scotland may be about forty thousand, and many of them want employment; this is great encouragement, both for setting up other manufactories, and the fishing trade among them: besides a great number of people may be expected from the opposite continent of the Highlands, and north; which from a late computation, by one who had an estimate of their numbers, from several ministers in the country, are reckoned to exceed the number of islanders above ten to one: and it is too well known that many of them also want employment. The objection, that they speak only Irish, is nothing: many of them understand English in all the considerable islands, which are sufficient to direct the rest in catching and curing fish; and in a little time the youth would learn English.

The commodiousness and safety of the numerous bays and harbours in those isles, seem as if Nature had designed them for promoting trade; they are likewise furnished with plenty of good water, and stones for building. The opposite mainland affords wood of divers sorts for that use. They have abundance of turf and peat for fuel: and of this latter there is such plenty in many parts, as might furnish salt-pans with fire all the year round. The sea forces its passage in several small channels through the land; so as it renders the design more easy and practicable.

The coast of each isle affords many thousand load of sea-ware, which, if preserved, might be successfully used for making glass, and likewise kelp for soap.

The generality of the bays afford all sorts of shellfish in great plenty; as oysters, clams, mussels, lobsters, cockles, etc. which might be picked and exported in great quantities. There are great and small whales of divers kinds to be had round the isles, and on the shore of the opposite continent; and are frequently seen in narrow bays, where they may be easily caught. The great number of rivers, both in the isles and opposite mainland, afford abundance of salmon, which, if rightly managed, might turn to a good account.

The isles afford likewise great quantities of black cattle, which might serve the traders both for consumption and export.

Strath in Skye abounds with good marble, which may be had at an easy rate, and near the sea.

There is good wool in most of the isles, and very cheap; some are at the charge of carrying it on horseback, about seventy or eighty miles, to the shires of Moray and Aberdeen.

There are several of the isles that afford a great deal of very fine clay; which, if improved, might turn to a good account for making earthenware of all sorts.

The most centrical and convenient places for keeping magazines of casks, salt, etc., are those mentioned in the respective isles; as one at Loch Maddy isles, in the isle of North Uist; a second in the isle Hermetra, on the coast of the isle Harris; a third in island Glass, on the coast of Harris; and a fourth in Stornvay, in the isle of Lewis.

But for settling a magazine or colony for trade in general, and fishing in particular, the isle of Skye is absolutely the most centrical, both with regard to the isles and opposite mainland; and the most proper places in this isle are island Isa in Loch Fallart, and Loch Uig, both on the west side of Skye; Loch Portree and Scowsar on the east side; and island Dierman on the south side; these places abound with all sorts of fish that are caught in those seas; and they are proper places for a considerable number of men to dwell in, and convenient for settling magazines in them.

There are many bays and harbours that are convenient for building towns in several of the other isles if trade were settled among them; and cod and ling, as well as fish of lesser size, are to be had generally on the coast of the lesser, as well as of the larger isles. I am not ignorant that foreigners, sailing through the Western Isles, have been tempted from the sight of so many wild hills that seem to be covered all over with heath, and faced with high rocks, to imagine that the inhabitants, as well as the places of their residence, are barbarous; and to this opinion, their habit, as well as their language, have contributed. The like is supposed by many that live in the south of Scotland, who know no more of the Western Isles than the natives of Italy, but the lion is not so fierce as he is painted, neither are the people described here so barbarous as the world imagines. It is not the habit that makes the monk, nor doth the garb in fashion qualify him that wears it to be virtuous. The inhabitants have humanity, and use strangers hospitably and charitably. I could bring several instances of barbarity and theft committed by stranger seamen in the isles, but there is not one instance of any injury offered by the islanders to any seamen or strangers. I had a particular account of seamen, who not many years ago stole cattle and sheep in several of the isles; and when they were found on board their vessels, the inhabitants were satisfied to take their value in money or goods, without any further resentment; though many seamen whose lives were preserved by the natives have made them very ungrateful returns. For the humanity and hospitable temper of the islanders to sailors, I shall only give two instances: Captain Jackson of Whitehaven, about sixteen years ago, was obliged to leave his ship, being leaky, in the bay within island Glass, alias Scalpa, in the isle of Harris, with two men to take care of her, though loaded with goods: the ship was not within three miles of a house, and separated from the dwelling places by mountains; yet when the captain returned, about ten or twelve months after, he found his men and the vessel safe.

Captain Lotch left the *Dromedary* of London, of six hundred tons burden, with all her rich cargo from the Indies; of which he might have saved a great deal, had he embraced the assistance which the natives offered him to unload her, but the captain's shyness, and fear of being thought rude, hindered a gentleman on the place to employ about seventy hands, which he had ready to unload her, and so the cargo was lost. The captain and his men were kindly entertained there by Sir Norman Macleod, and though, among other valuable goods, they had six boxes of gold dust, there was not the least thing taken from them by the inhabitants. There are some pedlars from the shire of Moray, and other parts, who of late have fixed their residence in the isle of Skye, and travel through the remotest isles without any molestation; though some of these pedlars speak no Irish. Several barks come yearly from Orkney to the Western Isles, to fish for cod and ling: and many from Anstruther in the shire of Fife, came formerly to Barra and other isles to fish, before the battle of Kilsyth, where most of them being cut off, that trade was afterwards neglected.

The magazines and fishing boats left by foreigners in the isles above mentioned, were reckoned secure enough, when one of the natives only was left in charge with them till the next season, and so they might be still. So that if a company of strangers from any part should settle to fish or trade in these isles, there is no place of greater security in any part of Europe; for the proprietors are always ready to assist and support all strangers within their respective jurisdictions. A few Dutch families settled in Stornvay, in the isle of Lewis, after King Charles II's restoration, but some cunning merchants found means by the secretaries to prevail with the king to send them away, though they brought the islanders a great deal of money for the products of their sea and land fowl, and taught them something of the art of fishing. Had they stayed the islanders must certainly have made considerable progress in trade by this time, for the small idea of fishing they had from the Dutch has had so much effect as to make the people of the little village of Stornvay to excel all those of the neighbouring isles and continent in the fishing trade ever since that time.

For the better government of those isles, in case of setting up a fishing trade here, it may perhaps be found necessary to erect the isles of Skye, Lewis, Harris, South and North Uist, etc. into a sheriffalty, and to build a royal burgh in Skye as the centre; because of the people's great distance in remote isles, from the head burgh of the shire of Inverness. This would seem much more necessary here than those of Bute and Arran, that lie much nearer to Dumbarton, though they be necessary enough in themselves.

It may likewise deserve the consideration of the government whether they should not make the isle of Skye a free port, because of the great encouragement such immunities give to trade; which always issues in the welfare of the public, and adds strength and reputation to the government. Since these isles are capable of the improvements above mentioned, it is a great loss to the nation they should be thus neglected.

This is the general opinion of foreigners, as well as of our own countrymen, who know them; but I leave the further inquiry to such as shall be disposed to attempt a trade there, with the concurrence of the government. Scotland has men and money enough to set up a fishery, so that there seems to be nothing wanting towards it, but the encouragement of those in power, to excite the inclination and industry of the people.

If the Dutch in their public edicts call their fishery a golden mine, and at the same time affirm that it yields them more profit than the Indies do to Spain, we have very great reason to begin to work upon those rich mines, not only in the isles, but on all our coast in general. We have multitudes of hands to be employed at a very easy rate; we have a healthful climate, and our fish, especially the herring, come to our coast in April or May, and into the bays in prodigious shoals in July or August. I have seen complaints from Loch Essort, in Skye, that all the ships there were loaded, and that the barrel of herring might be had there for fourpence, but there were no buyers.

I have known the herring fishing to continue in some bays from September till the end of January, and wherever they are, all other fish follow them, and whales and seals in particular, for the larger fish of all kinds feed upon herring.

XVI

A Brief Description of the Isles of Orkney and Shetland, etc.

THE isles of Orkney lie to the north of Scotland, having the main Caledonian ocean, which contains the Hebrides, on the west, and the German ocean on the east; and the sea towards the north separates them from the isles of Shetland. Pictland Firth on the south, which is twelve miles broad, reaches to Dungisbie Head, the most northern point of the mainland of Scotland.

Authors differ as to the origin of the name; the English call it Orkney, from Eric, one of the first Pictish princes that possessed them; and it is observed that *pict* or *pight* in the Teutonic language signifies a fighter. The Irish call them Arkive, from the first planter, and Latin authors call them Orcades. They lie in the northern temperate zone, and 13th climate; the longitude is between 22 degrees and 11 minutes, and latitude 59 degrees 2 minutes. The compass varies here 8 degrees. The longest day is about eighteen hours. The air is temperately cold, and the night so clear that in the middle of June one may see to read all night long; and the days in winter are by consequence very short. Their winters here are commonly more subject to rain than snow, for the sea air dissolves the latter. The winds are often very boisterous in this country. The sea ebbs and flows here as in other parts, except in a few sounds, and about some promontories; which alter the course of the tides, and make them very impetuous.

The isles of Orkney are reckoned twenty-six in number, the lesser isles, called *holms*, are not inhabited, but fit for pasturage: most of their names end in 'a' or 'ey' that in the Teutonic language signifies water, with which they are all surrounded.

The mainland, called by the ancients Pomona, is about twenty-four miles long, and in the middle of it, on the south side, lies the only town in Orkney, called Kirkwall, which is about three quarters of a mile in length; the Danes called it Cracoviaca. There has been two fine edifices in it, one of them called the King's Palace, which is supposed to have been built by one of the bishops of Orkney, because in the wall there is a bishop's mitre and arms engraven, and the bishops anciently had their residence in it.

The palace now called the bishop's, was built by Patrick Stewart, Earl of Orkney, anno 1606.

There is a stately church in this town, having a steeple erected on four large pillars in the middle of it; there are fourteen pillars on each side the church: it is called by the name of St Magnus's Church, being founded, as the inhabitants say, by Magnus, King of Norway, whom they believe to be interred there. The seat of justice for these isles is kept here; the steward, sheriff, and commissary do each of them keep their respective courts in this place. It has a public school for teaching of grammar learning, endowed with a competent salary.

This town was erected into a royal burgh when the Danes possessed it, and their charter was afterwards confirmed to them by King James III, anno 1486. They have from that charter a power to hold burgh courts, to imprison, to arrest, to make bylaws, to choose their own magistrates yearly, to have two weekly markets; and they have also power of life and death, and of sending commissioners to Parliament, and all other privileges granted to royal burghs. This charter was dated at Edinburgh the last day of March 1486, and it was since ratified by King James V, and

King Charles II. The town is governed by a provost, four bailiffs, and a common council.

On the west end of the main is the King's Palace formerly mentioned, built by Robert Stewart, Earl of Orkney, about the year 1574. Several rooms in it have been curiously painted with scripture stories, as the flood of Noah, Christ's riding into Jerusalem, etc., and each figure has the scripture by it, that it refers to. Above the arms within there is this lofty inscription, *'sic fuit, est, et erit'*. This island is fruitful in corn and grass, and has several good harbours; one of them at Kirkwall, a second at the bay of Kerston village, near the west end of the isle, well secured against wind and weather, the third is at Deer Sound, and reckoned a very good harbour, the fourth is at Grahamshall, towards the east side of the isle, but in sailing to it from the east side, seamen would do well to sail betwixt Lambholm and the mainland, and not between Lambholm and Burray, which is shallow.

On the east of the main land lies the small isle Copinsha, fruitful in corn and grass; it is distinguished by seafaring men for its conspicuousness at a great distance. To the north end of it lies the Holm, called the Horse of Copinsha. Over against Kerston Bay lie the isles of Hoy and Waes, which make but one isle, about twelve miles in length, and mountainous. In this island is the hill of Hoy, which is reckoned the highest in Orkney.

The isle of South Ronaldsha lies to the east of Waes, it is five miles in length, and fruitful in corn; Burray in the south end is the ferry to Duncansby in Caithness. A little further to the south lies Swinna isle, remarkable only for a part of Pentland Firth lying to the west of it, called the Wells of Swinna. They are two whirlpools in the sea, which run about with such violence, that any vessel or boat coming within their reach, go always round until they sink. These wells are dangerous only when there is a dead calm; for if a boat be under sail with any wind, it is easy to go over them. If any boat be forced into these wells by the violence of the tide, the boatmen cast a barrel or an oar into the wells; and while it is swallowing it up, the sea continues calm, and given the boat an opportunity to pass over.

To the north of the main lies the isle of Shapinsha, five miles in length, and has an harbour at Elwick on the south. Further to the north lie the isles of Stronsa, five miles in length, and Eda which is four miles; Ronsa lies to the north-west, and is six miles long. The isle Sanda lies north, twelve miles in length, and is reckoned the most fruitful and beautiful of all the Orcades.

The isles of Orkney in general are fruitful in corn and cattle, and abound with store of rabbits.

The sheep are very fruitful here, many of them have two, some three, and others four lambs at a time; they often die with a disease called the sheep-dead, which is occasioned by little animals about half an inch long, that are engendered in their liver.

The horses are of a very small size, but hardy, and exposed to the rigour of the season during the winter and spring: the grass being then scarce they are fed with sea-ware.

The fields everywhere abound with variety of plants and roots, and the latter are generally very large; the common people dress their leather with the roots of tormentil, instead of bark.

The mainland is furnished with abundance of good marl, which is used successfully by the husbandman for manuring the ground.

The inhabitants say there are mines of silver, tin, and lead in the mainland, South Ronaldsha, Stronsa, Sanda, and Hoy. Some veins of marble are to be seen at Buckquoy and Swinna. There are no trees in these isles, except in gardens, and those bear no fruit. Their common fuel is peat and turf, of which there is such plenty as to furnish a salt-pan with fuel. A south-east and north-west moon cause high water here.

The Finland fishermen have been frequently seen on the coast of this isle, particularly in the year 1682. The people on the coast saw one of them in his little boat, and endeavoured to take him, but could not come at him, he retired so speedily. They say the fish retire from the coast when they see these men come to it.

One of the boats, sent from Orkney to Edinburgh, is to be seen in the Physicians' Hall, with the oar he makes use of, and the dart with which he kills his fish.

There is no venomous creature in this country. The inhabitants say there is a snail there which has a bright stone growing in it. There is abundance of shellfish here, as oysters, mussels, crans, cockles, etc.; of this latter, they make much fine lime. The rocks on the shore afford plenty of sea-ware, as *Alga marina*, etc.

The sea abounds with variety of fish, but especially herring, which are much neglected since the battle of Kilsyth, at which time the fishermen from Fife were almost all killed there.

There are many small whales round the coast of this isle; and the amphibia here are otters and seals.

The chief products of Orkney that are yearly exported from thence are corn, fish, hides, tallow, butter, skins of seals, otter skins, lamb skins, rabbit skins, stuffs, white salt, wool, pens, down, feathers, hams, etc.

Some spermacetti and ambergris, as also the *os-oepier*, are found on the shore of several of those isles.

This country affords plenty of sea and land fowl, as geese, ducks, solan geese, swans, lyres, and eagles, which are so strong as to carry away children. There is also the cleck-goose; the shells in which this fowl is said to be produced are found in several isles sticking to trees by the bill; of this kind I have seen many: the fowl was covered by a shell, and the head stuck to the tree by the bill, but I never saw any of them with life in them upon the tree; but the natives told me that they had observed them to move with the heat of the sun.

The Picts are believed to have been the first inhabitants of these isles, and there are houses of a round form in several parts of the country, called by the name of Picts' houses; and for the same reason the firth is called Pictland or Pentland Firth. Our historians call these isles the ancient kingdom of the Picts. Buchanan gives an account of one Belus, King of Orkney, who, being defeated by King Ewen II of Scotland, became desperate and killed himself. The effigy of this Belus is engraven on a stone in the church of Birsa, on the mainland. Boethius makes mention of another of their kings, called Bannus, and by others Gethus, who being vanquished by Claudius Caesar, was by him afterwards, together with his wife and family, carried captive to Rome, and there led in triumph, Anno Christi 43.

The Picts possessed Orkney until the reign of Kenneth II of Scotland, who subdued the country, and annexed it to his crown. From that time Orkney was peaceably possessed by the Scots, until about the year 1099, that Donald Bane, intending to secure the kingdom to himself, promised both those and the Western Isles to Magnus, King of Norway, upon condition that he should support him with a competent force: which he performed; and by this means became master of these isles, until the reign of Alexander III, who by his valour expelled the Danes. The kings of Denmark did afterwards resign their title for a sum of money, and this resignation was ratified under the Great Seal of Denmark, at the marriage of King James VI of Scotland, with Anne, Princess of Denmark.

Orkney has been from time to time a little title of honour to several persons of great quality: Henry and William Sinclairs were called princes of Orkney; and Rothuel Hepburn was made Duke of Orkney; Lord George Hamilton (brother to the present Duke of Hamilton) was by the late King William created Earl of Orkney. The Earl of Morton had a mortgage of Orkney and Zetland from King Charles I, which was since reduced by a decree of the lords of Session, obtained at the instance of the king's advocate against the earl; and this decree was afterwards ratified by Act of Parliament, and the earldom of Orkney, and lordship of Zetland, have since that time been erected into a stewartry. The reason on which the decree was founded, is said to have been, that the earl's deputy seized upon some chests of gold found in the rich Amsterdam ship, called the *Carlmelan*, that was lost in Zetland, 1664.

There are several gentlemen of estates in Orkney, but the queen is the principal proprietor, and one half of the whole belongs to the crown, besides the late accession of the bishop's rents, which is about 9000 merks Scots per annum. There is a yearly roup of Orkney rents, and he that offers highest is preferred to be the king's steward for the time; and as such, he is principal judge of the country. But this precarious lease is a public loss to the inhabitants, especially the poorer sort, who complain that they would be allowed to pay money for their corn and meal in time of scarcity; but that the stewards carried it off to other parts, and neglected the interest of the country. The interest of the crown suffers likewise by this means, for much of the crown lands lie waste: whereas if there were a constant steward, it might be much better managed, both for the crown and the inhabitants.

There is a tenure of land in Orkney, differing from any other in the kingdom, and this they call Udal Right, from Ulas, King of Norway, who after taking possession of those islands, gave a right to the inhabitants, on condition of paying the third to himself; and this right the inhabitants had successively, without any charter. All the lands of Orkney are Udal lands, king's lands, or feued lands.

They differ in their measures from other parts of Scotland, for they do not use the peck or firlet, but weigh their corn in pismores, or pundlers; the least quantity they call a *merg*, which is eighteen ounces, and twenty-four makes a *leispound*, or *setten*, which is the same with the Danes that a stone weight is with us.

The Ancient State of the Church of Orkney

The churches of Orkney and Zetland isles were formerly under the government of a bishop; the cathedral church was St Magnus in Kirkwall. There are thirty-one churches, and about one hundred chapels in the country, and the whole make up about eighteen parishes.

This diocese had several great dignities and privileges for a long time, but by the succession and change of many masters, they were lessened. Dr Robert Reid their bishop, made an erection of seven dignities, viz.: 1. A provost, to whom, under the bishop, the government of the canons, etc., did belong; he had allotted to him the prebendary of Holy Trinity, and the vicarage of South Ronaldsha. 2. An archdeacon. 3. A precentor, who had the prebendary of Ophir, and vicarage of Stennis. 4. A chancellor, who was to be learned in both laws; to him was given the prebendary of St Mary in Sanda, and the vicarage of Sanda. 5. A treasurer, who was to keep the treasure of the church, and sacred vestments, etc., he was rector of St Nicholas in Stronsa. 6. A subdean, who was parson of Hoy, etc. 7. A subchanter, who was bound to play on the organs each Lord's day, and festivals; he was prebendary of St Colme. He erected seven other canonries and prebends; to which dignities he assigned, besides their churches, the rents of the parsonages of St Colme in Waes, and Holy Cross in Westra, as also the vicarages of the parish churches of Sanda, Wick, and Stromness. He erected, besides these, thirteen chaplains; every one of which was to have twenty-four miles of corn, and ten merks of money for their yearly salary; besides their daily distributions, which were to be raised from the rents of the vicarage of the cathedral church, and from the foundation of Thomas, Bishop of Orkney, and the twelve pounds ratified by King James III, and James IV of Scotland. To these he added a sacrist, and six boys to bear tapers. The charter of this erection is dated at Kirkwall, October 28th, anno 1544.

This was the state of the church under popery. Some time after the Reformation, Bishop Law being made Bishop of Orkney, and the earldom united to the crown (by the forfeiture and death of Patrick Stewart, Earl of Orkney), he, with the consent of his chapter, made a contract with King James VI, in which they resign all their ecclesiastical lands to the crown; and the king gives back to the bishop several lands in Orkney, as Horn, Orphic etc., and his majesty gave also the commissariat of Orkney to the bishop and his successors; and then a competent number of persons for a chapter were agreed on. This contract was made anno 1614.

The Ancient Monuments and Curiosities in these Islands are as follows:

In the isle of Hoy there's the Dwarfie Stone between two hills; it is about thirty-four feet long and above sixteen feet broad; it is made hollow by human industry: it has a small square entry looking to the east, about two feet high, and has a stone proportionable at two feet distance before the entry. At one of the ends within this stone there is cut out a bed and pillow capable of two persons to lie in, at the other opposite end there is a void space cut out resembling a bed, and above both these there is a large hole which is supposed was a vent for smoke. The common tradition is that a giant and his wife made this their place of retreat.

About a mile to the west of the mainland of Skealhouse, there is in the top of high rocks many stones disposed like a street, about a quarter of a mile in length, and between twenty and thirty feet broad. They differ in figure and magnitude, are of a red colour, some resemble a heart, some a crown, leg, shoe, last, weaver's shuttle, etc.

On the west and east side of Loch Stennis, on the mainland, there are two circles of large stones erected in a ditch; the larger, which is round on the north-west side is a hundred paces diameter and some of the stones are twenty feet high, and above four in breadth; they are not all of a height, nor placed at an equal distance, and many of them are fallen down on the ground.

About a little distance further there is a semi-circle of larger stones than those mentioned above. There are two green mounts at the east and west side of the circle, which are supposed to be artificial, and fibulae of silver were found in them some time ago which on one side resembled a horseshoe more than anything else.

The hills and circles are believed to have been places designed to offer sacrifice in time of pagan idolatry; and for this reason the people called them the ancient temples of the gods, as we may find by Boethius in the *Life of Manius*. Several of the inhabitants have a tradition that the sun was worshipped in the larger, and the moon in the lesser circle.

In the chapel of Clet, in the isle of Sanda, there is a grave of nineteen feet in length; some who had the curiosity to open it, found only a piece of a man's backbone in it, bigger than that of a horse. The minister of the place had the curiosity to keep the bone by him for some time. The inhabitants have a tradition of a giant there whose stature was such that he could reach his hand as high as the top of the chapel. There have been large bones found lately in Westra, and one of the natives who died not long ago was for his stature distinguished by the title of the Micle, or great man of Waes.

There are erected stones in divers parts of both of the main and lesser isles, which are believed to have been erected as monuments of such as distinguished themselves in battle.

There have been several strange instances of the effects of thunder here; as that of burning Kirkwall steeple by lightning in the year 1670. At Stromness a gentleman had twelve kine, six of which in a stall were suddenly killed by thunder, and the other six left alive; and it was remarkable that the thunder did not kill them all as they stood, but killed one and missed another. This happened in 1680, and is attested by the minister and others of the parish.

There is a ruinous chapel in Papa Westra called St Tredwels, at the door of which there is a heap of stones, which was the superstition of the common people, who have such a veneration for this chapel above any other that they never fail, at their coming to it, to throw a stone as an offering before the door: and this they reckon an indispensable duty enjoined by their ancestors.

Ladykirk, in South Ronaldsha, though ruinous, and without a roof, is so much reverenced by the natives, that they choose rather to repair this old one, than to build a new church in a more convenient place, and at a cheaper rate: such is the power of education, that these men cannot be cured of these superfluous fancies, transmitted to them by their ignorant ancestors.

Within the ancient fabric of Ladykirk, there is a stone of four feet in length, and two in breadth, tapering at both ends: this stone has engraven on it the print of two feet, concerning which the inhabitants have the following tradition; that St Magnus wanting a boat to carry him over Pentland Firth to the opposite mainland of Caithness, was made use of this stone instead of a boat, and afterwards carried it to this church, where it continues ever since. But others have this more reasonable opinion, that it has been used in time of popery for delinquents, who were obliged to stand barefeet upon it by way of penance. Several of the vulgar inhabiting the lesser isles, observe the anniversary of their respective saints. There is one day in harvest on which the vulgar abstain from work, because of an ancient and foolish tradition, that if they do their work, the ridges will bleed.

They have a charm for stopping excessive bleeding, either in man or beast, whether the cause be internal or external; which is performed by sending the name of the patient to the charmer, who adds some more words to it, and after repeating those words the cure is performed, though the charmer be several miles distant from the patient. They have likewise other charms which they use frequently at a distance, and that also with success.

The inhabitants are well proportioned, and seem to be more sanguine than they are; the poorer sort live much upon fish of various kinds and sometimes without any bread. The inhabitants in general are subject to the scurvy, imputed to the fish and salt meat, which is their daily food; yet several of the inhabitants arrive at a great age: a woman in Evie brought forth a child in the sixty-third year of her age.

One living in Kerston lately, was 112 years old, and went to sea at 110. A gentleman at Stronsa, about four years ago, had a son at 110 years old. One William Muir in Westra, lived 140 years, and died about eighteen years ago. The inhabitants speak the English tongue; several of the vulgar speak the Danish or Norse language; and many among them retain the ancient Danish names.

Those of distinction are hospitable and obliging, the vulgar are generally civil and affable. Both of them wear the habit in fashion in the Lowlands, and some wear a sealskin for shoes; which they do not sew, but only tie them about their feet with strings, and sometimes thongs of leather: they are generally able and stout seamen.

The common people are very laborious and undergo great fatigues, and no small hazard in fishing. The isles of Orkney were formerly liable to frequent incursions by the Norwegians, and those inhabiting the western isles of Scotland. To prevent which, each village was obliged to furnish a large boat well manned to oppose the enemy, and upon their landing all the inhabitants were to appear armed; and beacons were a general warning on the sight of an approaching enemy.

About the year 1634, Dr Graham being then Bishop of Orkney, a young boy called William Garioch, had some acres of land, and some cattle, etc. left him by his father, deceased: he, being young, was kept by his uncle, who had a great desire to obtain the lands, etc. belonging to his nephew; who being kept short, stole a setten of barley, which is about twenty-eight pound weight, from his uncle; for which he pursued the youth, who was then eighteen years of age, before the sheriff. The theft being proved, the young man received sentence of death; but going up the ladder to be hanged, he prayed earnestly that God would inflict some visible judgment on his uncle, who out of covetousness had procured his death. The uncle happened after this to be walking in the churchyard of Kirkwall, and as he stood upon the young man's grave, the bishop's dog ran at him all of a sudden, and tore out his throat; and so he became a monument of God's wrath against such covetous wretches. The account was given to Mr Wallace, minister there, by several that were witnesses of the fact.

Shetland

Shetland lies north-east from Orkney, between the 60th and 61st degree of latitude. The distance between the head of Sanda, which is the most northerly part of Orkney, and Swinburghead, the most southerly point of Shetland, is commonly reckoned to be twenty or twenty-one leagues; the tides running betwixt are always impetuous and swelling, as well in a calm as when a fresh gale blows; and the greatest danger is near the Fair Isle, which lies nearer to Shetland than Orkney by four leagues.

The largest isle of Shetland, by the natives called the Mainland, is sixty miles in length from south-west to north-east, and from sixteen to one mile in breadth. Some call these isles Hethland, others Hoghland, which in the Norse tongue signifies highland; Shetland in the same language signifies sealand.

This isle is for the most part mossy, and more cultivated on the shore than in any other part; it is mountainous, and covered with heath, which renders it fitter for pasturage than tillage. The inhabitants depend upon the Orkney isles for their corn. The ground is generally so boggy that it makes riding impracticable, and travelling on foot not very pleasant, there being several parts into which people sink, to the endangering the lives, of which there have been several late instances. About the summer solstice, they have so much light all night that they can see to read by it. The sun sets between ten and eleven, and rises between one and two in the morning, but then the day is so much the shorter, and the night longer in the winter. This, together with the violence of the tides and tempestuous seas, deprives the inhabitants of all foreign correspondence from October till April, and often till May, during which space they are altogether strangers to the rest of mankind, of whom they hear not the least news. A remarkable instance of this happened after the late revolution: they had no account of the Prince of Orange's late landing in England, coronation, etc., until a fisherman happened to land in these isles in

May following, and he was not believed, but indicted for high treason for spreading such news.

The air of this isle is cold and piercing, notwithstanding which many of the inhabitants arrive at a great age, of which there are several remarkable instances. Buchanan, in his history, lib. I, gives an account of one Laurence, who lived in his time, some of whose offspring do still live in the parish of Waes; this man, after he arrived at 100 years of age, married a wife, went out a-fishing when he was 140 years old, and upon his return, died rather of old age than of any distemper.

The inhabitants give an account of one Tairville, who arrived at the age of 180, and never drank any malt drink, distilled waters, nor wine. They say that his son lived longer than him, and that his grandchildren lived to a good age, and seldom or never drank any stronger liquors than milk, water, or bland.

The disease that afflicts the inhabitants here most is the scurvy, which they suppose is occasioned by their eating too much salt fish. There is a distemper here called bastard scurvy, which discovers itself by the falling of the hair from the people's eyebrows, and the falling of their noses, etc., and as soon as the symptoms appear the persons are removed to the fields, where little houses are built for them on purpose, to prevent infection. The principal cause of this distemper is believed to be want of bread, and feeding on fish alone, particularly the liver. Many poor families are sometimes without bread for three, four, or five months together. They say likewise that their drinking of bland, which is their universal liquor, and preserved for the winter as part of their provisions, is another cause of this distemper. This drink is made of butter milk mixed with water. There be many of them who never taste ale or beer, for their scarcity of bread is such that they can spare no corn for drink, so that they have no other than bland, but what they get from foreign vessels that resort thither every summer to fish.

The isles in general afford a great quantity of scurvy-grass, which, used discreetly, is found to be a good remedy against this disease. The jaundice is commonly cured by drinking the powder of shell-snails among their drink, in the space of three or four days. They first dry then pulverise the snails; and it is observable that though this dust should be kept all the year round, and grow into vermin, it may be dried again, and pulverised for that use.

The isles afford abundance of sea-fowl, which serve the inhabitants for part of their food during summer and harvest, and the down and feathers bring them great gain.

The several tribes of fowl here build and hatch apart, and every tribe keeps close together, as if it were by consent. Some of the lesser isles are so crowded with variety of sea-fowl that they darken the air when they fly in great numbers. After their coming, which is commonly in February, they sit very close together for some time, till they recover the fatigue of their long flight from their remote quarters; and after they have hatched their young, and find they are able to fly, they go away together to some other unknown place.

The people inhabiting the lesser isles have abundance of eggs and fowl, which contribute to maintain their families during the summer.

The common people are generally very dexterous in climbing the rocks in quest of those eggs and fowl; but this exercise is attended with very great danger, and sometimes proves fatal to those that venture too far.

The most remarkable experiment of this sort is at the isle called the Noss of Brassa, and is as follows: the Noss being about sixteen fathoms distant from the side of the opposite main; the higher and lower rocks have two stakes fastened in each of them, and to these there are ropes tied: upon the ropes there is an engine hung, which they call a cradle; and in this a man makes his way over from the greater to the lesser rocks, where he makes a considerable purchase of eggs and fowl; but his return being by an ascent makes it the more dangerous, though those on the great rock have a rope tied to the cradle, by which they draw it and the man safe over for the most part.

There are some rocks here computed to be about 300 fathoms high, and the way of climbing them is to tie a rope about a man's middle, and let him down with a basket, in which he brings up his eggs and fowl. The isle of Foula is the most dangerous and fatal to the climbers, for many of them perish in the attempt.

The crows are very numerous in Shetland, and differ in their colour from those on the mainland; for the head, wings, and tail of those in Shetland are only black, and their back, breast, and tail of a grey colour. When black crows are seen there at any time the inhabitants say it is a presage of approaching famine.

There are fine hawks in these isles, and particularly those of Fair Isle are reputed among the best that are to be had anywhere; they are observed to go far for their prey, and particularly for moorfowl as far as the isles of Orkney, which are about sixteen leagues from them.

There are likewise many eagles in and about these isles, which are very destructive to the sheep and lambs.

This country produces little horses, commonly called shelties, and they are very sprightly, though the least of their kind to be seen anywhere; they are lower in stature than those of Orkney, and it is common for a man of ordinary strength to lift a sheltie from the ground: yet this little creature is able to carry double. The black are esteemed to be the most hardy, but the pied ones seldom prove so good: they live many times till thirty years of age, and are fit for service all the while. These horses are never brought into a house, but exposed to the rigour of the season all the year round; and when they have no grass feed upon sea-ware, which is only to be had at the tide of ebb.

The isles of Shetland produce many sheep, which have two and three lambs at a time; they would be much more numerous did not the eagles destroy them: they are likewise reduced to feed on sea-ware during the frost and snow.

The Lesser Isles of Shetland are as follows:

The isle Trondra, which lies opposite to Scalloway town, on the west; three miles long and two broad.

Further to the north-east lies the isle of Whalsey, about three miles in length, and as many in breadth; the rase are very numerous here, and do abundance of mischief by destroying the corn.

At some further distance lie the small isles called skerries; there is a church in one of them. Those isles and rocks prove often fatal to seamen, but advantageous to the inhabitants, by the wrecks and goods that the wind and tides drive ashore; which often supplies them fuel, of which they are altogether destitute. It was here the *Carmelan*, of Amsterdam, was cast away, as bound for the East Indies anno 1664. Among the rich cargo she had several chests of coined gold; the whole was valued at 3,000,000 guilders; of all the crew four only were saved. The inhabitants of the small isles, among other advantages they had by this wreck, had the pleasure of drinking liberally of the strong drink, which was driven ashore in large casks for the space of three weeks.

Between the Brassa Sound and the opposite main, lies the Unicorn, a dangerous rock, visible only at low water, it is so called ever since a vessel of that name perished upon it, commanded by William Kirkcaldy, of Grange, who was in eager pursuit of the Earl of Bothwell, and was very near him when his ship struck.

On the east lies the island called Fisholm: to the north-east lies Little Rue, and on the west Mickle Rue; the latter is eight miles in length, and two in breadth, and has a good harbour.

Near to Esting lie the isles of Vemantry, which have several harbours – Orkney, little Papa, Helisha, etc.

To the north-west of the Ness lies St Ninian's Isle; it has a chapel and an altar in it, upon which some of the inhabitants retain the ancient superstitious custom of burning candles.

Papa Stour is two miles in length; it excels any isle of its extent for all the conveniences of human life: it has four good harbours, one of which looks to the south, another to the west, and two to the north.

The Lyra Skerries, so-called from the fowl of that name that abound in them, lie near this isle.

About six leagues west of the main, lies the isle Foula, about three miles in length; it has a rock remarkable for its height, which is seen from Orkney when the weather is fair; it has a harbour on the one side.

The isle of Brassa lies to the east of Tingwal; it is five miles in length, and two in breadth; some parts of the coast are arable ground; and there are two churches in it.

Further to the east lies the small isle called the Noss of Brassa.

The isle of Burray is three miles long, has good pasturage, and abundance of fish on its coast; it has a large church and steeple in it. The inhabitants say that mice do not live in this isle, when brought to it; and that the earth of it being brought to any other part where the mice are, they will quickly abandon it.

Haverot Isle, which is a mile and a half in length, lies to the south-east of Burray.

The isle of Yell is sixteen miles long, and from eight to one in breadth; it lies north-east from the main; there are three churches, and several small chapels in it.

The isle of Hakashie is two miles long, Samphrey isle one mile long, Biggai isle is a mile and a half in length; all three lie round Yell, and are reputed among the best of the lesser isles.

The isle of Fetlor lies to the north-east of Yell, and is five miles in length, and four in breadth; it has a church, and some of the Piets' houses in it.

The isle of Unst is eight miles long, and is the pleasantest of the Shetland isles; it has three churches and as many harbours; it is reckoned the most northern of all the British dominions. The inhabitants of the isle Vaila say that no cat will live in it, and if any cat be brought to it, they will rather venture to sea, than stay in the isle. They say that a cat was seen upon the isle about fifty years ago; but how it came there was unknown. They observed about the same time, how the proprietor was in great torment, and as they supposed by witchcraft, of which they say he then died. There is no account that any cat has been seen in the isle ever since that gentleman's death except when they were carried to it, for making the above-mentioned experiment.

The inhabitants say that if a compass be placed at the house of Udsta, on the west-side of the isle Fetlor the needle will be in perpetual disorder, without fixing to any one pole; and that being tried afterwards on the top of that house, it had the same effect. They add further that when a vessel sails near that house, the needle of the compass is disordered in the same manner.

There is yellow sort of metal, lately discovered in the isle of Uzia, but the inhabitants had not found a way to melt it; so that it is not yet turned to any account.

The Ancient Court of Justice

In these islands was held in Holm, in the parish of Tingwall, in the middle of the mainland. This Holm is an island in the middle of a freshwater lake; it is to this day called the Law Ting, and the parish, in all probability, hath its name from it. The entrance to this Holm is by some stones laid in the water, and in the Holm there are four great stones, upon which sat the judge, clerk, and other officers of the court. The inhabitants who had lawsuits attended at some distance from the Holm, on the other side the lake; and when any of them was called by the officer, he entered by the stepping stones; and being dismissed, he returned the same way. This was the practice of the Danes. The inhabitants have a tradition among them that after one had received sentence of death upon the Holm, he obtained a remission, provided he made his escape through the crowd of people on the lake side, and touched Tingwall steeple before any could lay hold on him. This steeple in those days was an asylum for malefactors and debtors to flee into. The inhabitants of this isle are all Protestants; they generally speak the English tongue, and many among them retain the ancient Danish language, especially in the more northern isles. There are several who speak English, Norse, and Dutch; the last of which is acquired by their converse with the Hollanders, that fish yearly in those isles.

The people are generally reputed discrete, and charitable to strangers; and those of the best rank are fashionable in their apparel.

Shetland is much more populous now, than it was thirty years ago; which is owing to the trade, and particularly that of their fishery, so much followed every year by the Hollanders, Hamburgers, and others. The increase of people at Lerwick is considerable; for it had but three or four families about thirty years ago, and is since increased to about three hundred families: and it is observable that few of their families were natives of Shetland, but came from several parts of Scotland, and especially from the northern and eastern coasts.

The fishery in Shetland is the foundation both of their trade and wealth; and though it be of late become less than before, yet the inhabitants by their industry and application, make a greater profit of it than formerly, when they had them nearer the coast, both of the larger and lesser isles; but now the grey fish of the largest size are not to be had in any quantity without going further into the ocean. The fish commonly bought by strangers here are cod and ling; the inhabitants themselves make only use of the smaller fish and herrings, which abound on the coast of this isle in vast shoals.

The fish called tusk abounds on the coast of Brassa; the time for fishing is at the end of May. This fish is as big as a ling, of a brown and yellow colour, has a broad tail; it is better fresh than salted. They are commonly sold at fifteen or sixteen shillings the hundred.

The inhabitants observe that the further they go to the northward, the fish are of a larger size, and in greater quantities. They make great store of oil, particularly of the large grey fish, by them called *seths*, and the younger sort *sillucks*; they say that the liver of one *seth* affords a pint of Scots measure, being about four of English measure. The way of making the oil is first by boiling the liver in a pot half full of water and when it boils the oil goes to the top and is skimmed off and put in vessels for use. The fishers observe of late that the livers of fish are less in size than they have been formerly.

The Hamburgers, Bremers, and others come to this country about the middle of May, set up shops in several parts, and sell divers commodities; as linen, muslin, and such things as are most proper for the inhabitants, but more especially beer brandy, and bread: all which they barter for fish, stockings, mutton, hens, etc. And when the inhabitants ask money for their goods, they receive it immediately.

In the month of June, the Hollanders come with their fishing busses in great numbers upon the coast for herring; and when they come into the Sound of Brassa, where the herring are commonly most plentiful, and very near the shore, they dispose their nets, etc., in order, but never begin till the twenty-fourth of June, for this is the time limited among themselves, which is observed as a law, that none will venture to transgress. This fishing trade is very beneficial to the inhabitants, who have provisions and necessaries imported to their doors; and employment for all their people, who by their fishing, and selling the various products of the country, bring in a considerable sum of money yearly. The proprietors of the ground are considerable gainers also, by letting their houses, which serve as shops to the seamen, during their residence there.

There have been two thousand busses, and upwards, fishing in this sound in one summer, but they are not always so numerous: they generally go away in August or September.

There are two little towns in the largest of the Shetland Isles; the most ancient of these is Scalloway; it lies on the west side of the isle, which is the most beautiful and pleasant part of it. It hath no trade, and but few inhabitants, the whole being about ninety in number. On the south-east end of the town stands the castle of Scalloway, which is four storeys high; it hath several conveniences and useful houses about it, and it is well furnished with water. Several rooms have been curiously painted, though the better part be now worn off. This ancient house is almost ruinous, there being no care taken to repair it. It served as a garrison for the English soldiers that were sent hither by Cromwell. This house was built by Patrick Stewart, Earl of Orkney, anno 1600. The gate hath the following inscription on it – *'Patricius Orchadiae et Zelandiae Comes'*. And underneath the inscription, *'Cujus fundamen saxum est, Domus ilia manebit; Labilis e contra si sit arena, perit'*. That house, whose foundation is on a rock, shall stand; but if on the sand, it shall fall.

The inhabitants say that this house was built upon the sandy foundation of oppression, in which they say the earl exceeded; and for that the other crimes were executed.

There is a high stone erected between Dingwall and Scalloway; the inhabitants have a tradition that it was set up as a monument of a Danish general who was killed there by the ancient inhabitants, in a battle against the Danes and Norwegians.

The second and latest built town is Lerwick; it stands on that side of the sound where the fishing is; the ground on which it is built is a hard rock, one side lies towards the sea and the other is surrounded with a moss, without any arable ground.

On the north is a citadel of Lerwick, which was built in the year 1665, in time of the war with Holland, but never completed; there is a little more of it now left than the walls. The inhabitants, about thirty years ago, fished up three iron cannons out of a ship that had been cast away near eighty years before; and being all over rust, they made a great fire of peats round them to get off the rust; and the fire having heated the cannon, all the three went off, to the great surprise of the inhabitants, who say they saw the ball fall in the middle of Brassa Sound, but none of them had any damage by them.

There are many Picts' houses in this country, and several of them entire to this day; the highest exceeds not twenty or thirty feet in height, and are about twelve feet broad in the middle; they taper towards both ends, the entry is lower than the doors of houses commonly are now, the windows are long and very narrow, and the stairs go up between the walls. These houses were built for watch-towers, to give notice of an approaching enemy; there is not one of them but what is in view of some other, so that a fire being made on the top of any one house the signal was communicated to all the rest in a few moments.

The inhabitants say that these houses were called burghs, which in the Saxon language signifies a town or castle fenced all round. The names of fortified places in the Western Isles are in several parts called *borg;* and the villages in which the forts stand are always named *borg.*

The inhabitants of Orkney say that several burying places among them are called burghs, from the Saxon word burying.

It is generally acknowledged that the Picts were originally Germans, and particularly from that part of it bordering upon the Baltic Sea. They were called Phightian, that is 'fighters': The Romans called them Picti. Some writers call them Pictavi, either from that name of Phightian, which they took to themselves, or from their beauty; and accordingly Boethius, in his character of them, joins both these together, *'Quod erant corporibus robustissimis candidisque'*; and Verstegan says the same of them.

The Romans called them Picti, because they had their shields painted of divers colours. Some think the name came from *pichk*, which in the ancient Scots language signifies pitch, that they coloured their faces with, to make them terrible to their enemies in battle; and others think the name was taken from their painted habit.

This isle makes part of the shire of Orkney; there are twelve parishes in it, and a greater number of churches and chapels. Shetland pays not above one-third to the crown of what Orkney does.

The ground being for the most part boggy and moorish, is not so productive of grain as the other isles and mainland of Scotland; and if it were not for the sea-ware, by which the ground is enriched, it would yield but a very small product.

There is lately discovered in divers parts, abundance of limestone, but the inhabitants are not sufficiently instructed in the use of it, for their cornland.

There is plenty of good peats, which serve as fuel for the inhabitants, especially on the main.

The amphibia in these isles, are seals and otters in abundance; some of the latter are trained to go a-fishing, and fetch several sorts of fish home to their masters.

There are no trees in any of these isles, neither is their any venomous creature to be found there.

There have been several strange fish seen by the inhabitants at sea, some of the shape of men as far as the middle; they are both troublesome and very terrible to the fishers, who call them sea devils.

It is not long since every family of any considerable substance in those islands, was haunted by a spirit they called Browny, which did several sorts of work; and this was the reason why they gave him offerings of the various products of the place: thus some when they churned their milk, or brewed, poured some milk and wort through the hole of a stone, called Browny's stone.

A minister in this country had an account from one of the ancient inhabitants who formerly brewed ale, and sometimes read his Bible, that an old woman in the family told him that Browny was much displeased at his reading in that book; and if he did not cease to read in it any more, Browny would not serve him as formerly. But the man continued his reading notwithstanding, and when he brewed refused to give any sacrifice to Browny; and so his first and second brewing miscarried, without any visible cause in the malt; but the third brewing proved good, and Browny got no more sacrifice from him after that.

There was another instance of a lady in Unst, who refused to give sacrifice to Browny, and lost two brewings; but the third proved good, and so Browny vanished quite, and troubled them no more.

I shall add no more, but that the great number of foreign ships which repair hither yearly upon the account of fishing, ought to excite the people of Scotland to a speedy improvement of that profitable trade; which they may carry on with more ease and profit in their own seas, than any foreigners whatever.

A LATE VOYAGE

TO

ST KILDA

Dedication

———➤●◄———

CHARLES MONTAGUE, Esq.

Chancellor of His Majesty's Exchequer, President
to the Royal Society, etc.

Sir,

The Royal Society (in which you so worthily at this time preside) having formerly done me the honour to public some of my observations in their celebrated *Transactions*, it has now encouraged me to presume on your patronage, and made me prefix your great name to this little essay.

The world is in general so well acquainted with those noble endowments and great abilities, for which our most wise and discerning monarch so early raised you to the highest places of trust and dignity, that only these poor islanders of whom I write, seem to be unhappily excluded from the knowledge of those many rare and excellent virtues, which under your administration do so signally bless mankind; of all which no one seems so necessary for me to implore, as that of your extraordinary goodness; which, I hope, will incline you to accept of this plain and humble address, as also to pardon the presumption of,

Sir,

Your most humble and obedient servant,

M. MARTIN.

253

Preface

M EN are generally delighted with novelty, and what is represented under that plausible invitation seldom fails of meeting with acceptance. If we hear at any time a description of some remote corner in the Indies cried in our streets, we presently conclude we may have some divertisement in reading of it; when in the meantime, there are a thousand things nearer us that may engage our thoughts to better purposes, and the knowledge of which may serve more to promote our true interest, and the history of Nature. It is a piece of weakness and folly merely to value things because of their distance from the place where we are born: thus men have travelled far enough in the search of foreign plants and animals, and yet continue strangers to those produced in their own natural climate. Therefore I presume that this following relation will not prove unprofitable or displeasing, unless the great advantages of truth and unaffected plainness may do it a prejudice, in the opinion of such as are more nice and childish than solid and judicious.

The ingenious author of this treatise is a person whose candour and integrity guard him against all affectation and vanity; and his great desire to propagate the natural history of the isles of Scotland, makes him relate, without any disguise, the several particulars that fell under his accurate observation. He was prompted by a generous curiosity to undertake a voyage through several isles to St Kilda (the particular account whereof you have in the following treatise) and that in an open boat, to the almost manifest hazard of his life, since the seas and tides in those rocky islands are more inconstant and ranging than in most other places. There is nothing related in the following account, but what he vouches to be true, either from his own particular observation, or else from the constant and harmonious testimony that was given him by the inhabitants; and they are a sort of people so plain, and so little inclined to impose upon mankind, that perhaps no place in the world at this day, knows such instances of true primitive honour and simplicity, a people who abhor lying tricks and artifices, as they do the most poisonous plants, or devouring animals.

The author, perhaps, might have put these papers into the hands of some who were capable of giving them the politest turns of phrase, and of making some pretty excursions upon several passages in them; but he thought the intelligent and philosophic part of mankind would value the truth more in such accounts, than anything that can be borrowed from art, or the advantages of more refined language; and such do contemplate the books of Nature with so much diligence and application that they may admire the original spring of power and wisdom, that first set Nature itself in motion, and preserves its regular course in all its wonderful and various phenomena; and therefore it may reasonably be hoped, that the meanness of its dress will not be made use of as any considerable objection against this preliminary essay.

He himself was born in one of the most spacious and fertile isles in the west of Scotland; and besides his liberal education at the university, had the advantage of seeing foreign places, and the honour of conversing with some of the Royal Society, who raised his natural curiosity to survey the isles of Scotland more exactly than any other, in prosecution of which design he has already brought along with him several curious productions of Nature, both rare and beautiful in their kind, which were never seen nor known here before; and, perhaps, there be few that have the same advantages of doing it to purpose, he being generally acquainted with most of the better sort, and nearly concerned in such as would very willingly encourage endeavours of this and the like nature.

I

THE various relations concerning St Kilda, given by those of the Western Isles, and continent, induced me to a narrow enquiry about it: for this end I applied myself to the present steward, who by his description, and the products of the island, which were brought to me, together with a natural impulse of curiosity, formed such an idea of it in my mind, that I determined to satisfy myself with the first occasion I had of going thither, it being never hitherto described to any purpose, the accounts which are given by Buchanan and Sir Robert Murray, being but relations from second and third hands, neither of them ever having the opportunity of being upon the place; which I attempted several times to visit, but in vain; until last summer, the Laird of MacLeod heartily recommending the care of the inhabitants of St Kilda to Mr John Campbel, minister of Harris, who accordingly went to St Kilda. This occasion I cheerfully embraced; and accordingly we embarked at the isle Esay in Harris the 29th of May, at six in the afternoon, 1697, the wind south-east.

We set sail with a gentle breeze of wind, bearing to the westward, and were not well got out of the harbour, when Mr Campbel observing the whiteness of the waves attended with an extraordinary noise beating upon the rocks, expressed his dislike of it, as in those parts a never-failing prognostic of an ensuing storm; but the same appearing sometimes in summer, before excessive heat, this was slighted by the crew. But as we advanced about two leagues further, upon the coast of the isle Pabbay, the former signs appearing more conspicuously, we were forced unanimously to conclude a storm was approaching, which occasioned a motion for our return; but the wind and ebb-tide concurring, determined us to pursue our voyage, in hopes to arrive at our desired harbour, before the wind or storm should rise, which we judged would not be suddenly; but our fond imagination was not seconded with a good event, as appears by the sequel; for we had scarce sailed a league further, when the wind inclined more southerly, and altered our measures; we endeavoured by the help of our oars to reach the Hawsker Rocks, some four leagues to the south coast, which we were not able to effect, we consumed the night in this vain expectation. By this time we are so far advanced in the ocean, that after a second motion for our return, it was not found practicable, especially since we could not promise to fetch any point of Scotland; this obliged us to make the best of our way for St Kilda, though labouring under the disadvantages of wind and tide almost contrary to us. Our crew became extremely fatigued and discouraged without sight of land for sixteen hours; at length one of our number discovered several tribes of the fowls of St Kilda flying, holding their course southerly of us, which (to some of our crew) was a demonstration we had lost our course, by the violence of the flood and wind both concurring to carry us northerly, though we steered by our compass right west.

The inhabitants of St Kilda take their measures from the flight of those fowls, when the heavens are not clear, as from a sure compass, experience shewing that every tribe of fowls bends their course to their respective quarters, though out of sight of the isle; this appeared clearly in our gradual advances, and their motion being compared, did exactly quadrate with our compass. The inhabitants rely so much upon this observation, that they prefer it to the surest compass; but we begged their pardon to differ from them, though at the same time we could not deny but their rule was as certain as our compass. While we were in this state, one of our number espied the isle Borera, near three leagues north of St Kilda, which was then about four leagues north of St Kilda, which was then about four leagues to the south of us; this was a joyful sight, and begot new vigour in our men, who being refreshed with victuals, lowering mast and sail, rowed to a miracle: while they were tugging at the oars, we plied them with plenty of aqua vitae to support them, whose borrowed spirits did so far waste their own, that upon our arrival at Borera, there was scarce one of our crew able to manage cable or anchor: we arrived there, and put in under the hollow of an extraordinary high rock, to the north of this isle, which was all covered with a prodigious number of solan geese hatching in their nests; the heavens were darkened by those flying above our heads; their excrements were in such quantity, that they gave a tincture to the sea, and at the same time sullied our boat and clothes: two of them confirmed the truth of what has been frequently reported of their stealing from one another grass wherewith to make their nests, by affording us the following and very agreeable diversion, and 'twas thus; one of them finding his neighbour's nest without the fowl, lays hold upon the opportunity, and steals of it as much grass as he could conveniently carry, taking his flight towards the ocean; from thence he returns after a short turn, as if he had made a foreign purchase, but it does not pass for such, as Fate would have it; for the owner discovered the fact, before this thief got out of sight, and being too nimble for his cunning, waits his return, all armed with fury, engages him desperately; this bloody battle was fought above our heads, and proved fatal to the thief, who fell dead so near our boat, that our men took him up, and presently dressed and eat him; which they reckoned as an omen and prognostic of good success in this voyage.

We proposed to be at St Kilda next day, but our expectation was frustrated by a violent storm, which did almost drive us to the ocean; where we had incurred no small risk, being no ways fitted for it; our men laid aside all hopes of life, being possessed with the belief that all this misfortune proceeded from the impostor (of whom hereafter) who they believed had employed the devil to raise this extraordinary storm against Mr Campbel, minister, who was to counteract him. All our arguments, whether from natural reason, or the providence of God, were not of force enough to persuade them to the contrary, until it pleased God to command a calm the day following, which was the first of June, and then we rowed to St Kilda; as we came close upon the rocks, some of the inhabitants, who were then employed in setting their gins, welcomed us with a God save you, their usual salutation, admiring to see us get thither contrary to wind and tide; they were walking unconcernedly on the side of this prodigious high rock, at the same time keeping pace with our boat, to my great admiration, insomuch that I was quickly obliged to turn away mine eyes, lest I should have the unpleasant spectacle of some of them tumbling down into the sea; but they themselves had no such fears, for they outrun our boat to the town, from thence they brought the steward and all the inhabitants of both sexes to receive us; we approached the outmost part of the low rock, called the Saddle; a parcel of the inhabitants were mounted upon it, having on their feet the usual dress on such occasions, i.e., socks of old rags sowed with feathers instead of thread; our boat being come pretty near, it was kept off this rock with long poles, some of their number coming by pairs into the sea received Mr Campbel and me upon their shoulders and carried us to land, where we were received with all the demonstrations of joy and kindness they were able to express; the impostor endeavouring to outdo his neighbours, and placing himself always in front of our attendants, discovered his hypocrisy, of which an account shall be given in the conclusion. All of us walking together to the little village where there was a lodging prepared for us, furnished with beds of straw, and according to the ancient custom of the place, the officer, who presides over them (in the steward's absence) summoned the inhabitants, who by concert agreed upon a daily maintenance for us, as bread, butter, cheese, mutton, fowls, eggs, also fire, etc., all which was to be given in at our lodging twice every day; this was done in the most regular manner, each family by turns paying their quota proportionably to their lands. I remember the allowance for each man per diem, beside a barley cake, was eighteen of the eggs laid by the fowl called by them *lavy*, and a greater number of the lesser eggs, as they differed in proportion; the largest of these eggs is near in bigness to that of a goose, the rest of the eggs gradually of a lesser size.

We had the curiosity after three weeks' residence, to make a calcule of the number of eggs bestowed upon those of our boat, and the Stewart's *birlin*, or galley, the whole amounted to sixteen thousand eggs; and without all doubt the inhabitants, who were treble our number, consumed many more eggs and fowls than we could. From this it is easy to imagine, that a vast number of fowls must resort here all summer, which is yet the more probable if it be considered; that every fowl lays but one egg at a time, if allowed to hatch.

The inhabitants live together in a little village, which carries all the signs of an extreme poverty; the houses are of a low form, having all the doors to the north-east, both on purpose to secure them from the shocks of the tempest of the south-west winds. The walls of their houses are rudely built of stone, the short couples joining at the ends of the roof, upon whose sides small ribs of wood are laid, these being covered with straw; the whole secured by ropes made of twisted heath, the extremity of which on each side is poised with stone to preserve the thatch from being blown away by the winds. This little village is seated in a valley surrounded with four mountains, which serve as so many ramparts of defence, and are amphitheatres, from whence a fair prospect of the ocean and isles is to be seen in a fair day.

This isle is by the inhabitants called Hirt, and likewise by all the Western Islanders; Buchanan calls it Hirta; Sir John Narbrough, and all seamen call it St Kilda; and in sea maps St Kilder, particularly in a Dutch sea map from Ireland to Zetland, published at Amsterdam by Peter Goas in the year, 1663, wherein the isle of St Kilda is placed due west betwixt fifty and sixty miles from the middle of the Lewis, and the isle answers directly to the fifty-eighth degree of northern latitude, as marked upon the ends of the map, and from it lies Rokol, a small rock sixty leagues to the westward of St Kilda; the inhabitants of this place call it Rokabarra; this map contains the soundings of some places near St Kilda; these not exceeding twenty or thirty fathom, it contains only the larger isle and a part of the lesser isles; this island is also called St Kilda, by a company of French and Spaniards, who lost their ship at Rokol in the year 1686, which they named to the inhabitants of St Kilda, whose latitude is fifty-seven degrees and three minutes.

The air here is sharp and wholesome; the hills are often covered with ambient white mists, which in winter are forerunners of snow, if they continue on the tops of the hills; and in summer, if only on the tops of the hills, they prognosticate rain; and when they descend to the valleys it is a prognostic of excessive heat. The night here about the time of the summer solstice exceeds not an hour in length, especially if the season is fair, then the sun disappears but for a short space, the reflex from the sea being all the time visible; the harvest and winter are liable to great winds and rain, the south-west wind annoying them more than any other, it is commonly observed to blow from the west for the most part of it, if not all July.

St Kilda is two miles long from east to west; from south to north one mile in breadth; five miles in circumference, and is naturally fenced with one continued face of a rock of great height, except a part of the bay, which lies to the south-east, and is generally well fenced with a raging sea. This bay is one half mile in length, and another in breadth; it is not ordinary for any vessel to anchor within this bay, in case of a storm, for this might endanger them; therefore they drop anchor without at the entry, judging it the securest place: the only place for landing here, is on the north side of this bay, upon a rock with a little declination, which is slippery, being clothed with several sorts of seaweeds; these, together with a raging sea, render the place more inaccessible, it being seldom without a raging sea, except under favour of a neaptide, a north-east or west wind, or with a perfect calm; when these circumstances concur, the *birlin* or boat is brought to the side of the rock, upon which all the inhabitants of both sexes are ready to join their united force to hale her through this rock, having for this end a rope fastened to the forepart; a competent number of them are also employed on each side; both these are determined by a crier, who is employed on purpose to warn them all at the same minute, and he ceases when he finds it convenient to give them a breathing.

At the head of the bay there's a plain sand, which is only to be seen in summer, the winter sea washing it all off the stones; there is no landing upon this place with safety, which the steward has learned to his cost. There is a little bay on the west side of this isle, all faced with an iron-coloured rock; some vessels take shelter here, when the wind is at south or north-east; there is a place of the rock here on the south side the rivulet, where you may land, if a neaptide or calm offer. The sea is very impetuous everywhere about this isle; they shewed me big stones which were lately removed out of their place, and cast into the Gallies Dock; I measured some of them which were in length seven, others eight foot, and three or four broad.

There is a little old ruinous fort on the south part of the south-east bay, called the Down. It is evident from what hath been already said, that this place may be reckoned among the strongest forts (whether natural or artificial) in the world; Nature has provided the place with store of ammunition for acting on the defensive; that is, a heap of stones in the top of the hill Oterveaul, directly above the landing place; it is very easy to discharge volley of this ammunition directly upon the place of landing, and that from a great height almost perpendicular, this I myself had occasion to demonstrate, having for my diversion put it in practice, to the great satisfaction of the inhabitants, to whom this defence never occurred hitherto. They are resolved to make use of this for the future, to keep off the Lowlanders, against whom of late they have conceived prejudices. A few hands may be capable of resisting some hundreds, if the above-mentioned weapons be but made use of. Those four mountains are faced on that side with regards the sea, with rocks of extraordinary height; the hill Conager on the north side, is about two hundred fathom height, perpendicularly above the sea.

There are round this isle four arches or vaults, through which the sea passes, as doth the daylight from either side, which is visible to any, though at a good distance; some of them representing a large gate: two of these look to the south, and two north-west; that on the point of the west bay is six fathom high above water, four in breadth, fifty paces in length, the top two fathom thick, and very strong, the cattle feeding upon it.

There are several veins of different stone to be seen in the rocks of the south-east bay; upon the north side of this rock is one as it were cut out by Nature, resembling a tarras walk. The crystal grows under the rock at the landing place; this rock must be pierced a foot or two deep, before the crystal can be had from the bed of sand where it lies; the water at the bottom is of a black colour, the largest piece is not above four inches long, and about two in diameter, each piece sexangular.

Upon the west side of this isle there is a valley with a declination towards the sea, having a rivulet running through the middle of it, on each side of which is an ascent of half a mile; all which piece of ground is called by the inhabitants, The Female Warrior's Glen. This Amazon is famous in their traditions: her house or dairy of stone is yet extant; some of the inhabitants dwell in it all summer, though it be some hundred years old; the whole is built of stone, without any wood, lime, earth, or mortar to cement it, and is built in form of a circle pyramid-wise towards the top, having a vent in it, the fire being always in the centre of the floor, the stones are long and thin, which supplies the defect of wood; the body of this house contains not above nine persons sitting; there are three beds or low vaults that go off the side of the wall, a pillar betwixt each bed, which contains five men apiece; at the entry to one of these low vaults is a stone standing upon one end fixed; upon this they say she ordinarily laid her helmet; there are two stones on the other side, upon which she is reported to have laid her sword: she is said to have been much addicted to hunting, and that in her time all the space betwixt this isle and that of Harris, was one continued tract of dry land. There was some years ago a pair of large deers' horns found in the top of Oterveaul Hill, almost a foot underground; and there was likewise a wooden dish full of deer's grease found in the same hill under ground. 'Tis also said of this warrior, that she let loose her greyhounds after the deer in St Kilda, making their course towards the opposite isles. There are several traditions of this famous Amazon, with which I will not further trouble the reader.

In this isle there are plenty of excellent fountains or springs; that near the female warrior's house is reputed to be the best, the name of it, Toubir-nimbuey, importing no less than the well of qualities or virtues; it runneth from east to west, being sixty paces ascent above the sea: I drank of it twice, an English quart at each time; it is very clear, exceeding cold, light, and diuretic; I was not able to hold my hands in it above a few minutes, in regard of its coldness; the inhabitants of Harris find it effectual against windy colics, gravel, headaches; this well hath a cover of stone.

There is a large well near the town, called St Kilder's Well; from which the island is supposed to derive its name; this water is not inferior to that above-mentioned; it runneth to the south-east from the north-west.

There is another well within half a mile of this, named after one Conirdan, an hundred paces above the sea, and runneth from north-west towards the south-east, having a stone cover.

Within twelve paces of this is a little and excellent fountain, which those of Harris and St Kilda, will needs call by the author's name, and were then resolved to give it a cover of stone, such as is above described.

There is a celebrated well issuing out of the face of a rock on the north side of the east bay, called by the inhabitants and

others, The Well of Youth, but is only accessible by the inhabitants, no stranger daring to climb the steep rock; the water of it is
received, as it falls, into the sea; it runs towards the south-east.
The taste of water of those wells was so pleasant, that for several weeks after the best fountains in the adjacent isles did not
relish with me. There is a rivulet runneth close by the town, and
another larger beyond St Kilder's Well; this last serves for washing linen, which it doth as well without soap, as other water does
with it; of this we had experience, which was a confirmation of
what had been reported to us concerning this water: we searched
if in the brinks we could discover any fuller's earth, but found
none; we discovered some pieces of iron ore in several places of
it; this rivulet drops form the mossy ground in the top of the hills.

The whole island is one hard rock, formed into four high
mountains, three of which are in the middle; all thinly covered
with black or brown earth, not above a foot, some places half
a foot deep, except the top of the hills, where it is above three
foot deep, and affords them good turf; the grass is very short
but kindly, producing plenty of milk; the number of sheep commonly maintained in St Kilda, and the two adjacent isles, does
not exceed two thousand, and generally they are speckled, some
white, some philamort, and are of an ordinary size; they do not
resemble goats in anything, as Buchanan was informed, except in
their horns, which are extraordinary large, particularly those in
the lesser isles.

The number of horses exceeds not eighteen, all of a red colour,
very low, and smooth skinned, being only employed in carrying
their turf and corn, and at the anniversary cavalcade, of which
hereafter. The cows that are about ninety head, small and great,
all of them having their foreheads white and black, which is discernable at a great distance, are of a low stature, but fat and
sweet beef; the dogs, cats, and all the sea-fowls of this isle are
speckled.

The soil is very grateful to the labourer, producing ordinarily
sixteen, eighteen, or twenty fold sometimes; their grain is only

bear, and some oats; the barley is the largest produced in all the Western Isles; they use no plough but a kind of crooked spade; their harrows are of wood, as are the teeth in the front also, and all the rest supplied only with long tangles of sea-ware tied to the harrow by the small ends; the roots hanging loose behind, scatter the clods broken by the wooden teeth; this they are forced to use for want of wood. Their arable land is very nicely parted into ten divisions, and these into subdivisions, each division distinguished by the name of some deceased man or woman, who were natives of the place; there is one spot called Multa Terra, another Multus Agris. The chief ingredient in their composts is ashes of turf mixed with straw; with these they mix their urine, which by experience they find to have much of the vegetable nitre; they do not preserve it in quantities as elsewhere, but convey it immediately from the fountain to the ashes, which by daily practice they find most advantageous; they join also the bones, wings, and entrails of their sea-fowls to their straw; they sow very thick, and have a proportionable growth; they pluck all their bear by the roots in handfuls, both for the sake of their houses, which they thatch with it, and their cows which they take in during the winter, the corn produced by this compost is perfectly free of any kind of weeds; it produces much sorrel where the compost reaches.

The coast of St Kilda, and the lesser isles, are plentifully furnished with variety of fishes, as cod, ling, mackerel, congers, braziers, turbat, graylords, sythes; these last two are the same kind, only differing in bigness, some call them black mouths; they are large as any salmon, and somewhat longer, there are also laiths, podloes, herring, and many more; most of these are fished by the inhabitants upon the rock, for they have neither nets nor long lines. Their common bait is the limpets or patellae, being parboiled; they use likewise the fowl called by them *bowger*, its flesh raw, which the fish near the lesser isles catch greedily; sometimes they use the *bowger's* flesh, and the limpets patellae at the same time upon one hook, and this proves successful also. In the month of July a considerable quantity of mackerel run themselves ashore, but always with a springtide. The amphibia seen here are the otters and seals; this latter the inhabitants reckon very good meat; there is no sort of trees, no, not the least shrub grows here, nor ever a bee seen at any time.

II

━━━━⮞●◀━━━━

LEVINIS, a rock about fourteen paces high, and thirty in circumference, narrower at the top; it stands about half a league to the south-east bay, and is not covered with any kind of earth or grass; it hath a spring of fresh water issuing out at the side; this rock, by an ancient custom, belongs to the galley's crew, but the above-mentioned allowance disposes them to undervalue it. Betwixt the west point of St Kilda, and the isle Soa, is the famous rock Stackdonn, i.e. as much, in their language, as a mischievous rock, for it hath proved so to some of their number, who perished in attempting to climb it; it is much of the form and height of a steeple; there is a very great dexterity, and it is reckoned no small gallantry to climb this rock, especially that part of it called the Thumb, which is so little, that of all the parts of a man's body, the thumb only can lay hold on it, and that must be only for the space of one minute; during which time his feet have no support, nor any part of his body touch the stone, except the thumb, at which minute he must jump by the help of his thumb, and the agility of his body concurring to raise him higher at the same time, to a sharp point of the rock, which when he has got hold of, puts him above danger, and having a rope about his middle, that he casts down to the boat, by the help of which he carries up as many persons as are designed for fowling at this time; the foreman, or principal climber, has the reward of four fowls bestowed upon him above his proportion; and, perhaps, one might think 14,000 too little to compensate so great a danger as this man incurs; he has this advantage by it, that he is recorded among their greatest heroes; as are all the foremen who lead the van in getting up this mischievous rock. Within pistol-shot from this place is the isle Soa; a mile and a half in circumference, but contracted narrower toward the top, being a full half mile in difficult ascent all round, most of it bare rock, some parts of it covered with grass, but dangerous to ascend; the landing is also very hazardous, both in regard of the raging sea, and the rock that must be climbed; yet the inhabitants are accustomed to carry burdens both up it and down, and of this I was once a witness. There is scarce any landing here, except in one place, and that under favour of a west wind and neaptide; the waves upon the rock discover when it is accessible; if they appear white from St Kilda, the inhabitants do not so much as offer to launch out their boat, in order to land in Soa, or any other isle or rock, though their lives were at the stake: this little isle is furnished with an excellent spring; the grass, being very sweet, feeds 500 sheep, each of them having generally two or three lambs at a birth, and every lamb being so fruitful, that it brings forth a lamb before itself is a year old. The same is also observed of lambs in the little isles adjacent to the isles of Harris and North Uist. The sheep in this isle Soa are never milked, which disposes them to be the more prolific: there are none to catch them but the inhabitants, whom I have seen pursue the sheep nimbly down the steep descent, with as great freedom as if it had been a plain field.

This isle abounds with infinite numbers of fowls, as *fulmar, lavy, falk, bowger,* etc.

There was a cockboat some two years ago came from a ship for water, being favoured by a perfect calm; the men discerned an infinite number of eggs upon the rocks, which charmed them to venture near the place, and at last purchased a competent number of them; so careful was one of the seamen as to put them into his breeches, which he put off on purpose for this use; some of the inhabitants of St Kilda happened to be in the isle that day; a parcel of them were spectators of this diversion, and were offended at it, being done without their consent, therefore they devised an expedient, which at once robbed the seamen of their eggs and breeches; and 'twas thus; they found a few loose stones in the superficies of the rock, some of which they let fall down perpendicularly above the seamen, the terror of which obliged them quickly to remove, abandoning both breeches and eggs for their safety; and those tarpaulin breeches were no small ornament there, where all wore girded plaids.

About two leagues and a half to the north of St Kilda, is the rock Stack Ly, two hundred paces in circumference, and of a great height, being a perfect triangle turning to a point at the top; it is visible above twenty leagues distant in a fair day, and appears blue; there is no grass nor earth to cover it, and it is perfectly white with solan geese sitting on and about it. One would think it next to impossible to climb this rock, which I expressed, being very close by it; but the inhabitants assured me it was practicable, and to convince me of the truth of it, they bid me look up near the top, where I perceived a stone pyramid-house, which the inhabitants built for lodging themselves in it in August, at which time the season proves inconstant there; this obliges the inhabitants in point of prudence to send a competent number of them to whose share the lots fall; these are to land in this rock some days before the time at which the solan geese use to take wing, and if they neglected this piece of foresight, one windy day might disappoint them of 5, 6, or 7,000 solan geese, this rock affording no less yearly; and they are so very numerous here, that they cannot be divided with respect to their lands, as elsewhere; therefore this is the reason why they send here by lots, and those who are sent act for the public interest, and when they have knocked on the head all that may be reached, they then carry them to a sharp point, called the casting point, from whence they throw them into the sea (the height being such that they dare not throw them in, but near the boat) until the boatmen cry, enough; lest the sea, which has a strong current there should carry them off, as it does sometimes, if too many are thrown down at once; and so by degrees getting all in, they return home; and after their arrival every man has his share proportionable to his lands, and what remains below the number ten, is due to the officer as a branch of his yearly salary. In this rock the solan geese are allowed to hatch their first eggs, but it is not so in the rocks next to be described; and that for this reason, that if all were allowed to hatch at the same time, the loss of the product in one rock would at the same time prove the loss of all the rest, since all would take wing almost at once.

The isle Borera lies near half a league from Stack Ly, to the north-east of it, being in circumference one mile and an half; it feeds about 400 sheep per annum, and would feed more, did not the solan geese pluck a large share of the grass for their nests.

This isle is very high and all rock, being inaccessible except in a calm, and there is only one place for landing, looking to the south: in the west end of this isle is Stallir House, which is much larger than that of the female warrior in St Kilda, but of the same model in all respects; it is all green without like a little hill; the inhabitants there have a tradition that it was built by one Stallir, who was a devout hermit of St Kilda; and had he travelled the universe he could scarcely have found a more solitary place for a monastic life.

There are about forty some pyramids in the isle, for drying and preserving their fowls, etc. These little houses are all of loose stones, and seen at some distance; there is also here a very surprising number of fowls, the grass as well as the rocks filled with them. The solan geese possess it for the most part; they are always masters wherever they come, and have already banished several species of fowls from this isle.

There was an earthquake here in the year 1686, which lasted but a few minutes; it was very amazing to the poor people, who never felt any such commotion before, or since.

To the west of Borera lies the rock Stack Narmin, within pistol-shot; this rock is half a mile in circumference, and is a possibility of landing only in two places, and that but in a perfect calm neither, and after landing the danger in climbing it is very great. The rock has not any earth or grass to cover it, and hath a fountain of good water issuing out above the middle of it, which runneth easterly: this rock abounds with solan geese and other fowls; here are several stone pyramids, as well for lodging the inhabitants that attend the seasons of the solan geese, as for those that preserve and dry them and other fowls, etc. The sea rises and rages extraordinarily upon this rock: we had the curiosity, being invited by a fair day, to visit it for pleasure, but it was very hazardous to us; the waves from under our boat rebounding from off the rock, and mounting over our heads west us all, so that we durst not venture to land, though men with ropes were sent before us; and we thought it hazard great enough to be near this rock; the wind blew fresh, so that we had much difficulty to fetch St Kilda again; I remember they brought 800 of the preceding year's solan geese dried in their pyramids; after our landing, the geese being cast together in one heap upon the ground, the owners fell to share out each man his own, at which I was a little surprised, they being all of a tribe; but having found upon enquiry that every goose carried a distinguishing mark on the foot, peculiar to the owner, I was then satisfied in this piece of singularity.

There is a violent current, whether ebb or flood, upon all the coasts of St Kilda, lesser isles and rocks. It is observed to be more impetuous with spring than neaptides; there are eddies on all the coasts, except at a sharp point where the tides keep their due course; the ebb southerly, and flood northerly.

A south-east moon causeth high tide; the springtides are always at the full and new moon, the two days following they are higher, and from that time decrease until the increase of the moon again, with which it rises gradually till the second after the full moon. This observation the seamen find to hold true betwixt the Mull of Kantyre, and the Farrow Head in the Strathnaver.

The landfowls produced here are hawks extraordinary good, eagles, plovers, crows, wrens, stonechaker, craker, cuckoo; this last being very rarely seen here, and that upon extraordinary occasions, such as the death of the proprietor MacLeod, the steward's death, or the arrival of some notable stranger. I was not able to forbear laughing at this relation, as founded upon no reason but fancy; which I no sooner expressed, then the inhabitants wondered at my incredulity, saying, that all their ancestors for a series of several ages had remarked this observation to prove true, and for a further confirmation, appealed to the present steward, whether he had not known this observation to have been true, both in his own and his father's time, who was also steward before him; and after a particular enquiry upon the whole, he told me, that both in his own and father's lifetime the truth of this observation has been constantly believed, and that several of the inhabitants now living have observed the cuckoo to have appeared after the death of the two last proprietors, and the two last stewards, and also before the arrival of strangers several times; it was taken notice of this year before our arrival, which they ascribe to my coming here, as the only stranger, the minister having been there before.

The sea-fowls are, first, gairfowl, being the stateliest, as well as the largest of all the fowls here, and above the size of a solan goose, of a black colour red about the eyes, a large white spot under each eye, a long broad bill; stands stately, its whole body erected, its wings short, it flieth not at all, lays its egg upon the bare rock, which, if taken away, it lays no more for that year, it is *palmypes,* or whole-footed, and has the hatching spot upon its breast, i.e., a bare spot from which the fathers have fallen off with the heat in hatching; its egg is twice as big as that of a solan goose, and is variously spotted, black, green, and dark; it comes without regard to any wind, appears the first of May, and goes away about the middle of June.

The solan goose, as some imagine from the Irish word *sou'l-er*, corrupted and adapted to the Scottish language, *'qui oculis irretortise longinquo respicit praedam'*: it equals a tame goose in bigness; it is by measure from the tip of the bill to the extremity of the foot, thirty-four inches long, and to the end of the tail, thirty-nine; the wings extended very long, there being seventy-two inches of distance betwixt the extreme tips; its bill is long, straight, of a dark colour, a little crooked at the point; behind the eyes the skin of the side of the head is bare of feathers; the ears of a mean size; the eyes hazel coloured; it hath four toes; the feet and legs black as far as they are bare; the plumage is like that of a goose. The colour of the old ones is white all over, excepting the extreme tips of the wings, which are black, and the top of the head, which is yellow, as some think the effect of age. The young ones are of a dark brown colour, turning white after they are a year old; its egg, somewhat less than that of a land goose, small at each end, and casts a thick scurf, and has little or no yolk. The inhabitants are accustomed to drink it raw, having from experience found it to be very pectoral, and cephalic. The solan geese hatch by turns; when it returns from its fishing, carries along with it five or six herrings in its gorget, all entire and undigested, upon whose arrival at the nest, the hatching fowl puts its head in the fisher's throat, and pulls out the fish with its bill as with a pincer, and that with very great noise; which I had occasion frequently to observe. They continue to pluck grass for their nests from their coming in March till the young fowl is ready to fly in August or September, according as the inhabitants take or leave the first or second eggs. It is remarkable of them, that they never pluck grass but on a windy day; the reason of which I enquired of the inhabitants, who said, that a windy day is the solan goose's vacation from fishing, and they bestow it upon this employment, which proves fatal to many of them; for after their fatigue they often fall asleep, and the inhabitants laying hold on this opportunity, are ready at hand to knock them on the head; their food is herring, mackerels, and syes; English hooks are often found in the stomachs both of young and old solan geese, though there be none of this kind used nearer than the isles twenty leagues distant; the fish pulling away the hooks in those isles go to St Kilda, or are carried by the old geese thither, whether of the two the reader is at liberty to judge.

The solan geese are always the surest sign of herrings, for wherever the one is seen, the other is always not far off. There is a tribe of barren solan geese which have no nests, and sit upon the bare rock; these are not the young fowls of a year old, whose dark colour would soon distinguish them, but old ones, in all things like the rest; these have a province, as it were, allotted to them, and are in a separated state from the others, having a rock two hundred paces distant from all other, neither do they meddle with, or approach to those hatching, or any other fowls; they sympathise and fish together, this being told me by the inhabitants, was afterwards confirmed to me several times by my own observation.

The solan geese have always some of their number that keep sentinel in the nighttime, and if they are surprised (as it often happens), all that flock are taken one after another, but if the sentinel be awake at the approach of the creeping fowlers, and hear a noise, it cries softly, 'grog, grog', at which the flock move not; but if this sentinel see or hear the fowler approaching, it cries quickly, 'bir, bir', which would seem to import danger, since immediately after, all the tribe take wing, leaving the fowler empty on the rock, to return home *re infecto*, all its labour for that night being spent in vain. Here is a large field of diversion for Apollonius Tyanaeus, who is said to have travelled many kingdoms over, to learn the language of beasts and birds.

Besides this way of stealing upon them in the nighttime, they are also catched in common gins of horsehair from which they do struggle less to extricate themselves than any other fowl, notwithstanding their bigness and strength; they are also caught in the herring lochs with a board set on purpose to float above water, upon it a herring is fixed, which the goose perceiving, flies up to the competent height, until it finds itself making a straight line above the fish, and then bending its course perpendicularly piercing the air, as an arrow from a bow, hits the board, into which it runs its bill with all its force irrecoverably, where it is unfortunately taken. The solan goose comes about the middle of

March with a south-west wind, warm snow, or rain, and goes away, according as the inhabitants determined the time, i.e., the taking away, or leaving its egg, whether at the first, second, or third time it lays.

The fulmar, in bigness equals the malls of the second rate; its wings very long, the outside of which are of a greyish white colour, the inside breast all white, a thick bill two inches long, crooked and prominent at the end, with wide nostrils in the middle of the bill, all of a pale colour, the upper mandible, or jaw, hangs over the lower on both sides and point, its feet pale, not very broad, with sharp toes, and a back toe; it picks its food out of the back of live whales, they say it uses sorrel with it, for both are found in its nest; it lays its egg ordinarily the first, second, or third day of May; which is larger than that of a solan goose egg, of a white colour, and very thin, the shell so very tender that it breaks in pieces if the season proves rainy; when its egg is once taken away, it lays no more for that year, as other fowls do, both a second and third time; the young fowl is brought forth in the middle of June, and is ready to take wing before the twentieth of July; it comes in November the sure messenger of evil tidings, being always accompanied with boisterous west winds, great snow, rain, or hail, and is the only sea-fowl that stays here all the year round, except the month of September and part of October. The inhabitants prefer this, whether young or old, to all other, the old is of a delicate taste, being a mixture of fat and lean; the flesh white, no blood is to be found but only in its head and neck; the young is all fat, excepting the bones, having no blood but what is in its head; and when the young fulmar is ready to take wing, it being approached, ejects a quantity of pure oil out at its bill, and will make sure to hit any that attacks it, in the face, though seven paces distant; this, they say, it uses for its defence; but the inhabitants take care to prevent this, by surprising the fowl behind, having for this purpose a wooden dish fixed to the end of their rods, which they hold before its bill as it spouts out the oil; they surprise it also from behind, by taking hold of its bill, which they tie with a thread, and upon their return home they untie it with a dish under to receive the oil; this oil is sometimes of a reddish, sometimes of a yellow colour, and the inhabitants and other islanders put a great value upon it, and use it as a catholicon for diseases, especially for any asking in the bones, stitches, etc. Some in the adjacent isles use it as a purge, others as a vomiter, it is hot in quality, and forces its passage through any wooden vessel.

The fulmar is a sure prognosticator of the west wind; if it comes to land, there is no west wind to be expected for some time, but if it keeps at sea, or goes to sea, or goes to sea from land, whether the wind blow from the south, north, or east, or whether it is a perfect calm, its keeping the sea is always a certain presage of an approaching west wind; from this quarter it is observed to return with its prey; its egg is large as that of a solan goose, white in colour, sharp at one end, somewhat blunt at the other.

The *scraber*, so called in St Kilda; in the Farn Islands, puffinet; in Holland, the Greenland dove; its bill small, sharp pointed, a little crooked at the end, and prominent; it is as large as a pigeon, its whole body being black, except a white spot on each wing; its egg grey, sharp at one end, blunt at the other.

It comes in the month of March, and in the nighttime, without regard to any winds; it's always invisible, except in the night, being all day either abroad at fishing, or all the day under ground upon its nest, which it digs very far under ground, from whence it never comes in daylight; it picks its food out of the live whale, with which, they say, it uses sorrel, and both are found in its nest. The young puffin is fat as the young fulmar, and goes away in August if its first egg be spared.

The *lavy*, so called by the inhabitants of St Kilda; by the Welsh, a *guillem*; it comes near to the bigness of a duck; its head, upper side of the neck all downwards of a dark brown, and white breast, the bill straight and sharp pointed; the upper chop hangs over the lower, its feet and claws are black.

Its egg in bigness is near to that of a goose egg, sharp at one end, and blunt at the other, the colour of it is prettily mixed with green and black; others of them are of a pale colour, with red and brown streaks; but this last is very rare; this egg for ordinary food is by the inhabitants, and others, preferred above all the eggs had here: This fowl comes with a south-west wind, if fair, the twentieth of February; the time of its going away depends upon the inhabitants taking or leaving its first, second, or third egg: if it stays upon land for a space of three days without intermission, it is a sign of southerly wind and fair weather, but if it goes to sea before the third expire, it is then a sign of a storm.

The bird, by the inhabitants called the *falk*, the 'razorbill' in the west of England, the 'awk' in the north, the 'murre' in Cornwall; *Alca hoeri*. It is a size less than the lavy; its head, neck, back, and tail are black; the inside to the middle of the throat, white; the throat under the chin of a dusky black; beyond the nostrils in the upper mandible, or jaw there is a furrow deeper than that in the coulterneb, the upper chop crooked at the end, and hangs over the lower, both having transverse furrows. It lays its egg in May, its young take wing the middle of July, if the inhabitants do not determine its stay longer, by taking the egg; which in bigness is next to the lavy, or guillem egg, and is variously spotted, sharp at one end, and blunt at the other.

The *bouger*, by those in St Kilda so called; 'coulterneb' by those in the Farn Islands; and in Cornwall, 'pope'; it is of the size of a pigeon, its bill is short, broad, and compressed sidewise, contrary to the bills of ducks, of a triangular figure, and ending in a sharp point, the upper mandible, or jaw, arcuate and crooked at the point; the nostrils are long holes produced by the aperture of the mouth; the bill is of two colours; near the head, of an ash colour, and red towards the point; the feet are yellow, the claws of a dark blue; all the back black, breast and belly white. They breed in holes underground, and come with a south-west wind about the twenty-second of March, lay their egg the twenty-second of April, and produce the fowl the twenty-second of May, if their first egg be not taken away; it is sharp at one end, and blunt on the other.

The assilag is as large as a lintwhite; black bill, wide nostrils at the upper part, crooked at the point like the fulmar's bill: it comes about the twenty-second of March, without any regard to winds, lays its egg about the twentieth of May, and produces the fowl towards the middle of October, then goes away about the end of November.

There are three sorts of sea-malls here, the first of a grey colour, in proportion near to a goose: the second sort of malls are considerably less, and of a grey colour, and the third sort is a white mall, less than a tame duck; the inhabitants call it *reddag*; it comes the fifteenth of April with a south-west wind, lays its egg about the middle of May, and goes away in the month of August.

The tirma, or seapie, by the inhabitants called *trilichan*, comes in May, goes away in August; if it comes the beginning of May, it is a sign of a good summer, if later, the contrary is observed. This fowl is cloven footed, and consequently swims not.

It is observed of all the sea-fowls here, that they are fatter in time of hatching than at other times, the solan geese excepted.

Every fowl lays an egg three different times (except the gair-fowl and fulmar, which lay but once); if the first or second egg be taken away, every fowl lays but one other egg that year, except the sea-malls, and they ordinarily lay the third egg, whether the first and second eggs be taken away, or no.

The inhabitants observe, that when the April moon goes far in May, the fowls are ten or twelve days later in laying their eggs, than ordinarily they used to be.

The inhabitants likewise say, that of these fowls, there first come over some spies, or harbingers, especially of the solan geese, towering about the islands where their nests are, and that when they have made a review thereof they fly away, and in two or three days after, the whole tribe are seen coming. Whither the fowls fly, and where they spend their winter, the inhabitants are utterly ignorant of.

The eggs are found to be of an astringent and windy quality to strangers, but, it seems, are not so to the inhabitants, who are used to eat them from the nest. Our men upon their arrival eating greedily of them became costive and feverish, some had the haemorrhoid veins swelled; Mr Campbel and I were at no small trouble before we could reduce them to their ordinary temper, we ordered a glister for them made of the roots of sedges, fresh butter, and salt, which, being administered, had its wished-for effect; the inhabitants reckoned this an extraordinary performance, being, it seems, the first of this kind they ever had occasion to hear of.

They preserve their eggs commonly in their stone pyramids, scattering the burnt ashes of turf under and about them, to defend them from the air, driness being their only preservative, and moisture their corruption; they preserve them six, seven, or eight months, as abovesaid; and then they become appetising and loosening, especially those that begin to turn.

That such a great number of wildfowls are so tame, as to be easily taken by the rods and gins, is not to be much admired by any who will be at the pains to consider the reason, which is the great inclination of propagating their species; so powerful is that σοργή or natural affection for their offspring, that they choose rather to die upon the egg, or fowl, than escape with their own lives (which they could do in a minute) and leave either of these to be destroyed.

It deserves our consideration to reflect seriously upon the natural propensity and sagacity of these animals in their kind; which if compared with many rational creatures, do far outstrip them, and justly obey the prescript of their natures, by living up unto that instinct that Providence has given them.

III

◆

THE inhabitants of this isle are originally descended of those of the adjacent isles, Lewis, Harris, South and North Uist, Skye: both sexes are naturally very grave, of a fair complexion; such as are not fair are natives only for an age or two; but their offspring proves fairer than themselves.

There are several of them would be reckoned among beauties of the first rank, were they upon a level with others in their dress.

Both men and women are well proportioned, nothing differing from those of the isles and continent. The present generation comes short of the last in strength and longevity. They shewed us huge big stones carried by the fathers of some of the inhabitants now living; any of which is a burden too heavy for any two of the present inhabitants to raise from the ground; and this change is all within the compass of forty years. But notwithstanding this, any one inhabiting St Kilda, is always reputed stronger than two of the inhabitants belonging to the isle of Harris, or the adjacent isles. Those of St Kilda have generally but very thin beards, and those too do not appear till they arrive at the age of thirty, and on some not till after thirty-five; they have all but a few hairs upon the upper lip, and point of the chin.

Both sexes have a lisp, but more especially the women, neither of the two pronouncing the letters, 'd', 'g', or 'r'. I remember a story of a craker that lisped (two years ago), the boys of the place took notice of, and were pleased to hear him, and to ape his cry; one of the steward's men beholding them, enquired the meaning of their noise, which he told them was ridiculous; they returned answer, that it was worth his while to behold the sport of a lisping craker, whom they aped; but the man replied, that they played the fool, for the craker diverted himself in lisping after them, and charged them with that imperfection; the boys no sooner heard this, but away they ran, and left the craker to cry and lisp as he pleased.

There are some of both sexes who have a genius for poetry, and are great admirers of music; the trump or Jewish harp is all the musical instrument they have, which disposes them to dance mightily. Their sight is extraordinary good, and they can discern things at a great distance; they have very good memories, and are resolute in their undertakings, chaste and honest, and the men reputed jealous of their wives. They argue closely, and with less passion than other islanders, or those inhabiting the Highlands on the continent.

They are reputed very cunning, and there is scarce any circumventing of them in traffic and bartering; the voice of one is the voice of all the rest, they being all of a piece, their common interest uniting them firmly together. They marry very young, the women at about thirteen or fourteen years of age; and are nice in examining the degrees of consanguinity before they marry. They give suck to their children for the space of two years. The most ancient person among them at present, is not above eighty years of age.

Providence is very favourable to them in this, that they are not infested with several diseases which are so predominant in the other parts of the world; the distemper that most prevails here, is a spotted fever, and that too confined to one tribe, to whom this disease is, as it were, become hereditary; others are liable to fluxes, fevers, stitches, the spleen; for all which they have but very few remedies; to get away their stitches, they commonly lie upon a warm hearth, with a side affected downwards; this they look upon to be almost infallible for dispelling the humour, or wind, that torments them. The smallpox hath not been heard of in this place for several ages, except in one instance, of two of the steward's retinue, who not having been well recovered of it, upon their arrival here, infected one man only.

The plants produced here, are *Lapathum vulgare,* the common dock, scurvy-grass round, being large as the palm of the hand, *mile-foil, Bursa pastoris,* silverweed, or argentine, plantine, sage, chicken-weed; sorrel, long, or the common sorrel; all-hail, or *siderites,* the sea-pink, *tormentil,* the scurf upon the stones, which has a drying and healing quality, and is likewise used for dyeing. The inhabitants are ignorant of the virtues of these herbs; they never had a potion of physic given them in their lives, nor know any thing of phlebotomy; a physician could not expect his bread in this commonwealth.

They have generally good voices, and sound lungs; to this the solan goose egg supped raw doth not a little contribute; they are seldom troubled with a cough, except as the steward's landing; which is no less rare, than firmly believed by the inhabitants of the adjacent isles.

Those of St Kilda, upon the whole, gave me this following account, that they always contract a cough upon the steward's landing, and it proves a great deal more troublesome to them in the night-time, they then distilling a great deal of phlegm; this indisposition continues for some ten, twelve or fourteen days; the most sovereign remedy against this disease, is their great and beloved catholicon, the *giben,* i.e. the fat of their fowls, with which they stuff the stomach of the solan goose, in fashion of a pudding; this they put in the infusion of oatmeal, which in their language they call *brochan;* but it is not so effectual now as at the beginning, because of the frequent use of it. I told them plainly that I thought all this notion of infection was but a mere fancy, and that, at least, it could not always hold; at which they seemed offended, saying, that never any, before the minister and myself, was heard doubt of the truth of it; which is plainly demonstrated

upon the landing of every boat; adding further, that every design was always for some end, but there was no room for any,
where nothing could be proposed; but for confirmation of the
whole, they appealed to the case of infants at the breast, who
were likewise very subject to this cough, but could not be capable
of affecting it, and therefore, in their opinion, they were infected
by such as lodged in their houses. There were scarce young or old
in the isle whom I did not examine particularly upon this head,
and all agreed in the confirmation of it. They add farther, that
when any foreign goods are brought thither, then the cough is
of longer duration than otherwise. They remark, that if the fever
has been among those of the steward's retinue, though before
their arrival there, some of the inhabitants are infected with it.
If any of the inhabitants of St Kilda chance to live, though but
a short space, in the isles of Harris, Skye, or any of the adjacent
isles, they become meagre, and contract such a cough, that the
giben must be had, or else they must return to their native soil.
This giben is more sovereign for removing of coughs, being used
by any other islanders, than those of St Kilda, because they love
to have it frequently in their meat as well as drink, by which too
frequent use of it, it loses its virtue; it was remarkable, that after
this infected cough was over, we strangers, and the inhabitants of
St Kilda, making up the number of about two hundred and fifty,
though we had frequently assembled upon the occasion of divine
service, yet neither young nor old amongst us all did so much as
once cough more.

Some thirteen years ago the leprosy broke out among them,
and some of their number died by it; there are two families at
present labouring under this disease. The symptoms of it are,
their feet begin to fail, their appetite declines, their faces become
too red, and break out in pimples, they get a hoarseness, and
their hair falls off from their heads, the crown of it exculcerates
and blisters, and lastly, their beards grow thinner than ordinary.

This disease may in a large measure be ascribed to their gross
feeding, and that on those fat fowls, as the fulmar and the solan

geese; the latter of which they keep for the space of a whole year, without salt or pepper to preserve them; these they eat roasted or boiled.

One of these lepers, being with me one day at the fulmar rock, importuned me to give him a remedy for his disease; I began to chide him for his ill diet in feeding so grossly; but finding the poor fellow ready and implicitly disposed to do whatever I should enjoin, I bid him take example from the fulmar who, they say, feeds sometimes on sorrel; this was a very surprising advise to him, but when he considered that the fulmar required sorrel to qualify the whale, he was the sooner persuaded that his *giben* and goose might require the same; I advised him further, to abstain from the *giben* and fat fowls, which was no small trouble to him, for he loved them exceedingly; I obliged him likewise to mount the hill Conager, a mile in height, once every morning and evening, and he was very careful to comply with those injunctions for the space of three days; in which short time he made some advances towards recovering his almost lost speech and appetite; for his throat was well nigh quite stopped up; he continued this practice a week longer, by which means he mended very considerably; and I left him fully resolved to proceed in this practice, until he was perfectly restored to his former state of health. I had the occasion to observe another of these lepers rave for some minutes, and when he was recovered to his right mind, he wrought at his ordinary employment.

The inhabitants are Christians, much of the primitive temper, neither inclined to enthusiasm nor to popery. They swear not the common oaths that prevail in the world; when they refuse or deny to give what is asked of them, they do it with a strong asseveration, which they express emphatically enough in their language to this purpose, 'You are no more to have it, than that if God had forbid it'; and thus they express the highest degree of passion. They do not so much as name the devil once in their lifetimes.

They leave off working after twelve of the clock on Saturday, as being an ancient custom delivered down to them from their ancestors, and go no more to it till Monday morning. They believe in God the Father, the Son and Holy Ghost; and a state of future happiness and misery, and that all events, whether good or bad, are determined by God. They use a set form of prayer at the hoisting of their sails: they lie down, rise, and begin their labours in the name of God. They have a notion, that spirits are embodied; these they fancy to be locally in rocks, hills, and wherever they list in an instant.

There are three chapels in this isle, each of them with one end towards the east, the other towards the west; the altar always placed at the east end; the first of these is called Christ Chapel, near the village; it is covered and thatched after the same manner with their houses; there is a brazen crucifix lies upon the altar, not exceeding a foot in length, the body is completely done, distended, and having a crown on, all in the crucified posture; they have it in great reverence, though they pay no kind of adoration or worship to it, nor do they either handle or see it, except upon the occasions of marriage, and swearing decisive oaths, which puts an end to all strife, and both these ceremonies are publicly performed. The churchyard is about a hundred paces in circumference, and is fenced in with a little stone wall, within which they bury their dead; they take care to keep the churchyard perfectly clean, void of any kind of nastiness, and their cattle have no access to it. The inhabitants, young and old, come to the churchyard every Sunday morning, the chapel not being capacious enough to receive them; here they devoutly say the Lord's prayer, Creed, and Ten Commandments.

They observe the festivals of Christmas, Easter, Good Friday, St Columba's Day, and that of All Saints; upon this they have an anniversary cavalcade, the number of their horses not exceeding eighteen; these they mount by turns, having neither saddle nor bridle of any kind, except a rope, which manages the horse only on one side; they ride from the shore to the house, and then after each man has performed his tour, the show is at an end. They are very charitable to their poor, of whom there are not at present above three, and these carefully provided for, by this little commonwealth, each particular family contributing according to their ability for their necessities; their condition is enquired into weekly, or monthly, as their occasions serve; but more especially at the time of their festivals, they slay some sheep on purpose to be distributed among the poor, with bread proportionable; they are charitable to strangers in distress, this they had opportunity to express to a company of French and Spaniards who lost their ship at Rokol in the year 1686, and came in, in a pinnace to St Kilda, where they were plentifully supplied with barley-bread, butter, cheese, solan geese, eggs, etc. Both seamen and inhabitants speaking only the Irish tongue, to which the French and the Spaniards were altogether strangers; upon their landing they pointed to the west, naming Rokol to the inhabitants, and after that, they pointed downward with their finger, signifying the sinking and perishing of their vessel; they shewed them Rokol in the sea map, far west off St Kilda. This, and much more, the masters of these ships told to a priest in the next island who understood French. The inhabitants acquainted me that the pinnace which carried the seamen from Rokol was so very low, that the crew added a foot height of canvas round it all, and began to work at it upon Sunday, at which the inhabitants were astonished, and being highly dissatisfied, plucked the hatchets and other instruments out of their hands, and did not restore them till Monday morning.

The inhabitants had occasion to shew great kindness to a boat's crew that was driven from the opposite isle South Uist, whither they themselves were driven afterwards, and where they were treated with no less civility and kindness than the above-mentioned had been by them; so that it may be said of them with great justice, that their charity is as extensive as the occasions of it.

The second of these chapels bears the name of St Columba, the third of St Brianan; both built after the manner of Christ's chapel; having churchyards belonging to them, and they are a quarter of a mile distance betwixt each chapel.

They told me of a ship that dropped anchor in the mouth of the bay the preceding year, and that the Lowlanders aboard her were not Christians; I enquired if their interpreter who they said spoke bad Irish, had owned this to be a truth, they answered, not; but that they knew this by their practices, and that in these three particulars; the first was the working upon Sunday, carrying several boats full of stones aboard for ballast; the second was the taking away some of their cows without any return for them, except a few Irish copper pieces; and the third was, the attempt made by them to ravish their women, a practice altogether unknown in St Kilda, where there has not been one instance of fornication or adultery for many years before this time; I remember they told me, that the bribe offered for debauching the poor women, was a piece of broad money, than which there could be nothing less charming in a place where the inhabitants cannot distinguish a guinea from a sixpence.

Their marriages are celebrated after the following manner, when any two of them have agreed to take one another for man and wife, the officer who presides over them, summons all the inhabitants of both sexes to Christ's chapel, where being assembled, he enquired publicly if there be any lawful impediment why these parties should not be joined in the bond of matrimony? And if there be no objection to the contrary, he then enquired of the parties if they are resolved to live together in weal and woe, etc. After their assent, he declares them married persons, and then desires them to ratify this their solemn promise in the presence of God and the people in order to which the crucifix is tendered to them, and both put their right hands upon it, as the ceremony by which they swear fidelity one to another during their lifetime.

Mr Campbel, the minister, married in this manner fifteen pair of the inhabitants on the seventeenth of June, who immediately after marriage, joined in a country dance, having only a bagpipe for their music, which pleased them exceedingly.

They baptise in the following manner, the parent calls in the officer, or any of his neighbours to baptise his child, and another to be sponsor, he that performs the minister's part being told what the child's name is to be, says, '—, I baptise thee to your father and your mother, in the Name of the Father, Son and Holy Ghost'; then the sponsor takes the child in his arms, as doth his wife as godmother, and ever after this there is a friendship between the parent and the sponsor, which is esteemed so sacred and inviolable, that no accident, how cross so-ever, is able to set them at variance; and it reconciles such as have been at enmity formerly.

This isle belongs in property to the Laird of MackLeod, head of one of the ancientest families of Scotland; it is never farmed, but mostly commonly bestowed upon some favourite, one of his friends or followers, who is called stewart of the isle. The present steward's name is Alexander MackLeod, who pays yearly to his master an acknowledgment of the various products of this isle. This steward visits St Kilda every summer, and upon his arrival he and his retinue have all the milk in the isle bestowed on them in a treat; there is another bestowed on them upon St Columba's Day, the fifteenth of June; we had a share of this second treat. The steward's retinue consist of forty, fifty, or sixty persons, and among them, perhaps the most meagre in the parish are carried thither to be recruited with good cheer, but this retinue is now retrenched, as also some of their ancient and unreasonable exactions.

The steward lives upon the charge of the inhabitants until the time that the solan geese are ready to fly, which the inhabitants think long enough; the daily allowance paid by them is very regularly exacted, with regard to their respective proportions of lands and rocks; there is not a parcel of men in the world more scrupulously nice and punctilious in maintaining their liberties and properties than these are, being most religiously fond of their ancient laws and statutes; nor will they by any means consent to alter their first (though unreasonable) constitutions; and we had a pregnant instance of this their genius for preserving their ancient customs; they have unchangeably continued their first and ancient measures, as the *maile, amir,* and *cubit;* this *maile* contains ten pecks; the *amir* which they at present make use of, is probably the Hebrew *omer,* which contains near two pecks; the *cubit,* or in their language, *lave keile,* i.e. an 'hand of wood', is the distance from the elbow to the finger's ends; this they only use in measuring their boats: the *amir,* or rather *half-amir* as they call it, is composed of thin boards, and as they confess has been used these four score years; in which tract of time it is considerably fallen short of the measure of which it was at first, which they themselves do not altogether deny; the steward to compensate this loss, pretends to a received custom of adding the hand of him that measures the corn to the *amir* side, holding some of the barley above the due measure, which the inhabitants complain of as unreasonable; the steward to satisfy them, offered to refer the debate to Mr Campbel's decision and mine, they themselves being to propose their objections, and two of his retinue, who were well seen in the customs of this place, in time of some of the former stewards, being appointed to answer them, and he promised that he would acquiesce in the decision, though it should prove to his prejudice; but they would not alter that measure if Mack-Leod did not expressly command the same to be done, being persuaded that he would not in the least alter that measure which his and their ancestors had had in such esteem for so many ages. So great was their concern for this *amir,* that they unanimously determined to send the officer as envoy (according to the ancient custom) to represent their case to MackLeod; this was the result of a general council, in which the master of every family has a vote, since every family pays this officer an *amir* of barley per annum, to maintain his character.

This officer as such, is obliged to adjust the respective proportions of lands, grass, and rocks, and what else could be claimed by virtue of the last tack, or lease, which is never longer than for three years, condescended to by the steward; nay, he is obliged always to dispute with the steward for what is due to any of them, and never to give over until he had obtained his demand, or put the steward into such a passion, that he gives the officer at least three strokes with his cudgel over the crown of his head; after these three strokes he has done the utmost that is required of him by their ancient customs. I enquired of the officer (who told me this passage) what if the steward give him but one blow over the crown, he answered, that the inhabitants would not be satisfied if he did not so far plead as to irritate the steward to give both a second and a third blow; I had the farther curiosity to enquire of the steward himself if he was wont to treat the officer in this manner, who answered, that it was an ancient custom, which in his short time he had not had occasion to practise, but if he should, he would not confine himself to the number of three blows, if the officer should prove indiscreet.

The steward bestows some acres of land upon the officer for serving him and the inhabitants; he gives him likewise the bonnet worn by himself upon his going out of the island; the steward's wife leaves with the officer's wife the *kerch*, or head-dress worn by herself, and she bestows likewise upon her an ounce of indigo. The steward has a large cake of barley presented to him by an officer at every meal, and it must be made so large as shall be sufficient to satisfy three men at a time, and by way of eminence it is baked in the form of a triangle, and furrowed twice round; the officer is likewise obliged to furnish the steward with mutton, or beef, to his dinner every Sunday during his residence in the island.

Notwithstanding these reciprocal acts of kindness, this officer must be allowed to go in quality of an envoy to MackLeod against the steward, upon extraordinary occasions, if the commonwealth have any grievances to redress, as that of the *amir* now depending; but the commission given him is limited, the whole boat's crew being joined in commission with him, and are a check upon him, lest his dependence upon the steward might be apt to bias him; he makes his entry very submissively, taking off his bonnet at a great distance when he appears in MackLeod's presence, bowing his head and hand low near to the ground, his retinue doing the like behind him one after another, making, as it were, a chain; this being their manner of walking both at home and abroad, for they walk not abreast as others do; and in making their purchase among the rocks, one leads the van, and the rest follow.

The number of people inhabiting this isle at present, is about one hundred and eighty, who in the steward's absence are governed by one Donald MackGillcolm, as their *meijre*, which imports an officer, this officer was anciently chosen, or at least approved of by the people, before the steward settled him in his office, but now the stewards have the nomination of him absolutely; he is president over them in all their debates, takes care that the lots be managed impartially, that none to whose share they fall may have cause to repine, whether it be fore the steward's service, or that of the commonwealths; the use of the lots, together with the crucifix, do mightily contribute to their peace and quiet, keeping every one within his proper bounds. It must needs be a very odd case indeed that falls not within the compass of either of these two to determine; when any case happens which does not fall under the decision of lots, and it is capable of being decided only by the oath of the parties, then the crucifix must determine the matter, and if it should prove to be a case of the highest importance, any of them is at liberty to refer it to his neighbour's oath, without any suspicion of perjury, provided the ceremony of touching the crucifix with their right hand be observed; and this is always publicly performed.

If any man is guilty of beating his neighbour, he is liable to a fine not exceeding the value of two shillings sterling; if any has beat his neighbour so as to draw blood from him; he is liable to a fine, but it must not exceed four shillings and six pence; these crimes are complained of by the officer to the steward upon his arrival, who either exacts the whole, or dispenses with the fines, as he judges convenient for their future quiet and peace.

They have only one common kiln, which serves them all by turns, as the lots fall to their share; he whose lot happens to be last does not resent it at all.

The officer by virtue of his place, is obliged through a point of honour to be the first that lands in the lesser isles and rocks, from whence they carry their fowls and eggs, and not within some trouble too. This notion of honour exposes him to frequent dangers; and, perhaps, it may not be unpleasant to describe it as I have seen it practised; and 'tis thus; when they have come as near to the rock as they think may consist with the safety of the boat, which is not a little tossed by the raging of the sea, those whose turn then it is, are employed with poles to keep off the boat, that is in great danger, in regard of the violence of the waves beating upon the rock, and they are to watch the opportunity of the calmest wave; upon the first appearance of which, the officer jumps out upon the rock; if there be any apparent danger, he ties a rope about his middle, with one end of it fasted to the boat; if he has landed safe, he then fixes his feet in a secure place, and by the assistance of this rope draws up all the crew to him, except those whose turn it is to look after the boat; but if in jumping out he falls into the sea (as his fortune is so to do sometimes) then he is drawn into the boat again by that part of the rope that is so fastened to it, and the next then whose turn it is must try his fortune, the officer after his fall being supposed to be sufficiently fatigued, so that he is not obliged to adventure his person again to a second hazard upon this occasion, especially he being exposed to the greatest danger that offers upon their landing when they return back again to the isle, where the sea often rages, he being obliged then by virtue of his office to stay in the boat, after the whole crew are landed, where he must continue employing his pole, until the boat be either brought safe to land, or else split upon the rocks.

They furnish themselves with ropes to carry them through the more inaccessible rocks; of these ropes there are only three in the whole island, each of them twenty-four fathoms in length; and they are either knit together and lengthen by tying the one to the other, or used separately as occasion requires; the chief thing upon which the strength of these ropes depends, is cows hides salted, and cut out in one long piece, this they twist round the ordinary rope of hemp, which secures it from being cut by the rocks; they join sometimes at the lower end two ropes, one of which they tie about the middle of one climber, and another about the middle of another, that these may assist one another in case of a fall; but the misfortune is, that sometimes the one happens to pull down the other, and so both fall into the sea; but if they escape (as they do commonly of late) they get an incredible number of eggs and fowls.

The ropes belong to the commonwealth, and are not to be used without the general consent of all; the lots determine the time, place, and persons for using them, they get together in three days a much greater number of fowls and eggs than their boat is able to carry away, and therefore what is over and above they leave behind in their stone pyramids: they catch their fowls with gins made of horsehair, these are tied to the end of their fishing rods, with which the fowlers creep through the rocks indiscernibly, putting the noose over their heads about their necks, and so draw them instantly; they use likewise hair gins which they set upon plain rocks, both the ends fastened by a stone, and so catch forty or fifty a day with them.

The inhabitants, I must tell you, run no small danger in the quest of the fowls and eggs, insomuch that I fear it would be thought an hyperbole to relate the inaccessibleness, steepness, and height, of those formidable rocks which they venture to climb. I myself have seen some of them climb up the corner of a rock with their backs to it, making use only of their heels and elbows, without any other assistance; and they have this way acquired a dexterity in climbing beyond any I ever yet saw; necessity has made them apply themselves to this, and custom has perfected them in it; so that it is become familiar to them almost from their cradles, the young boys of three years old being to climb the walls of their houses: their frequent discourses of climbing, together with the fatal end of several in the exercise of it, is the same to them, as that of fighting and killing is with soldiers, and so is become as familiar and less formidable to them, than otherwise certainly it would be. I saw two young men, to whose share the lots fell in June last, for taking the nest of a hawk (which was in a high rock above the sea) bringing home the hawks in a few minutes, without any assistance at all.

Their dogs are likewise very dextrous in climbing and bringing out from their holes those fowls which build their nests far underground, such as the scraber, puffinet, etc., which they carry in their teeth to their masters, letting them fall upon the ground before them, though asleep.

The inhabitants speak the Irish tongue only; they express themselves slowly but pertinently; and have the same language with those of Harris and other isles, who retain the Irish in its purity.

Their habit anciently was of sheepskins, which has been wore by several of the inhabitants now living; the men at this day wear a short doublet reaching to their waist, about that a double plait of plaid, both ends joined together with the bone of a fulmar, this plaid reaches no further than their knees, and is above the haunches girt about with a belt of leather, they wear short caps of the same colour and shape with the capuchins, but shorter, and on Sundays they wear bonnets; some of late have got breeches, and they are wide and open at the knees; they wear cloth stockings, and go without shoes in the summertime; their leather is dressed with the roots of tormentil.

The women wear upon their heads a linen dress, straight before, and drawing to a small point behind below the shoulders, a foot and a half in length, and a lock of about sixty hairs hanging down each cheek, reaching to their breasts, the lower end tied with a knot; their plaid, which is the upper garment, is fastened upon their breasts with a large round buckle of brass in form of a circle; the buckle anciently worn by the steward's wives were of silver, but the present steward's wife makes no use of either this dress or buckle. The women inhabiting this isle wear no shoes nor stockings in the summertime; the only and ordinary shoes they wear, are made of the necks of solan geese, which they cut above the eyes, the crown of the head serves for the heel, the whole skin being cut close at the breast, which end being sowed, the foot enter into it, as into a piece of narrow stocking; this shoe doth not wear above five days, and if the down side be next the ground, then not above three or four days; but, however, there is plenty of them; some thousands being catched, or, as they term it, stolen every March.

Both sexes wear coarse flannel shirts, which they put off when they go to bed; they thicken their clothes upon flakes, or mats of hay twisted and woven together in small ropes; they work hard at this employment, first making use of their hands, and at last of their feet; and when they are at this work, they commonly sing all the time, one of their number acting the part of a prime chantress, whom all the rest follow and obey.

They put the faces of their dead towards the east when they bury them, and bewail the death of their relations excessively, and upon those occasions make doleful songs, which they call laments. Upon the news of the late MackLeod's death, they abandoned their houses, mourning two days in the field; they kill a cow, or sheep, before the interment, but if it be in the spring, this ceremony then is delayed, because the cattle are at that time poor and lean, but, however, they are to be killed as soon as ever they become fat.

Their ordinary food is barley and some oatbread baked with water, they eat all the fowls, already described, being dried in their stone houses, without any salt or spice to preserve them; and all their beef and mutton is eaten fresh, after the same manner they use the *giben*, or fat of their fowls; this *giben* is by daily experience found to be a sovereign remedy for the healing of green wounds; it cured a cancer in an inhabitant of the isle of Lewis, and a fistula in one Nicholson of Skye, in St Maries Parish; this was performed by John MackLean, chirugeon there: they boil the seaplants, dulse, and slake, melting the giben upon them instead of butter, and upon the roots of silverweed and dock boiled, and also with their scurvy-grass stoved, which is very purgative, and here it is of an extraordinary breadth. They use this giben with their fish, and it is become the common vehicle that conveys all their food down their throats. They are undone for want of salt, of which as yet they are but little sensible; they use no set times for their meals, but are determined purely by their appetites.

They use only the ashes of sea-ware for salting their cheese, and the shortest (which grows in the rocks) is only used by them, that being reckoned the mildest.

Their drink is water, or whey, commonly: they brew ale but rarely, using the juice of nettle roots, which they put in a dish with a little barley-meal dough; these *sowens* (i.e. 'flummery') being blended together, produce good yeast, which puts their wort into a ferment, and makes good ale, so that when they drink plentifully of it, it disposes them to dance merrily.

They preserve the solan geese in their pyramids for the space, flitting them in the back, for they have no salt to keep them with. They have built above five hundred stone pyramids for their fowls, eggs, etc.

We made particular enquiry after the number of solan geese consumed by each family the year before we came here, and it amounted to 22,600 in the whole island, which they said was less than they ordinarily did, a great many being lost by the badness of the season, and the great current into which they must be thrown when they take them, the rock being of such an extraordinary height that they cannot reach the boat.

There is one boat sixteen cubits long, which serves the whole commonwealth; it is very curiously divided into apartments proportionable to their lands and rocks; every individual has his space distinguished to an hair's breadth, which his neighbour cannot encroach so much as to lay an egg upon it.

Every partner in summer provides a large turf to cover his space of the boat, thereby defending it from the violence of the sun, which (in its meridian height) reflects most vehemently from the sea, and rock, upon which the boat lies; at the drawing of it up, both sexes are employed pulling a long rope at the fore-end; they are determined in uniting their strength, by the cryer, who is therefore excepted from being obliged to draw the boat.

There is but one steel and tinder-box in all this commonwealth; the owner whereof fails not upon every occasion of striking fire in the lesser isles, to go thither and exact three eggs, or one of the lesser fowls from each man as a reward for his service; this by them is called the fire-penny, and this capitation is very uneasy to them; I bid them try their crystal with their knives, which when they saw it did strike fire, they were not a little astonished, admiring at the strangeness of the thing, and at the same time accusing their own ignorance, considering the quantity of crystal growing under the rock of their coast. This discovery has delivered them from the fire-penny tax, and so they are no longer liable to it.

They have likewise a pot-penny tax, which is exacted in the same manner as the fire-penny was, but is much more reasonable; for the pot is carried to the inferior isles for the public use; and is in hazard of being broken; so that the owners may justly exact upon this score, since any may venture his pot when he pleases. When they have bestowed some hours in fowling about the rocks, and caught a competent number, they sit down near the face of it to refresh themselves, and in the mean time, they single out the fattest of their fowls, plucking them bare, which they carry home to their wives, or mistresses, as a great present, and it is always accepted very kindly from them, and could not otherwise be, without great ingratitude, seeing these men ordinarily expose themselves to very great danger, if not hazard their lives, to procure those presents for them.

In the face of the rock, south from the town, is the famous stone, known by the name of the Mistress Stone; it resembles a door exactly; and is in the very front of this rock, which is twenty or thirty fathom perpendicular in height, the figure of it being discernable about the distance of a mile; upon the lintel of this door, every bachelor-wooer is by an ancient custom obliged in honour to give a specimen of his affection for the love of his mistress, and it is thus; he is to stand on his left foot, having the one half of his sole over the rock, and then he draws the right foot further out to the left, and in this posture bowing, he puts both his fists further out to the right foot; and then after he has performed this, he has acquired no small reputation, being always after it accounted worthy of the finest mistress in the world: they firmly believe that this achievement is always attended with the desired success.

This being the custom of the place, one of the inhabitants very gravely desired me to let him know the time limited by me for trying of this piece of gallantry before I designed to leave the place, that he might attend me; I told him this performance would have a quite contrary effect upon me, by robbing me both of my life and mistress at the same moment; but he was of a contrary opinion, and insisted on the good fortune attending it; but I must confess all his arguments were too weak to make me attempt the experiment.

They take their measures in going to the lesser islands from the appearance of the heavens; for when it is clear or cloudy in such a quarter, it is a prognostic of wind of fair weather, and when the waves are high on the east point of the bay, it is an infallible sign of a storm, especially if they appear very white, even though the weather be at that time calm.

If the waves in the bay make a noise as they break before they beat upon the shore, it is also an infallible forerunner of a west wind; if a black cloud appears above the south side of the bay, a south wind follows some hours afterwards. It is observed of the sea betwixt St Kilda and the isles Lewis, Harris, etc., that it rages more with a north wind, than when it blows from any other quarter. And it is likewise observed to be less raging with the south wind than any other.

They know the time of the day by the motion of the sum from one hill or rock to another, upon either of these the sun is observed to appear at different times; and when the sun doth not appear, they measure the day by the ebbing and flowing of the sea, which they can tell exactly, though they should not see the shoar for some days together, their knowledge of the tides depends upon the changes of the moon, which they likewise observe, and are very nice in it.

They use for their diversion short clubs and balls of wood; the sand is a fair field for this sport and exercise, in which they take great pleasure and are very nimble at it; they play for some eggs, fowls, hooks, or tobacco; and so eager are they for victory, that they strip themselves to their shirts to obtain it: they use swimming and diving, and are very expert in both.

The women have their assemblies in the middle of the village, where they discourse of their affairs, but in the meantime employing their distaff, and spinning in order to make their blankets; they sing and jest for diversion, and in their way, understand poetry, and makes rhymes in their language. Both men and women are very courteous; as often as they passed by us every day, they saluted us with their ordinary compliment of 'God save you'; each of them making their respective courtesies.

Both sexes have a great inclination to novelty; and, perhaps, anything may be thought new with them that is but different from their way of managing land, cattle, fowls, etc. A parcel of them were always attending the minister and me, admiring our habit, behaviour, and, in a word, all that we did or said was wonderful in their esteem; but above all, writing was the most astonishing to them; they cannot conceive how it is possible for any mortal to express the conceptions of his mind in such black characters upon white paper. After they had with admiration argued upon this subject, I told them, that within the compass of two years or less, if they pleased, they might easily be taught to read and write, but they were not of the opinion that either of them could be obtained, at least by them, in an age.

The officer in his embassy in July last, travelled so far as to land on the continent next to Skye, and it was a long journey for a native of St Kilda so to do, for scarce any of the inhabitants ever had the opportunity of travelling so great a way into the world.

They observed many wonderful things in the course of their travels; but they have a notion that MackLeod's family is equivalent to that of an imperial court, and believe the king to be only superior to him: they say this lady wore such a strange Lowland dress, that it was impossible for them to describe it; they admired glass windows hugely, and a looking-glass to them was a prodigy; they were amazed when they saw cloth hangings upon a thick wall of stone and lime, and condemned it as a thing very vain and superfluous.

They reckon the year, quarter, and month, as generally is done all Britain over. They compute the several periods of time by the lives of the proprietors and stewards, of whose greatest actions they have a tradition, of which they discourse with as great satisfaction, as any historian reflecting on the Caesars, or greatest generals of the world.

They account riding one of the greatest pieces of grandeur here upon earth, and told me with a strange admiration, that MackLeod did not travel on foot, as they supposed all other men did, and that they had seen several horses kept on purpose by him for riding.

One of their number landing in the isle of Harris, enquired who was the proprietor of those lands? They told him, that it was MackLeod, which did not a little raise his opinion of him; this man afterwards, when he was in the isle of Skye, and had travelled some miles there, one day standing upon an eminence, and looking round about him, he fancied he saw a great part of the world, and then enquired to whom those lands did belong, and when one of the company had acquainted him, that MackLeod was master of those lands also, the St Kilda man lifting up his eyes and hands to Heaven, cried out with admiration, 'O Mighty Prince, who art Master of such vast territories!' This he expressed so emphatically in the Irish language, that the saying from that time became a proverb whenever any body would express a greatness and plenitude of power.

One of the things they wondered most at, was the growth of trees; they thought the beauty of the leaves and branches admirable, and how they grew to such a height above plants, was far above their conception: one of them marvelling at it, told me, that the trees pulled him back as he travelled through the woods: they resolved once to carry some few of them on their backs to their boats, and so to take them to St Kilda, but upon second thoughts, the length of the journey, being through the greatest part of the isle of Skye, deterred them from this undertaking, for though they excel others in strength, yet they are very bad travellers on foot, they being but little used to it.

One of their number having travelled in the isle of Skye, to the south part of it, thought this a prodigious journey; and seeing in the opposite continent the shire of Inverness, divided from Skye only by a narrow sea, enquired of the company, if that was the border of England.

One of the St Kilda men, after he had taken a pretty large dose of aqua vitae, and was become very heavy with it, as he was falling into a sleep, and fancying it was to have been his last, expressed to his companions the great satisfaction he had in meeting with such an easy passage out of this world; 'For,' said he, 'it is attended with no kind of pain.' In short, their opinion of foreign objects is as remote from the ordinary sentiments of other mankind, as they are themselves from all foreign converse.

I must not omit acquainting the reader, that the account given of the seamen's rudeness to the inhabitants, has created great prejudices in them against seamen in general; and though I endeavoured to bring them into some good opinion of them, it will not be, I hope, improper here to deliver the terms upon which the inhabitants are resolved to receive strangers, and no otherwise; they will not admit of any number exceeding ten, and those too must be unarmed, for else the inhabitants will oppose them with all their might; but if any number of them, not exceeding that abovesaid, come peaceably, and with good designs, they may expect water and fire gratis, and what else the place affords, at the easiest rates in the world.

The inhabitants of St Kilda, are much happier than the generality of mankind, as being almost the only people in the world who feel the sweetness of true liberty: what the condition of the people in the Golden Age is feigned by the poets to be, that theirs really is, I mean, in innocency and simplicity, purity, mutual love and cordial friendship, free from solicitous cares, and anxious covetousness; from envy, deceit, and dissimulation; from ambition and pride, and the consequences that attend them. They are altogether ignorant of the vices of foreigners, and governed by the dictates of reason and Christianity, as it was first delivered to them by those heroic souls whose zeal moved them to undergo danger and trouble to plant religion here in one of the remotest corners of the world.

There is this only wanting to make them the happiest people in this habitable globe, viz., that they themselves do not know how happy they are, and how much they are above the avarice and slavery of the rest of mankind. Their way of living makes them condemn gold and silver, as below the dignity of human nature; they live by the munificence of Heaven; and have no designs upon one another, but such as are purely suggested by justice and benevolence.

There being about thirty of the inhabitants one day together in the isle Soa, they espied a man with a grey coat and plaid, in a shirt, floating on the sea upon his belly, and saw likewise a mall pecking at his neck; this vision continued above a quarter of an hour, and then disappeared; but shortly after, one of the spectators chanced to fall into the sea, and being drowned, resembled the forewarning vision in all things, and the mall was also seen upon his neck; this was told me by the steward some years before, and afterwards was confirmed to me by such as were themselves eyewitnesses of it.

None of the inhabitants pretended to the second sight, except Roderick the Impostor and one woman, and she told her neighbours that she saw, some weeks before our coming, a boat (different from that of the steward) with some strangers in it, drawing near to their isle.

An Account of one Roderick, supposed to have had Conversation with a Familiar
Spirit, and pretending to be sent by St John the Baptist with New Revelations and Discoveries

After our landing, the minister and I (according to our first resolution) examined the inhabitants apart by themselves concerning the new pretended religion delivered to them by their false prophet.

All of them, young as well as old, both men and women, unanimously agreed in this following account; they did heartily congratulate the minister's arrival, and at the same time declared their abhorrence of the imposter's delusions, and with repeated instances begged for the Lord's sake that he might be for ever removed out of the isle.

This impostor is a comely well-proportioned fellow, red-haired, and exceeding all the inhabitants of St Kilda in strength, climbing, etc. He is illiterate, and under the same circumstances with his companions, for he had not so much as the advantage of ever seeing any of the Western Isles; all his converse being only with the steward's retinue, who were as ignorant of letters as himself.

In the eighteenth year of his age, he took the liberty of going to fish on a Sunday (a practice altogether unknown in St Kilda); and he asserts, that in his return homeward, a man in Lowland dress, i.e., a cloak and hat, appeared to him upon the road; at this unexpected meeting, Roderick falls flat on the ground in great disorder, upon which this man desired him not to be surprised at his presence, for he was John the Baptist immediately come from Heaven with good tidings to the inhabitants of that place, who had been for a long time kept in ignorance and error, that he had commission to instruct Roderick in the laws of Heaven for the edification of his neighbours: Roderick answered, that he was no way qualified for so great a charge; the pretended John Baptist desired him to be of good courage, for he would instantly make him capable for his mission, and then delivered to him the following scheme, in which he so mixed the laudable customs of the church with his own diabolical inventions, that it became impossible for so ignorant a people as they, to distinguish the one from the other.

The first and principal command which he imposed upon them, was that of the Friday's fast, which he enjoined to be observed with such strictness, as not to allow one of them to taste any kind of food before night, no, not so much as a snuff of tobacco, which they love dearly; this bare fast, without any religious exercise attending it, was the first badge and cognizance of his followers. He persuaded the people, that some of their deceased neighbours were nominated saints in heaven, and advocates for them here who survived; he told, every one had his respective advocate; the anniversary of every saint was to be commemorated by every person under whose tutelage they were reputed to be. And this was observed by treating the neighbours with a liberal entertainment of beef or mutton, fowls, etc., the imposter himself being always the chief guest at the feast; where a share of the entertainment was punctually sent to his wife and children; the number of sheep ordinarily consumed on these occasions, was proportionate to the ability of him that bestowed them.

He imposed likewise several penances which they were obliged to submit to, under the pain of being expelled from the society of his fraternity in worship, which he pretended to be founded upon no less authority than that of St John the Baptist's and threatened to inflict the saddest judgments upon those as should prove refractory, and not obey his injunctions.

The ordinary penances he laid upon them, were to make them stand in cold water (without regard to the season, whether frost or otherwise) during his pleasure; and if there were any more of them upon whom this severity was to be inflicted, they were to pour cold water upon one another's heads until they had satisfied his tyrannical humour. This diabolical severity was evidence enough, that he was sent by him who is the father of lies, and was a murderer from the beginning.

He commanded that every family should slay a sheep upon the threshold of their doors, but a knife must not so much as touch it, he would have them only make use of their crooked spades for their instruments to kill them with; for which, if duly considered, there is nothing more improper the edge with which he commanded the sheep's neck to be cut being almost half an inch thick. Now this was to be done in the evening, and if either young or old had tasted a bit of the meat of it that night, the equivalent number of sheep were to be slain the following day, after the former manner.

He forbid the use of the Lord's Prayer, Creed, and Ten Commandments, and instead of them prescribed diabolical forms of his own. His prayers and rhapsodical forms were often blended with the names of God, our Blessed Saviour, and the Immaculate Virgin; he used the Irish word, *phersichin*, i.e. 'verses', which is not known in St Kilda, nor in the north-west isles, except to such as can read the Irish tongue. But that which seems to be most surprising, in his obscure prayers was his mentioning of ELI, with the character of our preserver. He used several unintelligible words in his prayers, of which he could not tell the meaning himself; saying only, that he had received them implicitly from St John Baptist, and delivered from before his hearers without any explication.

He taught the women a devout hymn, which he called the Virgin Mary's, as went from her, this hymn was never delivered in public, but always in a private house, or some remote place where no eye could see them but that of Heaven; he persuaded the innocent women that it was of such merit and efficacy, that any one who was able to repeat it by heart, would die in child-bearing: and every woman paid a sheep to the impostor for teaching her this hymn.

The place and manner of teaching this hymn afforded him a fair opportunity of debauching the simple women; and this some of their number acknowledged to the minister and me upon examination.

He prescribed to all his auditory, long rhymes, which he called psalms; these he ordinarily sung at his rhapsodical preachments.

He endeavoured to alter the common way of burying, which was by placing the faces of the dead to the east, and would have persuaded them to place them to the south, and that he might prevail the more with them so to do, he placed the bodies of those of his own family who happened to die, facing the south; yet the inhabitants would not follow his example in this, but continued in their former practice.

He persuaded the women, that if in all things they complied with his new revelation, they should be undoubtedly carried to Heaven; and that in their journey thither they were to pass through the firmament riding upon white horses. These and many more ridiculous things he imposed upon the people, of which this is but an abstract.

This unhappy fellow to consecrate his enterprise, pitched upon a little rising spot of ground, which he called John the Baptist's Bush; upon which he said these oracles were delivered by John Baptist to him. And this bush was from time forward believed to be holy ground, and must not be any further trod upon by any of their cattle, and if by chance one of them happen to touch it, it must be forthwith slain and eaten by Roderick and the owners; and if any proved refractory, and were resolved to spare their cattle, most dreadful commination was issued out against them, of being thenceforward excluded from any further fellowship with him, until they should acknowledge their faults, and comply with his luxurious desires, which to disobey he made them be-

lieve was damnable. It was reckoned meritorious if any body had
revealed who had transgressed the orders given by him.

This imposter continued for the space of several years, without control, to delude these poor innocent well-meaning people,
until at last his villainous design upon the women was found
out, I mean, that he intended to accomplish under the mask of
the devout hymn that he taught them, and was first discovered
by the officer's wife, who by the imposter was first proselted to
his false doctrines, and after that he would have debauched her
from her conjugal fidelity. This woman was so heroically virtuous, as to communicate his lewd design to her husband, who
ordered the matter so as to be in another room hard by at the
same time he supposed Roderick would be coming; there he stays
until this lecher began to caress his wife, and then he thought
himself obliged seasonably to appear for her rescue, and boldly
reproved the impostor for his wicked practices, which were so
widely contrary to his profession, and that upon the whole it
appeared he had no true mission.

The imposter was very much surprised at this unexpected and
fatal disappointment, which put him into an extreme disorder,
insomuch that he asked the officer's pardon, acknowledging his
crime, and promising never to attempt the like again. The officer
continued to upbraid him; telling him to his face, that he was
sent on by the devil; that innocence and chastity were always the
effects of true religion, and that the contrary practices were coun-
tenanced by false prophets; and that now they needed no other
proof of his being a notorious deceiver: however the imposter
being had in great reputation, prevailed with the officer to patch
up a friendship with him, who for the continuance of it, condescended to be the imposter's gossip, i.e., sponsor at the baptism
of one of his children; of which ceremony there is an account
already given: when there is no opportunity of being sponsor to
one another, and it is necessary to enter into bonds of friendship
at baptism; the inhabitants of the Western Isles, supplied this
ceremony by tasting a drop of each other's blood.

Notwithstanding this friendship thus patched up between these two, the imposter's miscarriages got air, which administered occasion to the most thinking among them, to doubt very much of his mission; his father, who was reputed a very honest man, told him frequently, that he was a deceiver, and would come to a fatal end. This imposter prophesied that one of the inhabitants (whose name I have forgotten) was to be killed in a battle in the isle of Harris, within a limited space of time; this poor unthinking man relying so much on one whom he thought an infallible oracle, ventured more desperately on the rock than ever before, fancying he could not fall, but it happened that he tumbled over and was drowned, at which the inhabitants were surprised; however the impostor continued in the exercise of his pretended mission.

One of the inhabitants called Muldonich, alias Lewis, cousin-german to the imposter, had a ewe which brought forth three lambs at once, they were seen to feed upon the bush pretended to be sacred, but Lewis would not comply with the order for killing the sheep, and had the boldness to aver, that it was an unreasonable piece of worship to destroy so many cattle, and deprive the owners of their use, adding withal, that he never heard any such thing practised in any of the Western Isles upon a religious account. The imposter insisted upon the heavenly command, which was to be observed by all his followers, adding the dreadful threatening against such as proved disobedient thereto; but Lewis would by no means be prevailed upon, choosing rather to be excluded from the pretended worship; than to kill his sheep.

The simple people looked for no less than a speedy judgment to befall this recusant, but when nothing ensued upon his disobedience, all of them began to have a less veneration for the imposter than before; nay, some said privately, that they might as well have ventured to run the same risk with Lewis, for the preservation of their cattle.

Notwithstanding all this villainy, the imposter continued to maintain his authority, until one night (for it was always at night that he kept his pretended religious meetings) by a special providence, a boy of the isle of Harris, called John (who had stayed with his father a year in St Kilda, and was employed in mending of their boat) happened to go into the house where Roderick was preaching after his usual manner, the boy lurked in the dark, and gave his father an account of what he had heard, so far as he could remember, all which the boy's father communicated to the steward upon his arrival, who being highly concerned at the relation given him, carried Roderick along with him to the isle of Skye before the late MacLeod, who being informed of this fellow's impostures, did forbid him from that time forward to preach anymore on pain of death.

This was a great mortification, as well as disappointment to the imposter, who was possessed with a fancy, that MacLeod would hear him preach, and expected no less than to persuade him to become one of his proselytes, as he has since confessed.

The imposter asserts, that every night after he had assembled the people, he heard a voice without saying, 'Come you out'; which when he heard he had no power to stay within; and that after his going forth, John the Baptist did meet him, and instructed him what he should say to the people at that particular meeting. he says, that John the Baptist used only to repeat the discourse to him once, of all which the imposter owns he could scarcely remember one sentence, and therefore he enquired of John the Baptist how he should behave himself in this case; and that John the Baptist returned this answer, 'Go, you have it', which the imposter believing, was upon his return would continue (after this his way of preaching) for several hours together, until he had lulled most of his hearers asleep.

When the above-mentioned earthquake was over, one of the inhabitants enquired of the imposter with admiration, how the rock was made to tremble? He answered, that it was the effect of pleasant music played by a devout saint in a church under ground; his neighbour owned his love for music, but heartily wished never to hear any more of this kind, which carried so great terror along with it.

The imposter owned the truth of all this account, first to the minister and me, and then he did the same publicly after divine service, in the presence of all the inhabitants, and such as were come to that place from the Isle of Harris. The minister and congregation jointly prayed for repentance and pardon to this poor wretch, which when ended, we carried him and all the inhabitants to the bush pretended to be sacred; he himself leading the van, was commanded to raze to the ground a part of that wall which he had ordered to be built round the said bush (which otherwise would in a time have proved such a purgatory, as might have robbed them of all their goods) which he and the inhabitants did in the space of an hour, we made them scatter the stones up and down in the field, lest their posterity might see such a monument of folly and ignorance. We reproved the credulous people for complying implicitly with such follies and delusions as were delivered to them by the imposter, and all of them with one voice answered, that what they did was unaccountable; but seeing one of their own number and stamp in all respects, endued, as they fancied, with a powerful faculty of preaching so fluently and frequently, and pretending to converse with John the Baptist, they were induced to believe his mission from heave, and therefore complied with his commands without dispute, and the rather, because he did not change their laws of neighbourhood.

They do now regret their wandering, and hope that God may pardon their error, since what they did was with a design (though a mistaken one) to serve Him.

They are now overjoyed to find themselves undeceived, and the light of the Gospel restored to them, as it was at first delivered to their ancestors by the first Christian monks, who had gone thither to instruct them.

This imposter is a poet, and also endued with that rare faculty of enjoying the second sight, which makes it the more probable that he was haunted by a familiar spirit. It hath been observed of him, before this imposture was discovered, that so often as he was employed by the steward to go to, or return from Harris, they were always exposed to the greatest dangers by violent storms, being at one time driven fifty leagues to the north-east, and by special providence were at last cast upon the little isle Rona, twenty leagues north-east of Lewis; the steward's wife, and all his crew making their reflections upon these dangers since the discovery of his imposture, could never be prevailed upon to receive him again into their boat. They often intreated Mr Campbel and me not to admit him into our boat, but we did not yield to these fears, for we received and brought him along with us, and afterwards delivered him to the steward's servants in the isle of Pabbay in Harris, where he remains still in custody in order to his trial.

DESCRIPTION
OF THE OCCIDENTAL
i.e.
WESTERN ISLES OF SCOTLAND

Introduction

R. W. Munro

Long before Martin Martin was gathering material for his book on the Western Islands of Scotland, a scholar of European reputation named George Buchanan completed his *Rerum Scoticarum Historia*, a work in flowing Latin prose published at Edinburgh in 1582. As the custom then was, a comprehensive account of the country and its people appeared as a prelude to his story. For details of the little-known isles, he would naturally turn to their former archdeacon, Donald Monro; they must have known each other in the early days of the reformed Church, when Buchanan had presided over its assembly as moderator.

From Man in the Irish Sea to North Rona and Sule Sgeir in the far north, Monro had listed some 250 islands scattered over 300 miles of sea off our western seaboard. Fortunately several copies of Monro's own description, based on a tour believed to have been made in 1549, have survived, as well as Buchanan's own summary. In adopting this tally of the Isles, the scholar was meticulous in acknowledging what he owed to the learned and pious churchman who provided it. The order in which the islands are marshalled is sometimes confusing to a modern reader 450 years later, but careful comparison of Monro's text with Buchanan's leaves no room for doubt that the arrangement was that chosen by the earlier writer. It may seem surprising, for example, to find Islay and Jura – only a short ferry crossing apart – separated by fifty-five intervening islands as far to the north as Lismore;

but to Monro, it seems, Jura went naturally with Gigha to the south and the scatter of islands off Knapdale and Lorn, while he saw Islay as part of the more distant Inner Hebrides – a concept contrary, as it happens, to the division between the separate dioceses of Argyll and the Isles.

Something must be said here of Donald Monro himself. It is not always easy to follow the career of a Scottish clergyman in the Reformation period. One of the laymen who attended the parliament in 1560 was Donald's cousin and clan chief, Robert Munro of Foulis, whose lands lay on the north side of the Cromarty Firth in Ross-shire; his own father Alexander held the small estate of Kiltearn, and his mother was a Maclean of Dochgarroch, near Inverness, and closely connected with Farquhar who was bishop of the Isles from 1530–44.

Although his roots were in the east, Donald thus had early associations with the Western Isles, and his family had a tradition of service in the Church. Archdeacons are not known in the presbyterian form of church government, and in the earliest dated copy of his writings (1642) Donald is styled 'High Dean of the Isles', through which (it adds) he travelled in 1549. That is apparently an informal version of the important office which he held. The Privy Seal register records that on 2nd March 1547/8 a Munro chaplain (tiresomely misnamed Archibald) was presented in the name of the child Queen Mary to the archdeaconry of the Isles, when it should become vacant by the demission of 'the venerable clerk Master Roderick Maclean'. Roderick was raised to the bishopric in 1550 – and there is documentary proof that it was indeed our Donald who filled his place: 'schir Donald Monroy, archdeane of the Isles' guided the pen of the Captain of Clanranald in 1553, when John Moidertach signed a contract at Ruthven in Badenoch with George, Earl of Huntly 'lieut-general in the North'; he appeared on record again in 1563, as *'archidiaconus Insularum'* when he witnessed charters at Foulis for his chief.

The rest of the pre-Reformation story is soon told, as least so far as the church is concerned, for we have glimpses only of what may have been Donald Monro's earlier ministry. It is generally supposed that he was the cleric of that name who in 1526 was made vicar of Snizort, in the Trotternish district of Skye, which was then held along with the charge of the island of Raasay. As vicar Monro would be the working incumbent, with the bulk of the parish revenue appropriated to the Bishop of the Isles. The parish of Snizort lay between Strath on the south and Uig to the north – that is, from Loch Sligachan to about Kingsburgh. The church stood on what is now an island in the River Snizort; this seems anciently to have been the seat of the bishopric of the Isles or Sodor, formerly in the Isle of Man. Monro makes no mention of the fact, but he does say that Raasay used to belong to the Bishop of the Isles 'in heritage', while in his day it pertained 'be the sword' to a branch of the MacLeods of Lewis. Later when he was archdeacon, Donald Monro was presented as parson (the Scottish equivalent of Latin *rector*) of Uig in Trotternish, which may have meant no more than that he was entitled to receive its revenues, along with those of another parish to which Uig was then united. This was in 1552, and the only other appearances of a cleric of the name are when he witnesses charters as parson of Y or Yi – probably Eye near Stornoway in Lewis – in 1549, 1552 and 1554, all in the east of Scotland.

So much, then, for what survives of Monro's place in the Church before the Reformation; but it must be seen against a background of almost constant civil disturbance. Attempts to restore the forfeited lordship of the Isles were frequent for nearly half a century, led first by Donald Dubh, grandson of John, the last lord, and after his capture by other leading members of clan Donald, supported by many of the island clans. During the minority which followed the king's death at Flodden, the crown had little influence in the Hebrides, and local feuds could be actively pursued. Trotternish was of course part of the forfeited lands of the lordship; it was a bone of contention between the MacLeod chiefs themselves and also with the MacDonalds of Sleat.

By 1528, the young James V had taken over control of affairs, and a new earl of Argyll wrote darkly of his family's long experience in the 'danting of the Isles'. But the king was ready to listen to those who were critical of Argyll's methods. Most of the 1530s passed in comparative tranquillity in the Isles, but hopes of restoring the lordship led to a brief insurrection under the chief of Sleat.

The king himself had hopes of bringing 'justice and good policy' to the Isles by a personal visit in the summer of 1540. His progress through the north and south Isles had sufficient force in men and artillery to overawe the disobedient chiefs, and enough pageantry to make a spectacle for the lesser men who (as one historian patronisingly put it) 'rushed from their muddy hovels to gaze at the lion of Scotland'. The MacLeods of Lewis and Harris came dutifully to the king, and in Skye a batch of MacDonalds met him in Trotternish. Unfortunately Monro has nothing to tell of this episode (he writes of 'Loch Portrigh' in what is only a passing reference, and this may well be a purely descriptive place-name and so not derived from the king's visit as has often been assumed).

James well knew that it would take time to achieve his aims, and he was not to live to see the last and potentially most formidable attempt to restore the old lordship. In the minority which followed his death, Donald Dubh was allowed to escape once more from custody; he was free by May 1543, and was well received in the islands. Styling himself Lord of the Isles and Earl of Ross, he issued commissions dated at Ellancharne on 28 July 1545 with consent of his barons and 'council of the Isles', throwing off any loyalty to the Scottish crown and taking the oath of allegiance to Henry VIII at Knockfergus in Ireland on 5 August, when he was said to have a fleet of 180 galleys and a force of 4000 men. After a brief return to Scotland, Donald died of a fever at Drogheda towards the end of 1545, leaving a 'base son' in that king's service. With him the direct line of the lords of the Isles expired, but an heir male was thought by some to be in the Islay family (Dunivaig and the Glens), descended from John Lord of the Isles by his marriage with Margaret Stewart.

Returning to Donald Monro from this necessary digression, in the protestant Church which emerged in 1560, it was not long before we find him in the higher councils of the reformers. Scotland was divided into ten districts in place of the old dioceses, over each of which a superintendent was to be appointed, answerable to the general assembly. Four of the bishops supported the reformation, and so did some holders of lesser offices. The former archdeacon was admitted to the charge of Kiltearn parish, later extended to include Limlair and Alness. Men suitable for the post of superintendent were rare, and commissions 'to endure only for a year' were granted to some ministers without releasing them from parish duties. Three such commissioners were appointed in the North by an assembly meeting at Perth in June 1563 – Donald Monro was to 'plant kirks' in Ross and help the Bishop of Caithness with preaching the gospel in the far north. Monro was the only Highlander selected, although it was complained that he 'was not prompt in the Scottish tongue'; but even with the high standards insisted upon, he was Commissioner of Ross for a dozen years. His last reappointment was in 1574 and another took his place, but the post became redundant with the election of Alexander Hepburn to replace the forfeited Bishop John Lesley.

Donald Monro was the first writer whose description of the Western Isles is known to have been based on personal observation. What follows is taken from the best of the three copies that have survived, first published in 1961. Careful comparison of it with Buchanan's text shows that there were considerable omissions in previous editions of Monro's work; these have been made good with the recovery of his account of more than forty islands, and of the 'Council of the Isles' which had hitherto been missing in his notice of Islay.

Unfortunately Monro says nothing of the purpose for which he was writing. The date 1549 is traditional and may not be exact, but it suggests that his information was gathered at an early stage in his appointment as archdeacon in the See of the Isles. One feature of his account is obvious, but another is less so. For nearly every island that he mentions, he tells us how far it is cultivated – 'fertile and fruitful', 'inhabit and manurit' being the most often repeated phrases; sometimes he is more specific on the products, such as sheep and cattle, corn crops and grazings, fish, wildfowl, rabbits, and so on.

Less readily noticed is the fact that Monro is careful to mention every parish church, and even in the larger islands he gives the number of these though not always the names – twelve in Skye, seven in Mull, five in the Uists, four each in Islay and Lewis, two in Tiree and others in Gigha, Colonsay, Coll, Canna, Eigg and Barra. His total of forty-five parish kirks in his diocese and two others in the neighbouring see of Argyll can be verified from other sources, and Monro's tally will not be found wanting.

Such exactness makes it highly probable that Monro's account was intended to enlighten any superior churchman unfamiliar with the diocese, or at least to remind himself of particulars which would be useful for such a dignitary. We know that Bishop Roderick held the see of the Isles only for a few years, and as one of an island clan he would have little need of information about the Hebrides from a subordinate; but Maclean's successor was Alexander Gordon, brother of the Earl of Huntly already mentioned (and himself a witness to the Clanranald contract).

Besides parish churches, references are frequent to the lairds' castles; deer and salmon, with opportunities for hunting and fishing, are often mentioned, and hawks' nests, seals, and birds' eggs also find a place. On a practical point of accessibility, Monro notes the islands which offer safe harbours and anchorages. In a carefully edited version of the pre-1961 text, Professor Hume Brown compared Monro's account favourably with Martin's more elaborate book, writing: 'We know more of the general appearance of these islands at the period with which we are dealing [Queen Mary's reign] than of any other part of the kingdom.'

An index of names as they appear on current Ordnance Survey maps has been included in this edition. There are, inevitably, some difficulties in identification, and several changes of name are worth noting. Scarpay na mult (162) near Barra has moved from Norse to Gaelic *Maol Domhnaich*, while the reverse appears to have happened with Eisell Ellan or Laich he (51) off Jura, where Pladda (=flat isle) has evidently displaced the Gaelic name. More recently, it seems, off Trotternish in Skye, Fladay (141) appears to be Staffin I., while Altavaig (Martin's 'Altig', 1934 p. 93, not in Monro) has become Eilean Flodigarry.

No holograph version of Monro's work is known to exist, but one of the incomplete copies was 'said to have been done from his papers'. In my 1961 edition I inserted my own numbering, which has been repeated in what follows; the numbers used in previous editions are added *in italics* to make comparison easier. When Monro explains the meaning of a Gaelic name (he calls it Irish or 'Erische'), I have been assured, he is usually accurate. Some of the mutilation and miscopying from which his reputation had suffered has been removed by the discovery of the fuller text, and a closer checking with Buchanan; any errors that remain may be caused either by islands or groups which he knew only from hearsay, or else by misreading (for example, 'n' for 'u' and 't' for 'c' are common). Further textual details and commentary appeared in the 1961 edition, and have not been repeated, but the manuscript has been checked and a few further islands identified.

Edinburgh, 1999

Description of the Occidental
i.e.
Western Isles of Scotland

by
Mr Donald Monro
who travelled through many of them in
Anno 1549

[1.*1*.] First in the Ireland-seas foregainst the points of Galloway, mid-sea nearest betwixt England, Ireland and Scotland lyes the first Isle of the foresaid Isles called in the Latine tongue Mona, sive Sodora, in English **Man**, and in Irish leid called Maniun; quhilk sometime (as auld auncient Historiographers shaws) was wont to be the seat first ordained by Finnan king of Scots to the Priests and Philosophers called in Latin Druides or Driudes; in English Culdees, or Worshippers of God; and in Irish leid Drache, quhilks were the first teachers of Religion in Albion. Whereinto is the Cathedral Kirk of the Bishoprey of Man and Isles dedicat in the honour of Peter Apostle. The Isle is 24 mile lang and 8 mile braid, with 2 Castles in it.

Title. 'Description of the Occidental i.e. Western Islands of Scotland' rewritten over original by another hand, and probably at the same time 'by Mr Donald Monro who travelled through many of them in Anno 1549' added. In other copies the title-page reads: 'A Descriptione of the Westerne Iies of Scotland called Hybrides. Compiled by Mr Donald Munro, Deane of the Iies. 1549'.

[2.2.] Northwart fra this Isle of Man 60 miles of sea lyes **Ellsay**
an Isle of ane mile lang, quharin is ane great heich hill round and
roche, and als abundant of Solan-geese,[1] and ane small point of ane
Ness quhairat the Fisher-boats lyes: for the same Isle is very good
for fishing, sic as Keiling, Ling and other white fishes. Forenent this
Isle lyes Carrick on the south-east part, Ireland on the southwest
part, and the Lands of Kintyre on the west and north-west part;
the said Ellsay being marchand midsea betwixt the said Marches.

[3.3.] Benorth or north-east fra this Isle 24 miles of sea lyes **Aran**
a great Isle full of great mountains and forrests good for hunting,
with part of woods; extending in length fra the Kyle of Aran to
Castle-Donan southwart to 24 mile, and fra Drum donin to the
West Kilbreid 16 mile braid, inhabite only at the sea-coasts. Here-
in are 3 Castles: ane callit Braizay pertaining to the Earle of Aran;
ane other auld house called the Castle of heid of Loch Ranesay
pertaining to the said Earle; and the third called Castle Donan
pertaining first to ane of the Stewarts of Buit his bluid called Mr
James, quha and his bluid are the best men in the countrey. In
Aran is an Loch callit Loch-Renasay with three or four small
Lochis and twa paroch-kirks, the ane callit Kilbreid, the other
called Kilmure. Forenent this Isle lyes the coast of Kyle in the east
and south-west be 10 or 12 mile of sea, in the north Buit be 8 mile
of sea, in the west Scibbenes pertaining to my Lord of Argile.[2]

[1] Buchanan (fol. 9) says: *frequens est cuniculis, auibusque marinis* (it abounds
with Conies and Sea-Fowls –1690 translation).

[2] Buchanan (fol. 9) adds: *Mare qua humilior est, irrumpens in ea sinum satis mag-
num facit: cuius aditum claudit insula Molas. Itaque montibus vndique se attollentibus,
ac ventorum impetum frangentibus portus nauibus intus est tutissimus: & in aquis per-
petuo tranquillis piscatio adeo copioso, vt si quid ultra, quam quod in vnum diem satis
capiatur, accolae in amre, tanquam in pisciniam id projiciant.* (Where it [the ground] is
lowest the sea forms a pretty large bay, whose entrance is protected by the island Molas,
besides which, the mountains towering on every side break the force of the wind, and
render it a very safe harbour for shipping. In these waters, perpetually tranquil, the
fishing is so abundant, that if more be caught than what are required, for one day, the
inhabitants throw them back again into the sea, as into a fish pond – Aikman's trans.).

[4.4.] Upon the shore of the Isle lyes **Flada** are little Isle full of Conyngis with ane other Isle called the Isle of

[5.5.] **Molass** quherein there was foundit be John of the Isles ane Monasterie of Friers which is decayed.

[6.6.] The Isle of **Buit** lyes (as we have said before) 8 miles of sea to the northeast fra this Isle of Aran ane mane Isle 8 mile lang fra the north to the south, and 4 mile braid fra the west to the east, very fertile ground, namely for aits with two strengths. The ane is the Round Castle of Buit callit Revsay of the auld; and about it ane Burrowstoun callit Buitt. Before the Town and the Castle is ane Kay[3] of the sea, quhilk is an gude heavin for schippis to ly on ankeris. That other Castle is callit the Castle of Kames, quhilk Kames in Irish is alsmekle to say as ane Bay in English: for under it is ane Bay of the sea, and sa should it be callit in English the Bay Castle. In this yle thair is twa paroche-kirks of that ane south callit the Kirk of Breid; the uther north in the Burrowstoun of Buitt callit Kilbrink, with twa chapellis, ane of thame above the toun of Buit, and the uther under the forsaid Castle of Kames. On the north and northwest of this lie be ane half mile of sea lyes the coast of Argile, the east side of it the coast of Cunyngham, be 6 myle of sea. On the west south-west of this Ile.

[7.7.] foirsaid lyes ane little Ile callit **Inismerog** twa myle of sea law main ground well inhabite and manurit, ane myle lang, half myle braid.

[8.8.] On the east and south-east of this Ile lyes ane Ile callit **Cumbray** inhabite and manurit, 3 myle lang, ane myle braid, with ane Kirk callit St Colms Kirk.

---

[3] Bay in other copies.

[9.*9*.] Besides this Ile of Cumbray lyes ane uther Ile callit **Cumbray of the Dais** because there is mony Dais in it.[4]

[10.*10*.] Before the south point of the Promonterie of Kintyre lyis be ane lang myle of sea ane Ile neirest ane myle lang callit the Ile of **Avoin,** quhilk Ile has obteinit that name fra the Armes of Denmark, quhilk Armes are callit in thair leid Havoin, inhabite and manurit, gude for schippis to ly on ankeris. Foranent this Ile on the schoir of Kintyre

[*11*.] lyes a stark Castell sumtime callit Carrik-steach with ane little water, wherein there is ane gude heavin for small boats, and this Avoin is ane common place for schippis.

[11.*12*.] On the south-west fra the Promonterie of Kintyre upon the coast of Irland be 4 myle to the land lyis an Ile callit **Rachlind** perteining to Irland and possest thir many zeiris by Clandonald of Kintyre, 4 myle lang, 2 myle braid, gude land inhabite and manurit.

[12.*13*.] Upon the north-west coast of Kintyre be 4 myle of the sea to the sun lyis ane little Ile callit **Caray** with ane chapell in it, gude for quhyte fisches, abundante of conyngis, inhabite and manurit, mair nor ane myle lang, half myle braid.

[13.*14*.] At the heid of this he lyand from this he in the north-east lyis ane Ile callit **Gighay** 6 myle lang, ane myle half mile breid with a Paroche-Kirk, gude fertile mane land, abundante of edderis in it. The auld Thane of Gighay sould be laird of the same callit M^{c}neill of Gighay, and now is possest be the Clandonald streker at the schoir of Kintyre from the south-west to the north-east, in length four myle of sea from Kintyre.

---

[4] 'It hath 2 houses on a little island with which at low water thair is communication', added by another hand. 'Dais' means deer, does.

[14.*15.*] Narrest that he layis **Diuray** ane uther fine forrest for deiris, inhabite and manurit at the coist side, part be Clandonald of Kintyre, part be M^cgillane of Doward part be M^cgillane of Loche of Boy, and part be M^cdufifithe of Collinsay, ane he of 24 mile of lenth, lyand from the south-west to the north-eist 12 mile of sea from Gighay above-written, and ane myle from Ila quhairin thair is twa lochis meittand utheris throw the mid-ile of salt water to the lenth of half myle. And all the deiris of the west part of the forrest will be callit be tynchells to that narrow entres, and the next day callit west again be tynchells throw the said narrow entres, and infinit deir slain there. Part of small woods in it. This Ile, as the Ancients alledges, sould be called Deray, taking the name from the deiris in norn leid, quhilk hes given it that name in auld tymes ago. In this Ile thair is twa gude Raid-is and safety for schippis; the ane callit Lubnalenray, the uther Lochcerbart. Foiranent uther is the greatest hills thairin [are chie-flie][5] Ben quheillis, Ben senta corben, Ben noir in Ardlayfasay. Ane chapell sumtyme the paroche kirk Kilernadill. The watter of Laxay thair, the water of Udergane, the water of Glengargaster, the water of Knokbrek and ill caray avin villi.[6] All this wateris salmond slane on thame. This Ile is full of noble cows [coillis] with certane fresche water Lochis nocht mekle of profeit.

[15.*16.*] Narrest this he be twa myle lyis ane Ile callit **Scarbay.** Betwixt thir 2 Ilis thair runs ane stream above the power of all sailing and rowing with infinite dangeris callit Arey brekan.[7] This

---

[5] Words and phrases printed within square brackets are not found in the copy used here, but have been supplied from other copies of Monro's manuscript (for details see 1961 edition, pp. 45, 148–51).

[6] The river names are unclear and not easily identified – other copies list the final four as Knockbraik, Lindill, Caray and Ananbilley. The mountain list given earlier included Ben Senta and Corben (Beinn Shiantaidh and Corre Bheinn, NR 5174 and 5275. The chapel but not the parish kirk was at Ardlussa, where a tombstone commemorated a descendant of Cilloiur MacCrain, the centenarian mentioned by Martin (p. 61 above).

[7] In other copies called 'Corybrekan'.

stream is 8 myle lang, quhilk may not be hantit but be certane tydes. This Scarbay is 4 myle lang from the west to the eist, ane myle braid, ane heich Roche Ile inhabite and manurit with some woods in it.

Efter this Scarbay lyis mony small Ilis not mekle of profit, notwithstanding thot neidfull to write all thair names as after followis.[8]

[16.*17*.] Narrest this layis [ane iyle, callit in Erische] **Ellan wellich** in the north-east.

[17.*18*.] Narrest this lyis ane [very] little Ile callit **Gewrastill.**

[18.*19*.] Narrest this Ile lyis ane little Ile callit **Lungay.**

[19.*20*.] Narrest this Ile lyis [ane iyle callit] **Fidlay chaillie.**

[20.*21*.] Narrest this he lyis ane little Ile callit [in Erische] **Fidlainrow.**

[21.22.] Narrest this he layis ane little he [in Erische] callit **Garvhelach skean.**[9]

[22.23.] Narrest this he lyis ane little Ile callit [in Erische] **Garvhelach na monaodh.**

[23.*24*.] Narrest this he lyis ane [verey] little Ile callit [in Erische] **Ellach nanaobh.**

---

[8] This connecting passage is not in other copies. Buchanan (fol. 9) says: *Post banc multae ignoblies insulae deinde sparguntur.*

[9] This and the next island, now known as Eilean Dubh Beag and Mor, were known as 'Garve-lach-na-skian' and 'Garve-lach-na-more' in Murdoch Mackenzie's chart 'The West Coast of Scotland from Ila to Mull' (1776).

[24.*25.*] Narrest this he lyis ane little Ile callit [in the Erische Leid] **Culbrenyn.**[10]

[*25.26.*] Narrest thir foirsaids small Iles lyis ane Ile callit **Dunchonill**[11] sa namet from Conill Kernoch ane strength, and alsmekle to say in English as ane round Castell.

[*26.27.*] Narrest this lyis ane Ile callit **Ellan a mhadi** [in Erische] callit in English the Wolfis Ile.

[*27.28.*] Narrest this layis [ane Iylland callit in Erische] **Belnachua** quhair thair is fair skailzie aneuch.

[*28.29.*] Narrest this lyis [the small Iyle of] **Ellan vickeran.**

[*29.30.*] Narrest this lyis [a small Iyland namitt in Erisch] **Ellan nagavna.**

[*30.31.*] Narrest this lyis ane Ile callit **Luyng,** 3 myle lang, lyand from the south-west to the north-eist 2 part myle breid with an paroche kirk, gude name land inhabite and manurit [guid for store and corne its possesit] be M^cgillane of Doward in feall fra my Lord of Argile, having sufficient for Hieland galies in it.[12]

[*31.32.*] Narrest this lyis ane Ile callit **Saoill** or **Seill** 3 myle lang half myle breid, lyand from the south-west to the north-eist, inhabite and manurit, gude for store and corn, perteining to my Lord of Argile.

---

[10] A Chuli, *Cuil Bhrianainn* (Brendan's Retreat) – for this group of islands see W. J. Watson, *Celtic Place-Names of Scotland* (1926), 81–2.

[11] Outlier of larger Garbh Eileach (omitted here), which gives name to the group.

[12] In other copies the last sentence reads: 'it is a heavin sufficient for heighland galayis in it' (see also note 44 on p. 326).

[32.*33*.] Narrest this lyis ane Ile callit **Sevnay**, 2 myle lang, half myle breid [from southwest to northeist], inhabite and manurit, gude for store and girsing, perteining to my Lord of Argile.

[33.*34*.] Narrest this lyis ane [little] Ile callit [in Erisch Leid] **Ellan Slait,** quhairin thair is abundance of skailzie to be wyn.[13]

[34.*35*.] Narrest this lyis ane [sma] he [in Erische] callit **Ellan Nagvisog.**

[35.*36*.] Narrest this lyis ane Ile callit [in the Erische Leid] **Ellan Eisdalf.**

[36.*37*.] Narrest this lyis ane Ile callit **Iniskenzie.**

[37.*38*.] Narrest this lyis ane Ile callit [in the Erische Leid] **Ellan anthian.**[14]

[38.*39*.] Narrest this lyis ane Ile[15] callit [in Erische Leid] **Ellan Uderga.**

[39.*40*.] Narrest this lyis [ane Iyle, callit in the Erische Leid] **Ellan [Righ],** or in English callit the Kings Ile.

[40.*41*.] Narrest this lyis [ane Ile, or rather a grate craige callit in the Erische Leid] **Ellan duff,** or callit in English the Black Ile.

[41.*42*.] Narrest this lyis [ane iyle callit in the Erische Leid] **Ellan naheglis,** callit in English the Kirk Ile.

[13] This may be the former Eilean na Beithich, submerged with the flooding of the slate ('skailzie') quarry (H. Shedden, *Story of Lorn, its Isles and Oban*, 107–8).

[14] Buchanan adds: *vocatur Thiana, ab herba frugibus noxia dissimili Luteae, nisi quod magis diluto sit colore* (called Tian, from an herb noxious to corn, somewhat like guild, but only not of such a bright yellow – Aikman's trans.).

[15] Others say 'ane uther verey smalle rocke'.

[42.*43*.] Narrest this lyis **Ellan Chriarache.**[16]

[43.*44*.] Narrest this lyis [ane Iyle callit in the Erische Leid] **Ellan ard,** callit in English the hich Ile.

[44.*45*.] Narrest this lyis [ane Iyle callit in the Erische Leid] **Ellan Iisall,** callit in English the laich Ile.

[45.*46*.] Narrest this [layes ane Iyle namitt in the Erische Leid] the **Glass Ellan,** callit in English the green Ile.

[46.47.] Narrest this lyis the [Iyle which in the Erische Leid is namitt] **Freoch Ellan,** callit in English the heder Ile.

[47.48.] Narrest this lyis [ane other which in the Erische Leid is callit] **Ellan na cravich,** the Hassile Isle.

[48.49.] Narrest this lyis [ane rockie scabrous Iyle callit in the Erische Leid] **Ellan na gobhar,** callit in English the Gaytis Ile.

[49.*50*.] Narrest this lyis [a verey prey litle sandey Iyle callit in the Erische Leid] **Ellan na gumyn,** callit in Eng. the Conyngis Ile.

[50.51.] Narrest this lyis [the iyle callit be the Erisch] **Ellan diamhoin,** callit in Eng. the Idle Ile.

[51.*52*.] [Narrest this isle lyes **Eisell ellan** or the laich isle a laich small isle.]

[52.*53*.] Narrest this lyis **Ellan Abhridich** in Irish Uridithe.

[53.*54*.] Narrest this lyis **Lismoir** ane fair mane Ile 8 myle lang from the north-eist to the south-west, 2 myle braid, with ane

---

[16] Triaracha (Buchanan).

paroche kirk quhilk sumtime was the cathedrall kirk seat of the
Bischop of Argyle, inhabite and manurit with ane castell callit
Achaadn or Bell buacheir all full of lyme stanes and mettal and
leid ovir lyand foiranent Doward.[17]

[54.] Narrest this lyis **Ellan na gaorach,** callit in English the Scheip
Ile, 2 myle lang, half myle braid, fertile and fruitfull, inhabite and
manurit.

[55.] Narrest this lyis **Suina 2** myle lang from the north-eist to the
south-west, half myle braid, inhabite and manurit.

[56.] Narrest this lyis **Iuichair** callit the Ferray Ile[18] half myle
lang, gude for corn store and fisching and girsing also.

[57.] Narrest this lyis **Garbh Ellan**, callit in English Roch Ile,
gude for store corn and fisching.

[58.] Narrest this lyis **Ellan Cloich** callit in English the Ile of the
stane, gude for store, corn and girsing.

[59.] Narrest this lyis **Flada**, gude for corn, store and fisching.

[60.] Narrest this lyis **Grezay**, gude for corn, store and fisching.

[61.] Narrest this lyis **Ellan Moir**, callit the great Ile, gude for
store and corn.

[62.] Narrest this lyis **Ardiasgar,** gude for corn, store and fisching.

---

[17] Buchanan says: *Lismora, in qua olim sedes Episcopate Argatheliae fuerat, longa octo millia P. lata duo. In ea praeter communia cum caeteris commoda, metalla inueniuntur* (Lismore, eight miles long, and two broad, which was formerly the seat of the Bishop of Argyle, and in which, bedsided the productions common to others, metals have been found – Aikman's trans.).

[18] The island at Lismore ferry is now called Inn I.

[63.] Narrest this lyis **Musadill,** half myle lang, gude for corn and fisching.

[64.] Narrest this lyis **Berneray** ane myle lang from the north-eist to the south-west, alsmekle braid, inhabite and manurit, gude for store, with ane wood for Ew in it.[19] This Ile was callit sumtime an holy Girth, very good for scheip.

[65.] Narrest this lyis **Ellan Inhologasgyr,**[20] full of pasture for store and full of rampis.

[66.] **Ellan drynachai** half myle lang, with mekle bourtrie and thornis, with auld mansis, quhair habitation of Bischops and Nobles were in auld times; gude for corn and store.

[67.] **Ransay** gude for corn and store, with mony thornis and bourtrie.

[68.] Narrest this lyis **Ellan Bhellnagobhan,** callit in English the Smith towns Iles, gude for store, with mekle wood.

[69.] Narrest this lyis **Kerveray** 3 myle lang, mair nor half myle braid, gude fertile fruitfull land, inhabite and manurit, very gude for store, perteining to M꜀covle of Lorn.

[70.55.] Narrest this forsaid Diuray on the west side of the same lyis **Ila,** ane Ile of 20 myle lang from the north to the south, and 16 myle braid from the eist to the west, fertil fruitfull and full of natural girsing pasture with mony great deiris, mony woods, with fair games of hunting besides every town, with mekle leid

---

[19] The yew tree that grew here was cut down (Ian Carmichael, *Lismore in Alba*, Perth 1947, 43).

[20] Presumably E. Loch Oscair of O.S. maps, may refer to Oscar son of Ossian (Carmichael, *Lismore*, 18), or perhaps from Gaelic *iasgair*, fishermen. Buchanan calls it 'Molochasgir'.

ovir in Moychaolis, with ane water callit Laxan whereupon
mony salmond are slane, with ane salt-water Loch there callit
Loch Gruynord, quhairin runs the waiter of Grunord with haich
sandy banks, upon the quhilk banks upon Eb sea lyis infinite
selchis quhilks are slane with doggis leirnit to the same effect.
In this Ile thair is ane gude raid for schippis callit Pollmoir in
Irish, and in English the meekle pool. This lyis at ane town callit Lantay vanych. Ane uther Ile lyis within Ellan Ruidard callit
in English the Ile of point of the Ness. The rade is callit Leo-
dannus [within this Iyle there is sundrie fresche water Lochis sic
as] Loch Moyburg, quhairin thair lyis an Ile perteining to the
Bishops of the Iles. The Loch of Ellan thairin,[21] quhairin thair is
ane Ile perteining to M^cgillane of Doward; Loch Sterotsa with
ane Ile perteining to the Abbot of Icolmkill. In this Ile thair is
strynthie castells: the first callit Dunavaig biggit on ane craig at
the sea side on the south-eist part of the cuntrey perteining to
the Clandonald of Kintyre. The second callit the castell of Loch-
gvrme, quhilk is biggit in ane Ile in the said fresh water loch
far fra land perteining to Clan-donald of Kintyre of auld, now
usurpit be M^cgillane of Doward. Ellan Finlagan in the middis of
Ila ane fair Ile in fresh water Loch.[22] Into this Ile of Finlagan the

[21] Other copies say 'raid' (harbour) for 'Ile', and a few lines later for 'thairin' they
have 'Charrin' (? Loch Ballygrant) and for Loch Sterotsa, 'Cherossa'.

[22] From this word 'Loch' (inclusive) to end of paragraph not in other copies.
Buchanan says: *Praeteria aquae dulcis lacum, in quo est insula Falangama dicta,
olim omnium Insulanorum regia, in qua insularum Regulus assumpto nomine regio
solebat habitare. Huic propinqua sed minor est inula Rotunda: cui etiam a consilio
nomen est inditum. In ea enim curia eraty in qua quatordecim e primorus ius assidue
dicebant, ac de summa rerum etiam agitabant consilia: quorum summa aequitas, &
moderatio pacem domini, forisque praestitit, & pads comitem rerum omnium afflu-
entiam* (There is also a fresh water loch, wherein stands the island named Falingania,
some time the chiefe seat of all the isles men. There the governor of the isles, usurping
the name of the king, was wont to dwell. Neere unto this island, and somewhat lesser than it, is the Round Island, taking the name from Counsell, for therein was the
justice seat, and fourteene of the most worthy of the countrie did minister justice unto
all the rest continually, and intrated of the weighty affaires of the realme in counsell,
whose great equitie and discretion kept peace both at home and abroad; and with
peace was the companion of peace, abundance of all things – Monipennie's trans.).

Lords of the Iles, quhen thai callit thame selfis Kings of the Iles, had wont to remain oft in this Ile forsaid to thair counsell: for thai had the Ile well biggit in palace-wark according to thair auld fassoun, quhairin thai had ane fair chapell. Besides this Ile be ane pennystane cast till it thair is ane uther Ile sumquhat les, fair and round, quhairin thai had thair Counsellhouse biggit, throw the quhilk the said Ile is callit in Irish Ellan na comharle, and in English is callit the Counsell-Ile. In this Ile thair conveinit 14 of the Iles best Barons, that is to say, four greatest of the Nobles callit Lords; to wit M^cgillane of Doward, M^cgillane of Lochbuy, M^ccloyde of Saray,[23] and M^ccloyde of Leozus. Thir four Barons forsaid might be callit Lords, and were haldin as Lords at sic time. Four Thanes of les living and estate; to wit, M^cginnihyn, M^cnaie,[24] M^cneill of Gighay and M^cneill of Barray. Uther four great men of living of thair royall blude of Clan-donald lineally descendit; to wit Clan-donald of Kintyre, M^cane of Ardnanmirquhame, Clan-Ronald, and Clan-Alister Carryche in Lochaber, with the Bishop and the Abbot of Icolmkill. Thir 14 persons sat down into the Counsell-Ile, and decernit, decreitit and gave suits furth upon all debaitable matters according to the Laws made be Renald McSomharkle callit in his time King of the Occident Iles, and albeit thair Lord were at his hunting or at ony uther games, zit thai sate every ane at thair Counsell ministring justice. In thair time thair was great peace and welth in the Iles throw the ministration of justice. In Ila thair is four paroche kirks, to wit Killmheny, Kilmorvin in the middis of the cuntrey, Kilchomain ane fair paroche kirk. In the town of Kilchomain the Lords of the Iles dwelt ofttymes. The kirk of Kildalltan lyand at the south side

[23] Monro's account of the Council of the Isles was first published in the 1961 edition, where at pp. 95–110 a special appendix was devoted to it with a further note on island charters at pp. 139–44 (pursued in Munros' *Acts of the Lords of the Isles*, Scottish History Society, 1986). 'Saray' should read 'Haray', for Harris.

[23] Initial letter changed to 'H' by another hand.

[24] The late Professor Angus Mathieson. of Glasgow University, in a useful review (*SHR* xliii, 48–51) was positive that this name stood for Mcguare or MacQuarrie of Ulva (see no. 103 below), after the name MacKinnon.

of the heichest hills in Ila. Ben Cargadh, Corben ben bhayne. This Ile pertenis to Clan-donald of Kintyre now pairtlie, and pairtlie to M^cgillane of Doward, with ane Falcon-nest in it.

[71.56.] At the Mouth of the Kyle of Ila betwixt it and Diuray lyis ane Ile callit **Ellan charne** and in English the Ile of Cairick.

Here begin we to cirkell Ila sungaittis aboute with litle Iles, as followis.

[72.57.] Narrest this southwart lyis ane Ile callit **Ellan na caltin,** callit in English the Hesill Isle.

[73.58.] Narrest that at the said schoir of Ila lyis [ane litle Iyle] **Ellan M^cmullynory** callit in English mullinoris Ile.

[74.59.] Narrest this at the said schoir lyis **Ellan Osrum** southwart.

[75.60.] Narrest this at the said schoir southwart lyis **Ellan bryd** callit in English Brydis Ile.

[76.61.] Narrest this at the said schoir lyis ane little Ile callit **Corsker,** callit in English the stay skeray or craig.

[77.62.] Narrest this at the said schore lyis ane [small] Ile callit **Ellan Isall,** callit in English the laich Ile.

[78.63.] Narrest this lyis [the litle] **Ellan Imersga.**

[79.64.] Narrest this lyis **Ellan Nabeathi.**

[80.65.] Narrest this at the south coist of Ila lyis ane Ile callit **Ellan teggsay** ane myle lang, gude mane land with ane Kirk in it, very gude for scheip and for fisching.

[81.66.] Narrest this lyis **Ellan na calrach,** callit in English the Scheips Ile, quhilk is very gude for the same and for corn also.

[82.67.] Narrest this lyis southwart **Ellan na naosg** callit in English the Myresnyppis Ile.[25]

[83.68.] Narrest this lyis **Ellan Rinard**[26] callit in English the Ile of the Ness point.

[84.69.] Narrest this lyis **Liach Ellan** callit in English the Lyart Ile.

[85.70.] Narrest this lyis **Tarskeray.**

[86.71.] Narrest this lyis ane Ile callit **Auchnarra.**

[87.72.] Narrest this lyis **Ellan moir** callit in English the great Ile, gude for store [and pastourage].

[88.73.] Narrest this lyis **Ellan dealloch dune** callit in English the Ile of the manis figure.

[89.74.] Narrest this lyis **Ellan Ean** callit in English John his Ile.

[90.75.] Narrest this lyis **Ellan stagbadis.**

[91.76.] Narrest this lyis at the west point of Ila ane Ile callit **Oversay** ane mile of lenth, with ane Kirk in it, gude land, verie gude for fisching, inhabite and manurit, with ane richt dangerous kyle and stream, callit Corie garnagh. Na man dare enter in it,

---

[25] Named after the mire or common snipe (see *DOST* ed. Craigie iv, 448; *SND* ed. Grant and Murison xi, 286; W. MacFarlane, *Geographical Coll.* iii, 191.

[26] Other copies say Rynahard, but Buchanan has Rinarda.

but at ane certain time of the tide, or else Ile man perish. This Ile lyis in lenth from the south-eist to the north-west.

[92.77.] Narrest this Ile [one the northwest coist of Ila] lyis ane Ile callit **Keanichis Ile** callit in English the Merchandis Ile.

[93.78.] Narrest this lyis ane Ile on the said north-west coist of Ila callit **Usabrast gude** for girs and fishing.

[94.79.] Narrest this [one the north coist of Iyla] lyis ane Ile callit **Ellan tanast**.

[95.80.] Narrest this lyis **Ellan nefe** on the north coist of Ila besides the enteres of Loch Grinord foirsaid, with ane Kirk in it. The Ile fair mane land, half mile lang, inhabite and manurit, gude for fisching.

[96.81.] Narrest this lyis ane Ile callit **Ellan na bany**, callit in English the Webstaris Ile.

[97.82.] Narrest this north fra Ila lyis ane Ile callit **Orvansay**, ane Ile of twa mile lang and neir alsmekle braid, quhairin thair is ane Monasterie of Channonis, mane laich land, full of hairis and fowmartis, with gude heavin for hieland Galayis and scheald at the schoiris. This Ile lyis aucht mile of sea northwart from Ila.

[98.83.] Narrest this before the Ile of Orvansay lyis ane Ile les nor it callit **Ellan na muk**, half mile lang, quhilk is gude for swine and uther bestiall.

[99.84.] North fra the Ile of Orvansay be ane half mile of sea lyis ane Ile callit **Colvansay** seven mile lang from the north-eist to the south-west, with twa mile breid, ane fertile Ile, gude for quhyte fishing, with ane paroche Kirk. This Ile is bruikit be ane gentle Capitane callit Mcduffyhe and perteinit to Clan-donald of Kintyre of auld.

[100.85.] Twelff mile northwart from the Ile of Colvansay lyis the Ile of **Mule,** ane great roch Ile; not the les it is fertile and fruit-full. This conteins in lenth from the north-eist to the south-west 24 mile, and in breid fra the eist south-eist to the north north-west under 24 mile, with certane woods, mony deiris and [verey] fair hunting games, with mony great montanes and cordis for hunting, with ane gude raid foiranent Icolmkill callit Polcarf. In this Ile thair is sevin paroche kirks and 3 Castells; to wit, the Cas-tell of Doward ane strenthie place biggit on ane craig at the sea side, the Castell of Lochbury perteining to Mᶜgillane of Lochbuy, the Castell of Aross, quihilk sumtime perteinit to the Lords of the Iies, and now is bruikit be Mᶜgillane of Doward foirsaid. In this Ile thair is twa gude [freche] waters callit Avinva and the water of Glenforsay full of salmond with sum uther waters that hes salmond on thame, but not in sic abundance of salmond as the waters foirsaid hes on thame, with certane salt water Lochs; to wit Loch Laois, ane little small Loch with gude tak of her-ing in it. This Loch lyis in the south-west of the cuntry. Next this Loch Leafan gude for hering. North west fra that Loch lyis loch Stafart[27] gude for hering. On the eist of the cuntrey lyis ane Loch callit Lochspelf. Narrest this Loch in the south south-eist lyis Lochbuy, ane fair braid Loch with ane gude tak of hering and uther fischingis. Within this Ile thair is twa freshwater Lochis: the ane is callit Loch strat stuaban, with ane Ile upon it callit Ellan strat stuaban; the uther Lochba, with ane Ile upon it. Thir Iles are laich inhabite and strenthis. This Ile perteinis pairtlie to Mᶜgillane of Doward, pairtlie to Mᶜgillane of Lochbuy, piartlie to Mᶜkinvin, and pairtlie to the Clan-donald of auld. This Ile lyis not four mile fra the ferme land of Morvarne.

[101.86.] At the south-west schoir of the Ile of Mule lyis ane little Ile callit **Ellan challmain,** callit in English the Dowis Ile, inhabite

---

[27] These two sea-lochs are now called Scridain and Loch na Keal.

and manurit, half mile lang, fruitfull for corn and girsing, with ane heavin for heiland boats, perteining to M^cgillane of Doward.

[102.*87*.] North-west fra this Ile lyis **Ellan Eray**, ane Ile of uther half mile lang, with ane mile narrest of breid, inhabite and manurit, gude mane land for corn store and [pastorage with aboundance of] fishing.

[103.*88*.] Narrest this be twa mile of sea lyis ane Ile callit in Irish leid **Icholum chille**, that is to say in English Saint Colms Ile, ane fair mayne Ile, of twa mile lang, mair nor ane mile breid, fertile and fruitfull for corn, store and fisching. Within this Ile thair was an Abbay of Monks and ane Monasterie of Nunnis with ane paroche kirk, with sundrie uther chapells dotit of auld be the Kings of Scotland and be the Clan-donald. This Abbey foirsaid was the Cathedral Kirk that the Bischoppis of the Iles had sen the time thai were banist out of the Ile of man be the Inglismen: for within this Ile of Man was thair Cathedral Kirk and thair living and thair dwelling als, as is foirsaid. Within this Ile of Colmkill thair was ane Sanctuarie or Kirkzaird callit in Irish Religoran, quhilk is ane fair Kirkzaird, well biggit about with stane and lyme. Into this Sanctuarie thair is three Tombs of stanes formit like little chapellis with ane braid gray [marble or] quhin stane in the gavill of ilk ane of the Tombs. In the stane of the mid Tomb thair is writtin [in Latin letters] *Tumulus Regum Scotiae*, that is to say, the Tomb or the Grave of the Scottis Kings. Within this Tomb, according to our Scottis and Irish Chronicles, thair lyis 48 crownit Scottis Kings, throw the quhilk this Ile has bene richlie dotit be the Scottis Kings, as we have hard. The Tomb on the south side of this foirsaid Tomb hes the subscription, to wit, *Tumulus Regum Hiberniae*, that is to say, the Tomb of the Irland Kingis: for we have in our Irish Chronicles that thair wes four Irland Kingis eirdit into the said Tomb. Upon the north side of our Scottis Tomb the inscription beiris *Tumulus Regum Norvegiae*, that is, the Tomb of the Kingis of Norway. In the quhilk Tomb we find in our ancient Irish Chronicles their lyis aucht Kingis of Norway. And als we find in our Irish Chronicles that Coelus King of Norway comandit his Nobles to tak him to Colmkill to be bureit, if it chansit him to die in the Ile[s]. But he was sa discomfite, that thair remanet not of his Army sa mony as wald bury him there: therefore he was bureit in Kyle, efter he strak a field against the Scottis and wes vincust be thame, as our Albin Scottis Chronicles beiris. Within this Sanctuarie also lyis for the maist [pairt of] the Lords of the Iles with thair linages, tuay Clane lane with thair linages, Mᶜkinvin and Mᶜguare with thair linage, with sundrie uther inhabitants of the haill Iles, because this Sanctuarie wes wont to be the sepulture of the best men of all the Iles, and als of our Kingis, as we have said; because it wes the maist honorable and ancient place that wes in Scotland in those dayis, as we reid.

[104.*89.*] At the south-west end of this Ile of Colmkill lyis ane Ile callit Soa, quhairin thair is infinite number of wild fowl nests, half mile lang, gude for scheip, perteining to Colmkill.

[105.*90.*] On the south-eist of this foirsaid Colmkill lyis ane Ile callit in Irish **Ellan namban,** and in Inglis the Women-Ile, gude for store, fishing and heder, perteining to Colmkill.

[106.*91.*] On the north north-eist end of Colmkill lyis ane little Ile callit **Ellan murudhain,** ane little laich mane [sandey] Ile, gude for scheip and for bent in time of zeir, perteining to Colmkill.

[107.*92.*] On the west north-west of this Ile of Colmkill lyis a little Ile callit **Ellan Reryng** ane profitable Ile of wild fowls eggis and for fisching, perteining to Colmkill.

[108.*93.*] On the north north-eist of this Colmkill lyis ane Ile be twelf mile of sea till it within the enteres of Loch stafart foirsaid callit **Iniskenzie,** uther half mile lang, les nor ane mile breid, ane fair Ile, fertile and fruitfull, inhabite and manurit, full of conyngis

about the schoiris of it, with ane paroche kirk, the maist pairt of
the parochin being upon the mane schoir of Mule foirsaid, ane
half mile distance of sea fra the said Ile. This Ile pertenit to the
Prior[28] of Colmkill, and the haill parochin of it.

[109.94.] Within this Ile of Iniskenzie in the said Loch of Stafart
be ane mile of sea lyis ane Ile callit **Eorsay,** ane fertile Ile, full of
corn, girsing and murens, ane mile lang, perteining to the Priore
of Colmkill.

[110.] Be twa mile of sea fra this Ellan of Eorsay lyis ane Ile to the
north-west callit **Ulvay** five mile lang, gude land with ane gude
Raid for hieland galeis in it.

[111.] Before this Ile of Ulvay on the south coist of it lyis ane little
Ile callit **Colvansay,** gude land for sa mekle with sum hesill wood
in it, and is manurit also.

[112.] Be ane quarter mile of sea to the west north-west fra this
Ulvay lyis ane Ile callit **Gomatra** two mile lang from the south to the
north, with half mile breid, with twa fair Raidis in it; ane of them on
the north side, the best in the south side, gude for mayne schippis to
ride on anker, gude land and well plenishit in corn and girsing.

[113.] Narrest this Gomatra be four mile of sea to the south lyis
ane Ile callit **Stafay**[29] half mile lang, abundante of girsing of the
meklevine, gude heavin for hieland Galayis, utter fyne for storme
and symmer and wynter scheiling also.

[28] Other copies say 'Priores'. Inchkenneth and Eorsa were Iona nunnery lands
(RCAHMS, *Argyll Inv.* iv, 147). Loch 'Stafart' is Loch na Kaal.

[29] As Staffa was among many islands missing in other copies of Monro's MS,
and not restored until my edition of 1961, Buchanan was for long credited with
being the first published writer to mention it (D. B. MacCulloch, *Wondrous Isle of
Staffa*, various edns.); Staffa has its Port an Fasgaidh, but MacCulloch was critical of
Monro's reference to a good sheltered haven. Monro was not concerned with scenery
or geology, and so Fingal's Cave is ignored.

[114.] Fra this Ile four miles of sea to the west north-west lyis twa Kerniborgis; the ane callit **Kerniborg moir,** the uther callit **Kerniborg beg;** baith strengthie craigis be nature biggit in the sea, and fortifeit about be the devise of man, lyand in the middis of it great stark streams of the sea, bruikit be M^cgillane of Doward, very perillous for shippis be reason of the starknes of the stream. Thir Craigis are easily made unwynable be craftie men, and namelie the greatest is strenthie but douth.

[115.] Narrest thir Iles be ane mile of sea to the west lyis ane Ile callit **Ellan na monadh;**[30] that is to say in Inglish, the fewall Ile quhilk furdis fewall to the strenthis foirsaid. Some manurit land in it, the rest of mure for fewall 2 pairt myle lang from the eist to the west, with a gude hieland heavin in it.

[116.] Narrest this lyis **Lungay** ane Ile of twa mile of lenth, gude for store, corn and fishing.

[117.] Narrest this lyis to the west south-west ane Ile callit the **Bak,** ane mile lang, very gude for store, namelie for stwidis, and als for fishing.

[118.] Narrest this toward the west be sax mile of the sea lyis **Thiridh** ane mane laich fertile fruitfull cuntrie, aucht mile lang from the north-eist to the south-west; three mile braid from the north-west to the south-eist. All inhabite and manurit with twa paroche kirkis in it, ane fresh water loch, with ane auld castell. Na cuntrie may be mair fertile of corn, and very gude for wild fowls and for fische, with ane gude heavin for heiland galayis.

---

[30] This island in the Treshnish group has become another Fladda; between the two Kerniborgs and Lunga. Buchanan says of it (in Aikman's translation): an island whose soil is almost wholly black, being a compound of rotten wood and old moss. The turf is dried for firing, and hence the island is called the Peat Island, for so they term that species of earth, which in English is called moss.

[119.] Be twa mile of sea from this Ile lies ane Ile callit **Gunna,** ane mile lang from the eist to the west, manurit and inhabite, gude for corn, store and fishing.

[120.] Be twa mile of sea northwart from Gunna lyis ane Ile of half a mile lang callit **Coll** tending in lenth from the south-west to the north-eist and twa mile braid. Ane mane fertile Ile inhabite and manurit, with ane castell and ane paroch kirk in it, gude for fishing and fowlers, with ane utter fine Falcons nest in it.

[121.95.] Upon the north north-eist coist of Mule lyis ane Ile callit **Calf,** ane mile lang, full of woods, sufficient raid for schippis perteining to M^cgillane of Doward.

[122.96.] Befor the castell of Aross foirsaid lyis twa Iles; the ane Glass Ellan moir, the uther **Glass Ellan beg;** and the south-eist fra that throw the Kyle of Mule lyis twa Iles of the foirsaid twa names perteining to M^cgillane of Doward.

[123.97.] From these Glass Ellans to the south-eist lyis ane Ile callit **Ellan Ardan ridir,** callit in Inglis the Knytis Ile, or the Ile of the Knytis Ness perteining to M^cgillane of Doward.

[124.98.] Southwart from Dowart lyis ane Ile upon the schoir side callit in Irish **Ellan amhadi,** and in Inglis the Wolfis Ile, gude for store, [being bentey] perteining to M^cgillane of Doward.

[125.99.] Southwart from Ellan amhadi upon the schore of Mule lyis ane Ile callit **Ellan moir,** gude for store and for fisching perteining to M^cgillane of Lochbuy.

[126.100.] Sixteen mile northwart fra the Ile of Coll lyis ane Ile callit **Rum,** ane Ile of 16 mile lang, 6 mile braid, in the neirest ane forrest full of heich montanes and abundante of little deiris in it, quhilk deiris will never be slane down-with but the principall settis man be in the heich of the hills, because the deir will be callit upwart ay be tynchellis, or without tynchellis they will up a forte.[31] In this Ile thair will be gottin about Beltane als mony wild fowl nestis full of eggis about the mure as men pleases to gadder, and that becaus the fowls hes few to start thame except deiris. This Ile stands fra the west to the eist in lenth, and perteins to the Laird of Coll callit M^cane abrie. Mony solenne geis are in this Ile. This land obeyis to M^cgillane of Doward instantlie.

[127.*101*.] Be four mile of sea towards the south-eist lyis ane little he half mile lang callit in Irish **Ellan na neach,** callit in Inglish the horse Ile, gude for horse and uther store, perteining to the Bischop of the Iles.

[128.*102*.] Be ane half mile of sea to this foirsaid Ile lyis ane Ile of twa mile lang, callit in Irish **Ellan na muk,** and in Inglish the Swines Ile, ane verie fertile frutfull Ile of cornis and girsing for all store, verie gude for fische, inhabite and manurit, with ane gude falcon nest, perteining to the Bischop of the Iles; with ane gude hieland heavin in it, the entrie at the west cheek of it.

[129.*103*.] Be twa mile of sea towards the north-west from this foirsaid Rum lyis ane Ile callit **Cannay,** fair mane land, four mile lang inhabite and manurit, with an paroch kirk in it, gude for corn, girsing and fisching, with an falcon nest in it. It perteins to the Abbot of Colmkill.

[130.*104*.] North fra this Ile callit Ellan na muk be four mile lyis ane Ile callit **Egge,** four mile lang, twa mile braid, gude mayne land, with ane paroch kirk in it, with mony solenne geis; very gude for store, namelie for scheip, with ane heavin for hieland Galayis.

---

[31] Other copies say 'will pass upwart perforce'; for further account of hunting deer by tinchell (circuit), see under Jura (no. 14).

[131.*105*.] North-eist fra this foirsaid Ile of Rum be twelf mile of sea lyis ane Ile uther half mile lang callit **Soabretill,** ane roch Ile quhairin deiris uses to be and hunting games, perteining to M^{c}cloyd of Herey.

[132.*106*.] North fra this be twa miles of sea lies the great Ile of **Sky** tending fra the south to the north to 42 miles, roch and lang; that is to say, fra the south point of Slait to the north point of Trouterness; and 8 mile braid [in some places] and in uther places 12 mile braid. In this Ile thair is 12 paroch kirks, inhabite and manurit fertile land, namely for aittis, excelland ony uther ground for girsing and pasture, abundante of store and of stwidis. In it mony woods, mony forrests, [maney deire], fair hunting games, mony great hills, principallie Cwillvelum and Glamok. Within this Ile thair is gude tak of salmond fische upon five principall wateris; to wit, the water of Snersport, the water of Sliggacham, the water of Straitsnarsdill, the water of Linlagallan, and the water of Killmartine, and seven or aucht uther small waters, quhairupon smaller salmond fische are slain. In this Ile thair is ane fresh water Loch, quhairupon thair is slane salmond and kipper callit the Loch of Glenmoir. Within this thair is five castles; to wit, the Castle of Dunvegane perteining to M^{c}cloyde of Hary, ane stark strenth biggit on ane craig; the Castell of Dumakin perteining to M^{c}kinvin; the Castell Dunringill perteining to the said M^{c}kynvin, the Castell of Cames in Slait perteining to Donald Gormesoun; and the Castell of Duntvillmen perteining to the said Donald Gormesoun within Trouternes: and the Castell of Dunskayt in Slait perteining to the said Donald Gormesoun. Within this Ile thair is seven sundrie cuntreys; to wit Slait perteining to Donald Gormesoun; Stratsnordill perteining to M^{c}kynvin, quhilk lyis next Slait; Mengzenes perteining to M^{c}cloyd of Haray; Braakadill perteining to the said M^{c}cloyd; Denrynes perteining to the said M^{c}cloyd; Waternes perteining to M^{c}cloyd of Leozus; and Trouternes perteining to Donald Gormesoun. Into this Ile thair is three principall salt water Lochis; to wit, Loch Sliggachan, Loch

Synort, and Loch Slaopan: gude tak of hering in thir three Lochis. By thir three Lochis, thair is within this Ile 13 salt water Lochis; to wit, Loch Stafayk, Loch Emort, Loche Vrakdill, [Loche] Kensale, Herlois, Loch Dunvegane, Loch Gristins, Loch Arnossort, Loch Wge, Loch Sneisport, Loch Portrigh, [Loche] Kenloch na-daladh in Slait:[32] gude tak of hering in mony of thir Lochis [sometymes bot nought sa guid by far as in the 3 first Loches]. This Ile is callit Ellan Skianach in Irish, that is to say in Inglish the wyngit Ile, be reason it hes mony wyngis and pointis lyand furth fra it, throw the deviding of thir foirsaid Lochis.

[133.*107*.] About this Ile of Sky thair lyis in ane circle certane Iles; to wit, at the coist side of Slait lyis ane Ile callit **Orandsay** ane mane land, inhabite and manurit gude land; perteining to Donald Gormesoun.

[134.*108*.] Foiranent Loch Ailis lyis ane Ile callit in Irish **Ellan na guyneyne,** that is to say in Inglish the Conyng Ile, full of wood and conyngis, half mile lang, perteining to M^ckenzie of Kintaill.

[135.*109*.] At the schoir of the Strat foirsaid lyis ane Ile callit **Pabay** west [neire] ane myle lang, full of woods, gude for fisching, and for thieves[33] to await on leill mennis geir, perteining to M^ckynvin.

[136.*110*.] Fra this Ile of Pabay south-west[34] be aucht mile of sea lyis ane Ile callit **Scalpay,** four mile lang, alsmekle braid, and fair hunting forrest full of deir, and certane little woods with certane towns, inhabite and manurit, with strenthie coves, gude for fisching, perteining to M^cgillane of Doward in heritage.

---

[32] Other copies list the following lochs: Skahauaik/Skahanaik, Emorte, Vrakdill, Kensale-serloss, Dunbegan, Gorsarinis, Arnossort, Snasporte, Portri, Ken Nadalae in Sleitt.

[33] Others say 'and a maine shelter for theeives and cutthrotts'.

[34] Actually north-west, only two miles.

[137.*111.*] Betwixt the mouth of Loch Caron and Raarsay lyis **Crowling** [ane small Ile zea rather a] gude raid for schippis.

[138.*112.*] Twa mile of sea fra this Ile of Scalpay foirsaid northwart lyis ane Ile callit **Raarsay** seven mile lang from the south to the north, lyand but ane mile of sea from Trouternes, twa mile of breid, with pairt of birkin woods, mony deir, pairt of profitable land, inhabite and manurit; with twa castellis, to wit, the castell of Kilmaluok and the castell of Brerkdill; with twa fair orcheartis at the saidis twa castellis; with ane paroche kirk callit Kilmaluok; ane roche cuntrie, but all full of frie stanes and gude querrellis, gude for fisching, perteining to M^cgillichallum of Raarsay be the sword, and all to the Bischop of the Iles in heritage. This M^cgillichallum sould obey Mccloyd of Leozus.

[139.*113.*] At the north end of this foirsaid Ile of Raarsay be ane half mile of sea fra it lyis ane Ile callit **Ronay,** mair nor ane mile lang, full of wood and hedder, with a heavin for hieland Galeis in the middis of it. And the said heavin is quiet for fostering of thieves, ruggaris and reevaris till await upon the pailing and spuilzeing of poor mens geir, perteining to M^cgillichallum of Raarsay be force and to the Bischop of the Iles be heritage.

[140.*114.*] **Ellan Gerloch** in the mouth of Gerloch: in it is gude raid for schippis.

[141.*115.*] To the north fra Ronay be six mile of sea lyis ane Ile callit **Fladay,**[35] ane meane roch Ile, half mile lang, inhabite and manurit, fruitfull in corn and girsing, perteining to Donald Gormsoun.

---

[35] Now apparently called Staffin I. Missing here is Altavaig, now Floddigarry (I. A. Nicolson, *Handbook of the Isle of Skye,* 22), isle Altvig of Martin's *Description* (p. 93 above), with a chapel.

[142.*116*.] Narrest this Fladay be twa myle of sea at the schoir of Trouternes lyis ane Ile callit **Ellan Tuylmen** half mile lang or thairby, manurit, gude for corn and store, perteining to Donald Gormsoun.

[*117*.] [Foure myle of sea fra this Ile Twilin northwart lyes ane Ile callit____.]³⁶

[143.*118*.] Upon the south side of Sky be ane half mile to the schoir of Braakadill foirsaid lyis ane Ile callit **Orandsay,** half mile lang, ane bonie Ile for corn and girsing, perteining to Mᶜcloyd of Haray.

[144.*119*.] Be ane mile of sea to this Ile of Orandsay lyis ane Ile callit **Bwya moir,** gude for corn and store, perteining to Mᶜcloyd of Harray.

[145–149.*120–3*.] Betwixt Bwya moir and **Ellan Isa** lyis five small Iles not mekle of profit.³⁷

[150–152.*124–6*.] [Before the castle of dunbegan lyes 3 small isles.]³⁸

[153.*127*.] At the schoir of Waternes lyis ane Ile callit **Ellan Isa,** ane fair laich mayne Ile inhabite and manurit, verie fertile

---

³⁶ This entry, supplied from other copies, might refer to Fladda-chuain, for which see Martin, p. 93 above; also no. 238 below.

³⁷ Other copies of Monro's MS say 'Narrest the Ile of Bwya moir Lyes 4 small Iles quhosse Names the author has Left blankes for'; Buchanan (fol. 10) has *deinde Buia maiorc deinceps quinque parvae insulae ignobiles*. These un-named islands, with Bwya moir and beag, were probably in Loch Bracadale, where O.S. map shows also Harlosh and Tamer Is.

³⁸ Inserted by a different hand, probably from other copies. Font's map names seven islands in Loch Faillord (the old name for L. Dunvegan) inside Isay (no. 153) – Yl. Cholbesk, Gravellan, Clash, Grinen, Heuf, Garra and Skiandel. O.S. names Gairbh E., E. Mor and E. Dubh.

and frutfull for corn and girsing, ane mile lang, half mile braid, havand beside it ane uther laich Ile full of scheip.[39] This Ile is gude for fishing, perteining to M^ccloyd of Leozus.

[154.*128.*] On the eist schoir of Waternes lyis Ile callit **Ellan Askerm**,[40] abundand of girsing and pasture, mair useit for scheling and store than for corn land, gude for fishing and slauchter of selchis, perteining to M^ccloyd of Leozus.

[155.*129.*] Upon the schoir of Lindill lyis ane Ile callit **Ellan Lindill**, verie gude for beir and scheip, perteining to M^ccloyd of Haray.

[156.*130.*] From this Isle of Sky toward the south-west be 80 miles of sea lyis ane Ile callit **Lingay,** gude for girsing and fisching, the Bischop of the Iles lands,[41] ane Ile of half mile lang, with ane falcon nest in it.

[157.*131.*] Bakwart to the north beside the Ile of Lingay is ane Ile callit **Gigarmen,** half mile lang, perteining to the Bischop of the Iles, with ane falcon nest in it.

[158.*132.*] Beside this Ile of Gigarmen towards the north lyis ane Ile callit **Berneray,** verie fertile land, inhabite and manurit, ane mile lang, gude for fishing, perteining to the Bischop of the Iles.

[159.*133.*] Beside the Ile of Bemeray towards the north lyis ane Ile callit **Megalay,** twa mile lang, inhabite and manurit, verie gude for corn and fishing, perteining to the Bischop of the Iles.

---

[39] Beside Isay O.S. map shows small islands Mingay and Clett, but not Ouia or Egg I. of Buchanan and his translator Aikman.

[40] Other copies have 'Askerin', but clearly 'Askerma' in Buchanan.

[41] There is no apparent reason to single out Lingay for mention as the first of the nine Bishop's Isles from Isle of Barra to Barra Head on Berneray (see also in Martin, p. 168 above).

[160.*134*.] Besides this Ile of Megalay, towards the north north-eist, lyis ane Ile callit **Pabay**, ane mile lang, inhabite and manurit, gude tak of fische in it, perteining to the Bischop of the Iles.

[161.*135*.] Besides this Ile lyis ane Ile to the northwart callit **Fladay**, ane mayne land, frutfull in corn, and als ane fishing, perteining to the Bischop of the Iles.

[162.*136*.] Besides this Ile of Fladay toward the north lyis ane Ile callit **Scarpay na mult**, twa mile lang, with ane halk nest in it, full of pasture, gude for fishing, perteining to the Bischop of the Iles.

[163.*137*.] Besides this Ile toward the north lyis ane Ile twa mile lang callit **Sanderay**, very gude for corn and fishing, inhabite and manurit, perteining to the Bischop of the Iles.

[164.*138*.] Besides this Ile northwart lyis ane Ile callit **Vatersay**, twa mile lang, ane mile braid, with ane excellent raid for mayne schippis that cumis thair to fische,[42] ane faire mayne Ile, inhabit and manurit, abundand of corn and girsing, gude pasture for scheip for the mekledome of it. All thir nine Iles foirsaid had ane chapell in everie Ile perteining to the Bischop of the Iles.

[165.*139*.] Besides this Ile of Vatersay towards the north, be twa mile of sea, lyis ane Ile callit **Barray**, seven mile lang from the southwest to the north-eist, four mile braid from the south-eist to the north-west; ane fertile and frutfull Ile for corn, and abundante of fisching of keiling, ling, and uther quhyte fisches,

---

[42] Buchanan (fol. 10) says: *Vatersa, quae praeter alia commoda plurimastationem habet multarum, & magnarum nauium* **capacem**, *in quarn ex omnibus circumia-centibus regionibus statis temporibus magna piscatorum frequentia conuenire solet* (Vatersa, which, besides a great many other advantages, possesses a capacious harbour capable of receiving ships of the largest size, in which a vast number of fishermen assemble at stated seasons, from all the surrounding regions – Aikman's trans.).

with ane paroche kirk callit Kilbaray. Within the south-west end of this Ile thair enteris ane salt water Loch, verie narrow in the entres, and round and braid within. Into the middis of the said Loch thair is ane castell in ane Ile upon ane strenthie craig callit Keselum perteining to Mcneill of Barray. In the north end of this cuntrey of Barray thair is ane round heich know mayne girs and grene about all to the heid thairof. Upon the heid of this know thair is ane spring and fresh water well. This well trewlie springis up certane little round quhyte things les nor the quantitie of ane quhyte virne,[43] likest to the shape, figure and form of ane little Cockle has appeirit to me. Out of this well thair rynnis ane little strype downwith to the sea; and quhair this strype enteris into the sea, thair is ane mile braid of sandis, quhilk ebbis ane mile, callit in Irish the Craimoir of Kilbaray, that is to say in Inglis, the great sandis of Baray. This sandis is all full of great Cockles, and alledgit be the ancient cuntrymen that all thay Cockles cumis down out of the foirsaid hill throw the said strype in the first small form as we have spoken, and eftir thair cuming into the sandis growis great Cockles, the confirmation quhairof I leif to Mr Hector Boyis. But alwayis thair is not ane fairer and mair profitable sandis for Cockles in ony pairt of the warld. This Ile perteins to Mcneill of Barray.

[166.*140.*] Betwixt Barray and Vyst thair lyis first **Orbandsay**, half mile lang, with ane falcon nest, ane gude profitable Ile inhabite and manurit, gude for scheip, perteining to Mcneill of Barray.

[167.*141.*] Besides this lyis **Ellan nahaonchaorach**, callit in Inglish the ane sheip Ile, ane little Ile full of girsing, gude for store, perteining to Mcneill of Barray.

[43] Corne, in other copies.

[*168.142.*] Besides this lyis **Ellan na hakersait,**[44] half mile lang, with ane heavin for heiland galayis, perteining to M^cneill of Barray.

[*169.143.*] Besides this lyis ane Ile callit **Garvlanga,** ane Ile full of girsing, gude for fisching, perteining to M^cneill of Barray.

[*170.144.*] Besides this lyis ane Ile callit **Fladay,** half mile lang, with ane falcon nest in it, fertile and frutfull, perteining to M^cneill of Barray.

[*171.145.*] Besides this lyis ane Ile callit **Buya beg,** half mile lang, gude for girsing and fisching, perteining to M^cneill of Barray.

[*172.146.*] Besides this lyis ane Ile callit *Buya moir,* twa mile lang, manurit, full of girsing and pasture, with a falcon nest in it, perteining to M^cneill of Barray.

[*173.147.*] Besides this lyis ane Ile **callit Hay,** half mile lang, fertile and frutfull, gude for fisching, perteining to M^cneill of Barray.

[*174.148.*] Besides this lyis ane Ile callit **Hellisay,** ane mile lang, fertile and frutfull, [weill manurit] gude for fisching, perteining to M^cneill of Barray.

[*175.149.*] Besides this lyis ane Ile callit **Gigay,** ane mile lang, fertile and frutfull, gude for store and fishing, perteining to M'neill of Barray.

[*176.150.*] Besides this lyis ane Ile callit **Lingay,** half mile lang, ane verie gude Ile for girsing, pasture and for scheling, perteining to M^cneill of Barray.

[44] This word, applied to a bay and insulated headland in NE of Barra, is from Gaelic *acarsaid* meaning harbour or anchorage, and is often used of havens suitable for the Highland galley (others being at nos 20, 97, 101, 110, 113, 115, 118, 128, 130, 139), while 'raids' or roads were for larger ships (nos 14, 70, 100, 112, 121, 137, 140, 164).

[177.*151*.] Besides this lyis ane Ile callit **Feray**, half mile lang, gude in corn and girsing, and als for fisching, perteining to M^cneill of Barray.

[178.*152*.] Besides this lyis ane mane sandie Ile callit **Fuday**, verie fertile and frutfull for beir and murens[45], the quhilk Ile payis murens zeirlie to M^cneill of Barray for pairt of thair mails and dewteis.

[179.*153*.] To the eist of this Ile of Fuday, be three mile of sea, lyis ane Ile callit **Eriskay** twa mile lang, inhabite and manurit. In this Ile thair is gottin [dylie] verie abaundant of [werey grate] pintill fisch at ebb seais, and als verie gude for uther quhyte fische: perteining to M^cneill of Barray.

[180.*154*.] Northwart fra this Ile foirsaid lyis the great Ile of **Vyist**,[46] 34 mile lang from the south south-west to the north north-eist, 6 mile braid, ane fertile cuntrie, ane mane laich land, full of heich hills and forrests on the eist coist or south-eist, and all plenishit laich land on the north north-eist, with five paroche kirkis. This cuntrie is bruikit be sundrie Capitanes; to wit, the south southwest end of it callit Vaghastill be M^cneill of Barray. Within his south pairt of Vyist on the eist coist of the same lyis ane salt water Loch callit Loch Wagcastell. The rest of the Ile callit Peiteris parochin, the parochin of Howf, and the mane land of the mid cuntrey callit Matherhanach perteins to Clan-Renald, haldin of the Clan-Donald of Kintyre; and at the end thairof the sea enteris, and cuttis the cuntrie be ebbing and flowing throw it. And in the northside of this thair is ane parochin callit Vlmdbhadhla

---

[45] Prof. Matheson (see note 24 on p. 310 above) saw nothing surprising in a duty paid in bent grass (see nos 106,109), useful for thatching, etc. E. Murudhain (previously Moroan) near Iona has not been identified.

[46] The name here includes North Uist (Cean Tuath), Benbecula (Vlindbhadhla, ?Vlmdbhadhla) and South Uist, incl. Loch Boisdale (Vaghastill), with the North and South Fords (now bridged) between.

perteining to the said Clan-Donald. At the north end thereof the sea cuttis the cuntrie agane, and that cutting of the sea is callit the Faghill of Caraness. And be north this the cuntrie is callit kean tuathe of Vyist, that is to say in Inglis, the north heid of Vyist, quhilk conteins to twa paroch kirks, and is mair of profit than the rest of the haill Vyist, perteining to Donald Gormesoun. In this Ile thair is infinite number of fresh water Lochis: but thair is ane [maine] Loch intill it callit Loch Vi three mile lang. Ane arm of the sea hes worn the earth that wes at the tane end of this Loch, quhilk ze sea hes gottin entres to the said fresh water Loch; and in that narrow entres that the sea hes gottin to the said Loch foirsaid the cuntriemen hes biggit up ane thik dyke of great roche stones, and penniestane cast lang narrest; notwithstanding the flowing streams of the sea enteris in throw the said dyke of stanes in the said fresh water Loch, and sa thair is gottin amang the roch stanes of the dyke foirsaid flewkis, podlokis, schaytis and little hering stikand fast amang the stanes. Upon this Loch thair is gottin ane kind of fish the quantitie and shape of ane salmond without skaills, the uther half narrest his womb quhyte of it and the u[p]maist half narrest his bak jeat blak, with finnis like ane salmond. Into this north heid of Vyist thair is sundrie coves and holes under the earth coverit with hedder above, quhilk fosteris money rebellis in the cuntrey of the north heid of Vyist, and in the said cuntrie of Vyist thair is sundrie halk nestis.

[181.*155*.] [Betwixt the Kentnache and Benvalgha lyes ane werey small Ile callit_____.]

[182.*156*.] Be aucht mile of sea from this Ile towards the west lyis ane Ile four mile lang, half mile braid, laich mane land, callit **Helsker na caillach,** perteining to the Nunnis of Colmkill, gude corn land not well fyrit.

[183.*157*.] To the north-west of the Keantuach of Vyist lyis ane Ile be 12 mile of sea callit **Haifsker,** quhairin infinite slauchter of selchis is maid at certane times in the zeir, perteining to Donald Gormesoun.

[184.*158*.] To the west north-west of this Ile out of the mane Ocean seais be 60 mile of sea lyis ane Ile callit **Hirta**, mane laich sa far as is manurit of it, abundand in corn and girsing, namelie for scheip, for thai are fairer and greater scheip thair and langer taillit than thair is in ony uther Ile thairabout. The inhabitants thairof are simple creatures, scant learnit in ony Religion: but Mccloyd of Haray his Stewart, or quhom he deputtis in sic office, sayles anes in the zeir at midsymmer with sum chaiplane to baptize bairns thair, and gif they want ane chaiplane, thai baptize thair bairns thameselfis. The said Stewart, as himself tald me, usit to tak ane mask of malt thair with ane maskein fat and mask his malt, and or the fat be readie, the commons of the town baith men, women and bairns puttis thair hand in the fat, and finding it sweit greynes eftir the sweitnes thairof, quhill neither wort nor draff are left unsuppit out thair, quhill baith men, women and bairns were deid drunkin, so that thai could nocht stand on thair feit. The saids Stewards ressaves thair maillis in maill and reistit muttonis, wild reistit foullis and selchis. This Ile is mair nor ane mile lang narrest, almsekle breid, quhilk is not seen of ony land or of ony schoir, But at the schoir side of it lyis three great hills, quhilk are ane pairt of Hirt, quhilk are seen far off from the forlands. In thir roch Iles are infinite fair scheippis, with ane falcon nest and wild foullis biggand. But the seais are stark and verie evill entering in ony of the saids Iles. This Ile perteinit to Mccloyd of Haray of auld.

[185.*159*.] At the north-west coist of this forsaid Kentuath lyis ane Ile callit **Valay**, twa mile lang from the north to the south, ane mile braid, ane fair mayne Ile, [inhabit and manurit], perteining to Donald Gormesoun.

[186.*160*.] Betwixt this Kentuath and the Harey lyis certane profitable Iles, to wit, **Soa,**[47] inhabite and manurit, ane mile lang, mayne land, perteining to Donald Gormsoun.

[187.] Besides this lyis ane Ile callit **Stroma** inhabite and manurit, gude land, les nor ane mile lang.

[188.] Besides this lyis ane maist profitable Ile callit **Pabay,** four mile lang, ane mile braid, maist plentifull of beir, girsing and fisching.

[189.] Besides this lyis ane Ile callit **Bemeray** als lang, als braid, als plentifull.

[190.] Besides this lyis ane Ile callit **Enisay,** quhairin M^cloyd of Harey hes a dwelling place, ane fair mayne land, weill inhabite and manurit, ane mile lang, half mile braid.

[191.] Beside this lyis ane Ile callit **Keligir,** inhabite and manurit, half mile lang, fertile and frutfull for the mekledome.

[192.] Beside this lyis ane Ile callit **Sagha beg,** manurit, fertile and frutfull.

[193.] Beside this lyis ane Ile callit **Sagha moir,** half mile lang, fertile and frutfull, inhabite and manurit.

[194.] Beside this lyis **Hermodray,** half mile lang, fertile and frutfull.

[195.] Beside this lyis **Scarvay,** fertile and frutfull, inhabite and manurit.

[47] In the Sound of Harris several larger islands are omitted, particularly Boreray, and the name Soa is not on O.S. maps.

[196.] Beside this lyis **Grya,** verie profitable for feiding and fostering of gudes.

[197.] Besides this lyis **Linga,** verie profitable also for feeding and fostering of gudes.

[198.] Beside this lyis **Gillinsay,** inhabite and manurit, verie profitable for girsing and fishing.

[199.] Beside this lyis **Heyia,** verie profitable for girsing and fishing.

[200.] Beside this lyis **Hoya,** verie profitable for store and fishing.

[201.] Besides this lyis **Ferelay,** inhabite and manurit, fertile and frutfull for corn, store and fishing.

[202.] Besides this lyis **Soya beg,** manurit, fertile and frutfull for corn, store and fishing.

[203.*185.*] Besides this lyis ane Ile callit **Soya moir,** manurit, fertile and frutfull, gude for fishing, ane mile lang.

[204.*186.*] Besides this lyis **Ellan Isay,** manurit, fertile and frutfull, gude for fishing.

[205.*187.*] Besides this lyis **Seuna beg,** manurit, fertile and frutfull, gude for corn, store and fishing, half mile lang.

[206.*188.*] Besides this lyis **Seuna moir,** mair nor ane mile lang, half mile braid, inhabite and manurit, gude for corn, store and fishing.

[207.*189.*] Besides this lyis **Tarandsay,** ane Ile of five mile lang, half mile braid, inhabite and manurit; ane roch Ile with certane townis. But all this tilth is delvit with spaidis, except sa mekle as ane hors pleuch will teill; and zit thay have maist abundante of beir, and maist myth of corn, store and fishing; perteining to M^ccloyd of Haray.

[208.*190*.] Besides this lyis the Ile of **Slegain**, manurit, gude for corn, store and fishing, perteining to M^ccloyd of Haray.

[209.*191*.] Besides this lyis **Tuemen**, gude for corn, store and fishing, perteining to M^ccloyd of Haray.

[210.*192*.] Besides this out in the sea above Usiemes in Heray lyis ane Ile callit the **Scarp**, manurit, fertile and frutfull, gude for corn, store and fishing, perteining to M^ccloyd of Haray.

[211.*193*.] Above the north-west coist of Leozus towards the mayne Occident seas lyis certane Iles, of whom I will make mention, or we begin Heray and Leozus: to wit, first fiftie mile in the occident seais, from the coist of the parochin of Vige in Leozus, towards the west north-west iyis the 7 Iles of **Flavain**, callit with thame girth and halie Iles, verie naturall girsing. Within thir saidis Iles is infinite wild scheip, quhilks na man knawis quha pat in the said scheip of thame that lives this day of the cuntriemen. But M^ccloyd of Leozus at certane times in the zeir sendis men and houndis thair, and huntis mony of the said scheip to deid. The flesh of thir scheip may not be eittin be honest and clene men for fatnes: for thair is na flesh on thame but all quhyte like talloun, and wild gustit thairwith. The saidis Iles are nather manurit nor inhabite, but great heich grene hillis full of wild scheip in thai 7 Iles foirsaid quhilk may not be ovircumein, perteining to M^ccloyd of Leozus.

[212.*194*.] Besides the coist of Leozus towards the said north-west lyis ane Ile callit **Garvellan**, gude for store and fishing, perteining to M^ccloyd of Leozus.

[213.*195*.] Besides this lyis ane Ile callit **Lambay**, gude also for store and fishing, perteining to Mᶜcloyd of Leozus.

[214.*196*.] Besides this lyis **Fladay**, gude for store and fishing, ane bony laich Ile, perteining to Mᶜcloyd of Leozus.

[215.*197*.] Besides this lyis **Keallasay**, ane gude Ile, narrest ane mile lang, frutfull for store and fishing, and als manurit, perteining to Mᶜcloyd of Leozus.

[216.*198*.] Besides this Keallasay lyis **Berneray beg**, ane half mile lang narrest, [ane] mile braid, ane laich roch Ile, full of little laich craigis and holvis[48] betwixt, of naturall fertile earth, and infinite for wair on every schoir of the same. This Ile is well inhabite and manurit, and will gif zeirlie mair nor 200 bollis beir with delving only, perteining to Mᶜcloyd of Leozus.

[217.*199*.] Beside this lyis **Berneray** moir, ane Ile of five mile lang, inhabite and manurit, fertile and frutfull, with mony pastures and mekle store, gude for fishing and fewall also, perteining to Mᶜcloyd of Leozus.

[218.*200*.] Besides this lyis **Kirtay**, inhabite and manurit, ane mile lang, fertile and fruitfull, gude for store and fishing, perteining to Mᵉcloyd of Leozus.

[219.*201*.] Besides this lyis **Bwya beg,** inhabite and manurit, gude for store, corn and fishing, perteining to Mᶜcloyd of Leozus.

[220.*202*.] Besides this lyis **Bwya moir**, mair nor ane mile lang, inhabite and manurit, gude for store, corn and fishing, perteining to Mᶜcloyd of Leozus.

---

[48] Other copies have 'how', holes or hollows.

[221.*203*.] Besides this lyis **Vexay,** ane gude mane Ile, ane mile lang, inhabite and manurit, verie naturall pastures for store, fishing and fewall, perteining to M^cloyd of Leozus.

[222.*204*.] Besides this lyis **Pabay,** ane Ile mair nor ane mile lang, ane frutfull, fertile mane Ile full of corn and scheip, quhairn thair wes a kirk, quhairin also M^cloyd of Leozus uses to dwell, quhan he wald be quiet or feirit. This Ile is gude for fishing also, perteining to M^cloyd of Leozus.

[223.*205*.] Besides this Pabay lyis **Sigrame moir na guneyne,** that is to say, the great Conyngis Ile, quhairin thair are mony conyngis, gude for girsing and fishing, perteining to M^cloyd of Leozus.

[224.*206*.] Besides this lyis **Sigram beg,** manurit, gude for corn, girsing and fishing, half mile lang, perteining to M^cloyd of Leozus.

[225.*161*.] At the north point of Leozus thair is ane little Ile callit the **Pygmies Ile,** with ane little kirk in it of thair awn handie wark. Within this kirk the ancients of the cuntrie of Leozus sayis that the saids Pygmeis hes bene earthit thair. Mony men of divers cuntries hes delvit up deiply the fluir of the said kirk, and I my-self amangis the lave, and hes fundin in it deip under the earth certane banes and round heids of verie little quantitie, alledgit to be the banes of the saids Pygmeis, quhilk may be licklie according to sindrie storeis that we reid of the Pygmeis. But I leave this far of it to the ancients of the Leozus. This Ile perteins to M^cloyd of Leozus.

In the south-eist coist of Leozus thair enteris twa great salt water Lochis of quhyte fischings; to wit the north Loch of the Y, and the south Loch of the Y. Thir twa Lochis are full of quhyte fische everie time in the zeir, perteining to Mccloyd of Leozus.[49]

[226.*162*.] Besides[50] this at the south-eist schoir of Leozus lyis ane Ile callit **Ellan Fabill**, very gude for vayk store and fishing, perteining to M^ccloyd of Leozus.

[227.*163*.] South fra this said coist lyis **Ellan Adam**, manurit, and gude for vaik bestiall, perteining to M^ccloyd of the Leozus.

[228.*164*.] Upon the said schoir, towards the west, lyis **Ellan na nuan** callit in Inglish the Lambs Ile, quhairin all the vaik lambs of that end of the cuntrie uses to be fed and fosterit, perteining to M^ccloyd of the Leozus.

[229.*165*.] Betwix this Ile and Steornvay thair lyis **Ellan Huilmen**, manurit and gude for store and corn, perteining to M^ccloyd of the Leozus.

[230.*166*.] Southwart fra this Ile lyis **Ellan Viccowill**, ane gude Ile for corn, store and fisching, perteining to M^ccloyd of the Leozus.

[231.*167*.] Besides this lyis **Havreray**, ane gude Ile for corn, girsing and fisching, ane mile lang, perteining to M^ccloyd of the Leozus.

[232.*168*.] Besides this lyis **Laxay**, ane gude Ile full of corn, girsing and fishing, perteining to M^ccloyd of the Leozus.

---

[49] This paragraph not in other copies. Buchanan (Aikman's trans.) says: 'On the south-east coast of Lewis are two bays, styled the one the South and the other the North Loch, in both of which abundance of fish may be taken during the whole year'. The ruined church of Y or Eye (see p. 293 above) stands on the neck of the peninsula of that name.

[50] Other copies say 'Besouth'; Buchanan agrees.

[233.*169*.] Besides this lyis **Ere**, quhilk is in Inglish callit Irland, laich mane land, full of corn and girsing, perteining to M^cloyd of the Leozus.

[234.*170*.] Within the Lochis foirsaid lyis **Ellan Cholmkle** callit in Inglish St Colmis Ile. Within this Ile M^cloyd of the Leozus hes ane fair Orcheard, and Ile that is Gardiner hes that Ile frie; gude mane land for corn, girsing and fishing, perteining to M^cloyd of the Leozus.

[235.171.] Besides this lyis **Torray**, ane Ile manurit, gude for corn, girsing and fisching, perteining to M^cloyd of the Leozus.

[236.*172*.] Southwart from this Ile lyis ane Ile callit **Ellan Iffurt**,[51] sum manurit land, with gude pasture and scheling of store, with fair hunting of Ottiris out of thair bowris, perteining to M^cdoyd of the Leozus.

[237.*173*.] Southwart from this Ile lyis ane Ile callit **Scalpay** of Haray, twa mile lang, ane profitable Ile for corn and girsing [and fischinge], perteining to M^cloyd of the Haray.

[238.*174*.] Towards the north-eist be 20 mile of sea lyis ane Ile in the sea callit **Fladay**, half mile lang, ane profitable Ile in corn and girsing, and als in fishing, perteining to Donald Gormesoun.

[239.*175*.] Northwart fra this Ile lyis the Ile callit **Ellan Senta**,[52] callit in Inglish the saynt Ile, mair nor twa mile lang, verie profitable for corn, store and fisching, perteining to M^cloyd of the Leozus.

---

[51] O.S. have moved from Iuvard to Liubhaird; other copies of MS call this island at the mouth of Loch Shell 'E. Hurte', but Buchanan has 'Iffurta'.

[52] This must be Garbh Eilean in the Shiant group, from the reference to the rock archway at the E end (Toll a Roimh).

On the eist side of this Ile thair is ane Bow made like ane Volt, mair nor ane arrow shot of any man, in manner of ane Volt under earth, throw the quhilk Volt we useit to row or sail with aire [our] boats, for feir of the horrible brak of seais that is on the outwart side of the point quhair that Bow is, but na great schippis may cum thair, perteining to M^ccloyd of the Leozus.

[240.*176.*] Be eist this lyis ane Ile callit **Senchastell**, callit in Inglish the auld castell, ane strenth full of corn and girsing, and wild fowl nests in it, and als fisching, perteining to M^ccloyd of the Leozus.

[241.*177.*] Upon the schoir of Loch Briene[53] lyis **Ellan Eu**, half mile lang, full of woods to await upon leill mens geire and gude for theves to the same effect, perteining to M^ckenzie.

[242.*178.*] Northwart from this Ile lyis **Ellan Gruinord**, mair nor ane mile lang, full of wood, gude for fostering of rebells, perteining to M^ckenzie.

[243.*179.*] Northwart from this Ile lyis **Ellan na clerach**, half mile lang, gude for girsing and wild fowl eggis, perteining to M^ckenzie.

[244.*180.*] Narrest this lyis **Ellan af vill**[54], gude for store and fishing.

[245.*181.*] Narrest this lyis **Havreray moir**.

[246.182.] Narrest this lyis **Havreray beg**.

[247.*183.*] Besides this lyis **Ellan na neach**.

---

[53] Actually in Loch Ewe.
[54] Other copies have 'Afuil'; Buchanan 'Afulla'.

[248.*184.*] Besides this lyis **Ellan Mertack**.[55]

All thir 8 Iles abovewrittin is in the mouth of Loch bryne.[56]

[249.*207.*] North, or north-west fra this Ile lyis the **Haray** and **Leozus**, quhilk is but ane Ile baith togidder extending in lenth fra the south-west to the north-east to 60 miles, and from the northwest to the south-eist 16 mile in bried. Within the south part of this said Ile lyis ane Monasterie with ane steipill, quhilk was foundit and biggit be M^{c}cloyd of Haray callit Roadill. This south part of the cuntrie callit Haray is verie fertile and frutfull for corn, store and fisching, and tways mair of delvit nor of teillit land in it. Within this end of the cuntrie thair is ane water with ane gude tak of salmond fische in it, with ane heich grene hill callit Copefeall maist excellent for scheip in these parts, quhairin thair wes (quhan I was thair) scheip without awineris and very auld. In this cuntrie of Haray north-wart, betwix it and the Leozus are mony forrests, mony deir but not great of quantitie, verie fair hunting games without any woods, with infinite slauchteris of Otteris and Martrikis.[57] This Ile hes nather wolfis,

---

[55] That this must be Isle Martin near the Summer Is. at the mouth of Loch Broom is made clear by Buchanan and his translator Aikman (where the name appears as 'Mertaika') by the connecting paragraph which follows (not in other copies of Monro). Prof. W. J. Watson at first derived the name from St Martin, but later admitted that he had no proof of any connection *(Place Names of Ross and Cromarty, 255, Celtic Place-Names of Scotland*, 291). The word martric, mertrick, or mertrik figures in dictionaries such as *DOST* and *SND*, and Monro's references to slaughter of 'otteris and martrikis' in Harris (see no. 249) is cited; Martin's *Description* at p. 34 above refers to the 'mertrick' there, 'about the size of a big cat', and the smaller pine marten was widely recorded in Lochbroom parish and elsewhere (F. Fraser Darling and J. Morton Boyd, *The Highlands and Islands* (Collins' new naturalist series, 1964), 66–8).

[56] This sentence not in other copies. Buchanan says: *Hae octo proximae insulae ante ostium sitae sunt sinus, quern vulgo lacum Briennum vocant* (These eight neighbouring islands are situated at the north of Loch Brien or Broom – Aikman's trans.).

[57] Buchanan here inserts the source of his information: *Narrat Donaldus Monrous homo doctus, & pius se cum illic esset, vidisse oues admodum annosas, utin eo pecoris genere, sine certis dominis vagas* (Donald Monro, a pious and well-informed man, mentions, that he saw when there, old sheep, old for that species of cattle, wandering about without any particular owner – Aikman's trans.).

toddis nor edderis in it. The Leozus is in the north pairt of this Ile, and the maist, also fair and well inhabite at the sea coist, ane fertile frutfull cuntrie, for the maist pairt all beir with four paroche kirks, and with ane Castell callit Steornvay, with three principall salt water Lochis, verie gude for tak of hering; to wit, Loch Selga farrest to the south-west; Loch Sifort northwart fra that; ane Loch that is lang, and certane small Lochis in it, quhilk is callit the Lochis for the same cause. By this thair are three Lochis not evil for tak of herring; to wit, Loch Steornvay [with] infinite [fresche] water Lochis. In this Leozus thair are 8 waters with great tak of salmond, with 12 waters having ane gude tak of smaller salmonds. In this cuntrie thair is mony scheip, for it is ane verie gude cuntrie for the same: for they ly furth evir on mures and glennis, and enteris nevir in ane house and thair wool is but anes in the zeir clippit aff thame in some fauldis. In this cuntrie all is peitmosland at the sea coist, and the place quhair Ile wynis his peittis this zeir thair he sawis his beir the next zeir: eftir that he gudes it weill with sea wair. Ane great tak of quhaillis is oft-times in this cuntrie, swa that be relation of the maist ancient in the cuntrie thair come [26 or] 27 quhaillis young and auld to the teind anes thair. Thair is ane Cove in this cuntrie, quhairin the sea fillis and is twa faddom deip at ebb sea, and four faddom and mair at full sea. Within this Cove thair uses quhyles to be slane with hwikis verie mony haddokis and quhyttingis by men with thair wandis sittand on the craigis of that Cove and Laddes and lasses and women also. Thair is verie mony halk nestis in Leozus and Haray.

[250.208.] Towards the north-eist or north north-eist from Leozus 60 miles of sea lyis ane little Ile callit **Ronay**, laich mane land, inhabite and manurit be simple people scant of ony Religion. This Ile is half mile lang, half mile braid: abundand of corn growis in it be delving, abundante of natural claver girs for scheip. Thair is ane certane number of ky and scheip ordanet for this Ile be thair awin auld rycht, extending to sa mony as may be sufficient upon the said girsing; and the cuntrie is sa fertile of girsing, that the superexcrescens of the said ky and scheip baith feidis thame in flesche and als payis thair dewties with the same for the maist pairt. Within this Ile thair is sic fair quhyte beir meill maid like flowir, and quhan thay slay thair scheip [they slay them] belly flauchts and stuffis the said skynnis fresche of the beir meill. They send thair dewtie aftirwart to M^{c}cloyd of Leozus, with certane reistit muttonnis, and mony reistit wild fowls. Within this Ile thair is ane chapell callit St Ronans chapell, into the quhilk chapell (as the ancients of that cuntrie alledgis) thay use to leave ane spaid and ane schoole quhan ony deid, and upon the morn findis the place of the grave taiknit with ane spaid (as thai alledge). In this Ile thay use to tak mony quhaillis and utheris great fisches.

[251.209.] Be sixteen mile of sea towards the west of this Ile lyis ane Ile callit **Swilskeray**, ane mile lang, without girs or hedder, with heich blak craigis and blak fog upon pairt of thame. This Ile is full of wild fowls, and quhan the fowls hes thair birds ripe, men out of the parochin of Niss in Leozus uses to saill thair and tarry thair 7 or 8 dayis and to fetch with thame hame thair boatfull of dry wild fowls with wild fowl fedderis. In this Ile thair hantis ane fowl callit the Colk,[58] little les nor ane goose, quha cummis in vair to the land to [lay] his eggis and to cleck his birdis quhill he bring thame to perfection, and at that time his fleiss of fedderis fallis off him all haillelie, and Ile flasses [saylis] to the mayne sea again, and cummis nevir to land quhill the zeiris end again, and than he cummis with his new fleiss of fedderis. This fleiss that he laves zeirlie upon his nest hes na banes in the fedderis nor any kind of hard thing in thame that may be felt or graipit but uttir fine downis.

[58] This bird was the eider duck; 'his' and 'he' in this paragraph appear as 'her' and 'she' in other copies.

INDEX

Island names only are listed here, where these have been identified. If there is any doubt about identity, this is indicated by an asterisk * after the name. The form used is that of the Ordnance Survey maps (usually the 1:50 000 Landranger series, but when taken from another edition this is indicated by a double**), followed by grid reference, to show the islands' location. As these maps are under constant revision, including the spelling of place-names with a Gaelicised element, changes made in the latest issues have not always been noted. Islands named by Monro which have not so far been satisfactorily identified (particularly in the Outer Hebrides) are listed at the end of the index, with their apparent locations.

UNIDENTIFIED ISLANDS

Off Argyll mainland:

26	E. a Mhadi
34	E. Nagvisog
36	Iniskenzie
37	E. anthian
38	E. Uderga
42	E. Chriarache
43	E. Ard
44	E. Iisall
45	Glass Ellan
46	Freuch Ellan
47	E. na Cravich

Near Lismore:

62	Ardiasgar

Off Islay:

72	E. na caltin
77	E. Isall
79	E. Nabeathi
82	E. na naosg
83	E. Rinard
86	Auchnarra

93	Usabrast
96	E. na bany

Near Iona:

106	E. Murudhain
107	Reidh E.

Off Barra:

167	E. nahaonchaorach
168	E. na hakersait
173	Hay

Sound of Harris:

200	Hoya
201	Ferelay
205	Seuna beg
206	Seuna moir

Off Harris/Lewis:

208	Slegain
209	Tuemen
213	Lambay
227	E. Adam
233	Ere
238	Fladay

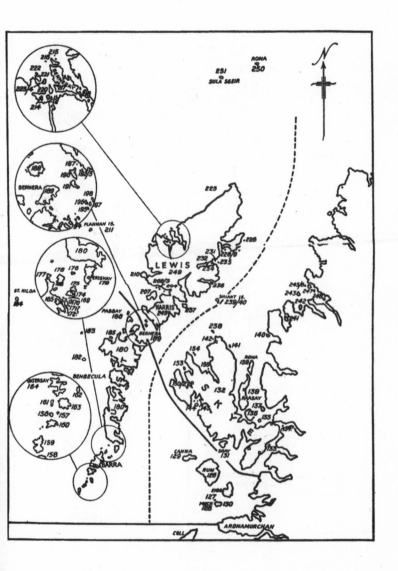

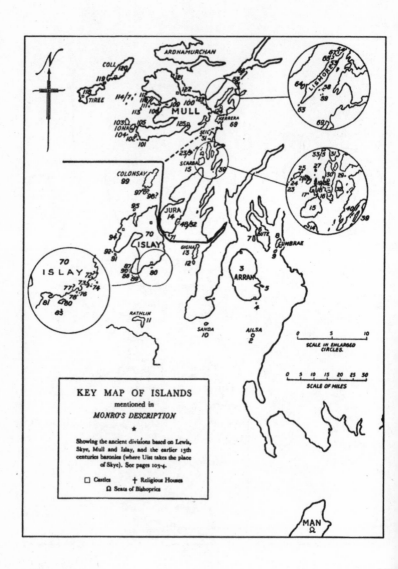

KEY MAP OF ISLANDS
mentioned in
MONRO'S DESCRIPTION

★

Showing the ancient divisions based on Lewis,
Skye, Mull and Islay, and the earlier 13th
centuries baronies (where Uist takes the place
of Skye). See pages 103-4.

☐ Castles   + Religious Houses
Ω Seats of Bishoprics